"A remarkable book. By clearing conceptual ground, synthesizing ~~~~ ~es and debates, formulating challenges and first-hand reflections, the book will stand as a key book for researchers and students dealing with MIL."

Ulla Carlsson
Professor, University of Gothenburg, UNESCO
Chair on Freedom of Expression, Sweden

"Media and information literacies are becoming ever more important for society worldwide. Haider and Sundin provide an original, and insightful analysis, balancing theoretical considerations and practical implications, which will be a valuable and timely resource for anyone researching or teaching in these areas."

David Bawden
Professor, Department of Information Science,
City, University of London, UK

"Haider and Sundin brilliantly explain how a digital culture fraught with fragmentation, emotionalization and distrust turns to media/information literacy. By revealing the invisibility of our information systems, they allow us to ponder the contradictions, assumptions, and unintended consequences of such solutions."

Francesca Tripodi
PhD, School of Information and Library
Science and senior researcher at the Center for Information, Technology
and Public Life, UNC-Chapel Hill, USA

"Our current epistemic crisis has thrown long-standing contradictions in media and information literacy into high relief. Haider and Sundin identify and illuminate key paradoxes that must be grappled with to reorient our teaching policies and practices. This foundational text is bound to spark fruitful conversations now and for years to come."

Barbara Fister
Scholar-in-Residence, Project Information Literacy, USA

"With this book Jutta Haider and Olof Sundin contribute cutting-edge insights into the subject of Media and information literacy, indispensable to academics and professionals in the field, essential to policy-makers."

Louise Limberg
Professor Emerita, Swedish School of Library
and Information Science, University of Borås, Sweden

PARADOXES OF MEDIA AND INFORMATION LITERACY

Paradoxes of Media and Information Literacy contributes to ongoing conversations about control of knowledge and different ways of knowing. It does so by analysing why media and information literacy (MIL) is proposed as a solution for addressing the current information crisis.

Questioning why MIL is commonly believed to wield such power, the book throws into sharp relief several paradoxes that are built into common understandings of such literacies. Haider and Sundin take the reader on a journey across different fields of practice, research and policymaking, including librarianship, information studies, teaching and journalism, media and communication and the educational sciences. The authors also consider national information policy proposals and the recommendations of NGOs or international bodies, such as UNESCO and the OECD. Showing that MIL plays an active role in contemporary controversies, such as those on climate change or vaccination, Haider and Sundin argue that such controversies challenge existing notions of fact and ignorance, trust and doubt, and our understanding of information access and information control. The book thus argues for the need to unpack and understand the contradictions forming around these notions in relation to MIL, rather than attempting to arrive at a single, comprehensive definition.

Paradoxes of Media and Information Literacy combines careful analytical and conceptual discussions with an in-depth understanding of information practices and of the contemporary information infrastructure. It is essential reading for scholars and students engaged in library and information studies, media and communication, journalism studies and the educational sciences.

Jutta Haider is Professor at the Swedish School of Library and Information Science (SSLIS), University in Borås. She has published widely on information practices and digital cultures' emerging conditions for production, use, and distribution of knowledge and information. This includes work on algorithmic information systems and on knowledge institutions, including encyclopaedias and search engines. She is co-author of *Invisible Search and Online Search Engines: The Ubiquity of Search in Everyday Life* (Routledge, 2019).

Olof Sundin is Professor in Information Studies at the Department of Arts and Cultural Sciences, Lund University, Sweden. He has extensive experience of researching the configuration of information in contemporary society, the construction of trustworthiness, as well as practices of media and information literacy in schools and in everyday life. He is co-author of *Invisible Search and Online Search Engines: The Ubiquity of Search in Everyday Life* (Routledge, 2019).

PARADOXES OF MEDIA AND INFORMATION LITERACY

The Crisis of Information

Jutta Haider and Olof Sundin

Routledge
Taylor & Francis Group

LONDON AND NEW YORK

Cover Image: © Diana Miller / Getty Images

First published 2022
by Routledge
4 Park Square, Milton Park, Abingdon, Oxon OX14 4RN

and by Routledge
605 Third Avenue, New York, NY 10158

Routledge is an imprint of the Taylor & Francis Group, an informa business

© 2022 Jutta Haider and Olof Sundin

British Library Cataloguing-in-Publication Data
A catalogue record for this book is available from the British Library

Library of Congress Cataloging-in-Publication Data
Names: Haider, Jutta, author. | Sundin, Olof, author.
Title: Paradoxes of media and information literacy : the crisis of information / Jutta Haider and Olof Sundin.
Description: New York, NY : Routledge, 2022. | Includes bibliographical references and index.
Identifiers: LCCN 2021057848 (print) | LCCN 2021057849 (ebook) | ISBN 9780367756215 (hardback) | ISBN 9780367756192 (paperback) | ISBN 9781003163237 (ebook)
Subjects: LCSH: Information literacy. | Media literacy.
Classification: LCC ZA3088 .H35 2022 (print) | LCC ZA3088 (ebook) | DDC 028.7--dc23/eng/20220308
LC record available at https://lccn.loc.gov/2021057848
LC ebook record available at https://lccn.loc.gov/2021057849

ISBN: 978-0-367-75621-5 (hbk)
ISBN: 978-0-367-75619-2 (pbk)
ISBN: 978-1-003-16323-7 (ebk)

DOI: 10.4324/9781003163237

Typeset in Bembo
by SPi Technologies India Pvt Ltd (Straive)

CONTENTS

FIGURES

PREFACE

Having worked on information literacy for many years, and more recently also on media and information literacy, we have struggled with the many paradoxes we have encountered. Even our research seemed to be built on a paradox, caught between being asked for advice on how to develop and teach media and information literacy and studying this extremely heterogeneous field from a critical distance. As a researcher, one would have the obvious choice of either accepting the contradictions and moving forward in research to make a difference or changing focus and examining the field as such. Since we sometimes overcomplicate things, we decided to try and do both at the same time. To paraphrase a famous saying: We want to have the apple and eat it, comment on how the symbol-laden fruit of knowledge and temptation is rotting as we speak and provide means to intervene.

The book contains questions and ideas that we have been developing and carrying around for a long time, but the book is mainly an outcome of the project "Algorithms and Literacies: Young People's Understanding and Society's Expectations" (The Swedish Research Council, 2017-03631). We also build on material created in two other research projects, although to a lesser extent. In "Search critique and the critical assessment information in compulsory school" (funded by The Swedish Internet Foundation) Hanna Carlsson was a co-researcher and in "Algorithm awareness between generations" (funded by the National Library of Sweden) Lisa Ohlsson Dahlquist was a co-researcher. Thank you very much, Hanna and Lisa! Your contributions were very important, and without your insights this book would not have been the same. We also want to thank Johan Frid at the Humanities Laboratory at Lund University for his help.

Some of the ideas and empirical material we draw on and elaborate in the book have been previously presented in earlier shorter versions in the following publications. "Information literacy as a site for anticipation: Temporal tactics for infrastructural meaning-making and algo-rhythm awareness" in *Journal of Documentation*, 2021;

"Information literacy challenges in digital culture: Conflicting engagements of trust and doubt" in *Information, Communication & Society*, published online 2020; "Where is Search in Information Literacy: A Theoretical Note on Infrastructure and Community of Practice" in *Sustainable Digital Communities: 15th International Conference, iConference 2020, Boras, Sweden, March 23–26, 2020, Proceedings*; *Algoritmmedvetenhet i mötet mellan generationer: En forskningsrapport inom ramen för Digitalt först med användaren i focus*, 2020 (with Lisa Ohlsson Dahlquist); "Skolan och biblioteken som aktörer för demokratiska samtal" in *Det demokratiska samtalet i en digital tid: En antologi om desinformation, propaganda och näthat*, 2020; "How Do you Trust? On Infrastructural Meaning-making and the Need for Self-reflection" in *Understanding Media and Information Literacy (MIL) in the Digital Age: A question of Democracy*, 2019; *Sök – och källkritik i grundskolan: En forskningsrapport*, 2018 (with Hanna Carlsson).

We have also presented some of the ideas at seminars and conferences in Sweden and internationally. We would like to mention the keynote "Algorithms and Platforms: Is there a Place for Information Literacy?" that Olof Sundin gave at the ECIL European Conference in Information Literacy in 2021. Olof Sundin was also invited to give the talk "Literacy, Open data and the Crisis of Information" at the Data Literacy in Context – DaLiCo.Virtual Summer School on Open Governmental Data (2020) where he presented some initial thoughts on the crisis of information. These two talks developed ideas that became part of the first and second chapters. Jutta Haider presented earlier versions of Chapters 2 and 6 at higher seminars at the Department of Culture and Media Studies, Umeå University, and at the Centre for Nordic Media Research at Gothenburg University (Nordicom). Jutta Haider also gave a talk entitled "From what to when: On representations of information inequality and the role of time" at the *Symposium on Theories of Information Disparities in Society* (2017), Nankai University, China. This was the first time the ideas that are presented in Chapter 4 were tested.

To our colleagues at Lund University and at the Swedish School of Library and Information Science in Borås: rather than risking forgetting anyone, we would like to thank you all. The research seminars at our respective universities have been particularly important: Research Seminar for Mediated Culture and Information at Lund University and Research Seminar in Library and Information Science as well as the Information Practices and Digital Cultures research group at the University of Borås. We would also like to thank all the students, teachers, and librarians we met in lectures, workshops, and conversations inside and outside the university. As we prepare for these activities, many of our ideas take on an understandable format.

A special thanks to Mathias Cederholm, whose tireless work mediate everything important concerning media and information literacy in the Swedish Facebook group "Källkritik, fake news och faktagranskning" [Source criticism, fake news, and fact checking]. The efforts that Mathias makes on a daily basis, together with the other administrators and members, have been absolutely indispensable for our environmental scanning. We also want to extend our gratitude to the many participants in the different research projects this book draws on. You talked to us about everything from literacy, to Google, to algorithms and different aspects of your everyday or professional lives and provided many thought-provoking perspectives on the challenges society faces.

During the last months' work with the book, we asked some colleagues to read chapters at short notice. Thank you for reading and commenting parts of the book: Fredrik Bertilsson, Hanna Carlsson, Ulf Dalquist, Alison Gerber, Joacim Hansson, Heidi Julien, Dirk Lewandowski, Karin Linder, and Lisa Olsson Dahlquist. You have generously shared your expertise with us, for which we are very grateful. Special thanks go to Ola Pilerot and Louise Limberg, who read and commented on most of the chapters in the book. With your long and extensive experience in the field, your insightful comments were extremely valuable. Getting a "thumbs up" from you was more important to us than you can imagine. At the same time, any weaknesses, mistakes, or problems in the book are definitively not the fault of any of our colleagues.

1
INTRODUCTION TO THE LITERACY PARADOXES

Can injecting disinfectant help you recover from a viral infection? Obviously, it cannot, but it was what former US President Donald Trump recommended scientists investigate, live at a press conference in April 2020. In the pandemic years of 2020 and 2021, the world exploded with information about a new respiratory disease, COVID-19, that was caused by a novel coronavirus. We encountered highly complex scientific information, advice issued by public authorities, rules and regulations provided by various authorities, different types of health information, speculation about prevention and treatment, a flurry of statistics, in addition to rumours and numerous conspiracy theories and purposefully spread, potentially harmful content. We also encountered tweets by concerned citizens and Facebook updates with interpretations of information they had read, as well as TikToks from all around the world about life under lockdown. Datasets from different countries and international organisations were made available. Soon, anyone with an internet connection and a spreadsheet program could act as an amateur epidemiologist, seemingly without any need for a contextual understanding of the production of data. Information on this new disease and the virus causing it was everywhere. The various strategies different countries chose, as well as the responses to them, came to be considered not merely through the lenses of epidemiology and public health, or even international relations and policymaking, but also as symbols of ideological or even national identity. Counting and comparing the number of cases, ICU admissions, and even the death toll across different countries developed into a competitive sport, a cynical new activity for some to engage in when all else was shut down.

This book is not about COVID-19, but many information challenges became acutely apparent in the wake of this pandemic. These are brought together with examples from other areas and used to locate what we propose to call an ongoing crisis of information in contemporary society. This crisis, we argue, is characterised by a volatility of information that manifests differently across various domains, but which

DOI: 10.4324/9781003163237-1

taken together presents a number of challenges to the precariously balanced networks of institutions, knowledge systems, and practices that have traditionally – but of course, imperfectly – constituted democracies in the West. Much is to be said, and has been said, about this crisis, and there are diverse disciplinary contributions to be made to the analysis and understanding of it. Our contribution to this conversation is a modest one, but one which we hope adds a unique dimension. We focus our attention on one specific attempt at containing this crisis of information, namely media and information literacy, a multifaceted and malleable concept whose plasticity makes it an ideal device for interrogating the current information landscape. It appears in different guises in various fields, and – as we will explore in due course – it is loaded with different, often contradictory values, norms, and ideals. At the most basic level, what unites the otherwise profoundly different understandings of media and information literacy is the assumption that certain understandings, competences and resources enable people to proficiently engage with information and media and that these are involved in arranging an individual's relation to society.

Clearly, in many ways, this is a valid assumption. At the same time, information in contemporary society is characterised by great instability, carrying with it an increasingly profound uncertainty regarding the control over public knowledge. Where does this leave us? We want to bring to the fore effects and manifestations of this volatility. This crisis of information has many shapes, forms, and facets, but through the prism of media and information literacy we can identify a number of information-related challenges that constitute this situation. These include fragmentation, individualisation, emotionalisation, and the erosion of the collective basis for trust, all with implications for not just the individual, but also for democracy, and ultimately the organisation of society. We will provide some clarification on our use of these concepts in the next section. Of course, different aspects of the state of information in contemporary society have been studied, argued over, and theorised in myriad ways, from different disciplinary, political, legal, or economic perspectives. The flow of publications is unlikely to ebb any time soon. This is an expression of the urgency of the concern being felt; an urgency that is amplified by the realisation that the crisis of information cannot be divorced from its social and experiential foundations and effects: it is thus – simultaneously a health crisis, a climate crisis, a crisis of trust, a crisis of democracy and participation, and even a crisis of the future.

The crisis of information

Does alcohol protect you against a virus?

The English-language Wikipedia article now named "COVID-19 misinformation" has a version history going back to early February 2020, a good month before the World Health Organisation (WHO) even declared the outbreak of a pandemic (Wikipedia 9-9-2021). Since then, the article has grown long and rich in content, and similar articles exist in over 30 other languages on Wikipedia. It includes well-known and widespread conspiracy theories such as that the spread of the virus is caused by electromagnetic fields from 5G mobile networks, or less popular ones such as the idea that the virus arrived in the Wuhan region of China with a meteorite.

The article also contains a section on the misinformation that drinking pure alcohol supposedly protects people against the virus. This false claim has led to the deaths of hundreds in Iran as a result of drinking methanol (Islam et al., 2020). CNN reports how the former US President Donald Trump alone made 654 false claims about the virus in just 14 weeks during spring 2020 (Dale and Subramaniam, 2020). Some of the false information circulating about the virus is easy to debunk; for example, the danger of 5G mobile communications masts, an idea that has resulted in sabotage of such masts and threats against people working with the network. The idea that cocaine use can prevent COVID-19 was so widely spread at one point that the French Ministry of Health found itself officially disparaging the claim. Other theories or false claims arise from a lack of context. This complicates comparison between different countries and leads to certain explanations or statements changing their meaning when transferred from one country or context to another. Some theories are based on unsubstantiated correlation, while yet others might even start from actual science-based observations which are then interpreted and developed further in ways that are unsupported by the scientific study in question. What Wikipedia's taxonomy of COVID-19 misinformation and similar taxonomies show is less how many and which different types of misinformation and conspiracy theories exist about COVID-19, but rather that what we call misinformation is by no means a homogenous entity, neither are so-called conspiracy theories. We will return to this important point in due course.

Before the WHO classified the outbreak of the then-novel coronavirus as a pandemic and even before said virus and the disease it causes had been assigned their official names, SARS-CoV-2 and COVID-19, the organisation issued a warning about the new coronavirus being "accompanied by a massive 'infodemic'" (WHO, 2020). This, they explained, is "an over-abundance of information-some accurate and some not-that makes it hard for people to find trustworthy sources and reliable guidance when they need it" (ibid.). Since then, talk of an infodemic has joined the older image of information overload (Bawden and Robinson, 2020) in public debate and media reporting. Infodemic makes for a powerful metaphor, yet it invites problematic oversimplification of a complex social phenomenon by biologising it (Simon and Camargo, 2021). The image fuses well with already established analogies and images, such as those of computer viruses and memes or other content going viral on social media, and engenders new ones, including the notion that people can inoculate themselves against fact resistance, that psychological vaccinations are possible, or that so-called 'fake news' can be stopped by creating herd immunity to it. The term "fake news", in particular, has come to be used by politicians and other public persons to describe news they reject or discredit positions they disagree with. It is in the current debate best understood as a "floating signifier", as Farkas and Schou (2018) suggest, which is also why we refrain from using the notion as an analytical concept.

That said, if acted on, certain types of incorrect health information can be directly lethal. For example, the American Center for Disease Control (CDC) reported deaths that had resulted from people drinking hand sanitiser in attempts to treat or prevent COVID-19. Drinking urine, on the other hand, may not be lethal or even dangerous by itself, but using it to treat COVID-19 can still set in motion chains of events leading to deadly outcomes and add to an already ongoing destabilisation of trust in healthcare professions and government institutions more broadly (Islam et al., 2020).

Crisis, co-constitution, and digital culture

Paradoxes of Media and Information Literacy: The Crisis of Information is a book about media and information literacy in digital culture. The word *crisis* marks a turning point, and in its original Greek meaning it denotes the turning point in a disease. While we want to be careful not to simplify complex, multi-layered social phenomena using poorly understood medical metaphors, there is a certain appeal in describing the extreme volatility of information that characterises contemporary society as just that: a crisis and a potential turning point. The appeal lies in the way that crisis, in such an understanding, conjures up the possibility of hope on the one hand, but also leaves open the possibility of different outcomes on the other. And further, that it is not a sudden event that comes out of nowhere, but one that has multiple causes, different developments and, regardless of how it unfolds, inevitably leaves traces or even scars, and opens up new paths. The crisis of information cuts through numerous social arrangements and reveals (and also challenges) their interdependence in new and profound ways. In the process, many taken-for-granted assumptions – not only about what counts as information, but also about how information should be produced, questioned, organised, and sustained – are being challenged. But what are the most tangible facets of this crisis, and how can they be traced out for our exploration of media and information literacy?

During the COVID-19 pandemic, the increased volatility of information has become ever more palpable. Rumours, governmental information, research reports, pre-prints, policy documents, official statistics, research data, journal articles, and conspiracy theories, all amalgamate on the same platforms, detached from their original context and imbued with different meanings. Often, it is near impossible to confidently establish the origin or status of the fast-changing, continuously updated information that is aggregated in social media feeds, in search engine results, or even in spreadsheets. Fragmentation describes how a complex body of knowledge is arranged into a continuously shifting shape provided by networks of ever fewer corporate information platforms. Not only is information becoming more fragmented, but access to information is also becoming more individualised, depending on, for example, who you are, who you follow, and who you interact with. The extent of personalisations and their societal effects are invisible to the individual user. Nobody knows for sure what others encounter, which unique combination of apps, search engines, and social media make up other people's information ecosystem, how they arrive at which terms to enter into which search engine, or how the feed will recon-figure itself in the next reload, in response to the next swipe, after the next search or engagement. Positioning the fragmentation of information at the level of experience highlights how intimately the ongoing fragmentation of the collective understanding of society's knowledge base relates to the information infrastructure within which everything from everyday life to politics plays out. Both the foundations of trust and the possibilities for the creation of shared meaning are called into question.

This points to a number of interrelated challenges that contribute to the desta-bilisation of information – fragmentation, individualisation, emotionalisation, and the erosion of the collective basis for trust – all of which are, clearly not created, yet exacerbated by society's commercial, algorithmic information infrastructure, and a qualitatively new form of politicisation of information, where information is increas-ingly tailored to the form provided by multi-sided platforms and their specific logic of amplification. The importance of algorithms, user data, and increasingly AI-based systems for contemporary culture, more specifically for multi-sided platforms such as search engines, recommender systems, intelligent household assistants, streaming services, or dating apps, cannot be overstated. It is becoming increasingly important to understand how algorithmic systems work and how they are trained to perform in specific situations, while at the same time they are becoming ever more elusive and embedded in society and everyday life at all levels. One way to approach this is to use the term "digital culture", not as a historical period with a clear definition at the expense of other understandings of culture and society, but as a perspective that allows us to foreground the prevalence of certain socialities and ways of knowing and being in the world that are embedded in the organisation of society at differ-ent levels. To borrow from media researcher Ted Striphas, "algorithmic culture" is one where "human beings have been delegating the work of culture – the sorting, classifying and hierarchizing of people, places, objects and ideas – to data-intensive computational processes" (Striphas, 2015, p. 396; see also Lloyd, 2019). Digital cul-ture as a perspective takes this into account, but also how algorithms, along with the platforms in which they are embedded, and the data extracted from users, exist within wider rationalities and programmes of social change (see also Beer, 2017).

Like all knowledge organisation and information systems, multi-sided platforms, algorithms, and data are always contingent and never impartial. In other words, algo-rithmic configurations, and multi-sided platforms are active and co-constitutive of the wider social fabric. Co-constitutive implies not only that this is not a one-way relation, but also that people, society, algorithms, data, platforms, regulators and so on are all constitutive of each other (Barad, 2003; 2007; Orlikowski and Scott, 2015). For the purpose of understanding society from the vantage point of digital culture, they cannot be meaningfully separated. People create meaning from platforms and algorithms in the various practices they are involved in, but they also resist them in more or less consequential ways. Platforms and their algorithms not just influ-ence people in one direction, but through their interactions with these systems people also change them. Fragmentation, individualisation, and emotionalisation are integral to how commercial algorithmic information systems operate, at least in the sense that the categorisations applied to cluster, target, and extract data from people is intentionally invisible to those subjected to it. Trust in public knowledge, on the other hand, requires collectively shared and societally accepted methods for producing, challenging, and vetting knowledge, which fragmentation obscures and undercuts.

Facts and opinions

In a seminal text published in *The New Yorker* in the 1960s, Philosopher Hanna Arendt describes how "factual truth, if it happens to oppose a given group's profit or pleasure, is greeted today with greater hostility than ever before" (Arendt, 2000[1967], p. 552). As a result, she maintains, facts are often ideologised, and this way turned into opinions, or to use a contemporary term, into "alternative facts", a notion popularised by Donald Trump's former senior counsellor. These opinions can then be legitimately disagreed upon. Therefore, the strategic blurring of the line between facts and opinions is a political move that makes sense. It allows the transformation of facts into opinion, which can then be represented as negotiable information and circulated in ways that are easily scaled up and politicised. In Arendt's words, "[u]nwelcome opinion can be argued with, rejected, or compromised upon, but unwelcome facts possess an infuriating stubbornness that nothing can move except plain lies" (Arendt, 2000 [1967], p. 556). Opinions are not only easier to dispute; such dispute is legitimate and expected in political deliberation (Davies, 2018, p. 159–165). Opinions cannot be deemed true or false; they can only be more or less popular, more or less shared between people or groups.

While not originating it, the commercial logic of algorithmic information systems certainly contributes to escalating the strategic transformation of facts into opinions, and thus of what can be called the networked mass production of the tactical politicisation of facts. Donald Trump, whose presidency coincided with the start of the COVID-19 pandemic, has become the epitome of this move. Everything became a matter of opinion, or at least ambiguous, and thus, also easily dismissible by others: climate change, sexual integrity, medical treatments, and so on. However, when Trump attempted to delegitimise the result of the 2020 presidential election, he went further. The legitimately vetted numbers that confirmed him losing the US presidential election were not only challenged in the way intended by the system, which they also were, but more importantly they were transformed to support a different fact, namely the 'fact' of vast fraud and conspiracy. Only then, the accuracy of the voting results could be questioned, and a new fact could be established through its circulation and repetition in various social media. This lie – at odds with all empirical evidence – was so difficult to uphold, that, to borrow Arendt's words, expressed more than 50 years earlier:

> if the modern political lies are so big that they require a complete rearrangement of the whole factual texture – to the making of another reality, as it were, into which they will fit without seam, crack, or fissure, exactly as the

facts fitted into their own original context – what prevents these new stories, images, and non-facts from becoming an adequate substitute for reality and factuality?

Arendt, 2000 [1967], p. 566

The presidency of Donald Trump – covered in detail, as US politics often are, by media across the globe – made this rearrangement of the *factual texture* more visible and tangible. It became a part of political commentary in the media and in everyday life. Lies and semi-lies, or alternative facts and ambiguities, were constantly cabled out through social media, in particular Twitter. There, at the end of his four years as US president and before he was banned from the platform, Trump's account had almost 90 million followers. Professional journalists with their ethos to "seek truth and report it" (Society of Professional Journalists, n.d.) found themselves passing on tweets and commenting their outrageousness.

The 45th president of the United States is definitely not the only person to have politicised facts in this way, and the USA is not the only country where this occurs. Yet, US politics have global reach and ramifications that are normative beyond their national borders. Many other examples, and this list could be made very long, can be identified, regarding issues such as climate science and the politics of climate change, reproductive and sexual health, structural discrimination of historically oppressed and excluded communities, public health responses to diseases, and how slave trade, colonisation, the Holocaust, and other genocides are presented and also questioned. Today's platformised information infrastructure – such as it exists through social media, search engines, or various recommender systems – tends to increase and scale up this politicising of information through algorithmic reinforcement, allowing for amplification of content that attracts emotions, engagement, and, not least, habitual enragement. This in itself does not necessarily imply that only lies or counter-factual information have this effect. Evidently, this is not always the case and the use of social media platforms for organising in productive, community-building ways, clearly also happens, yet we argue that this happens despite, not because of the means for interaction these services provide.

Still, it has been shown that social media have, as for instance media studies researcher Richard Rogers (2021) suggests, a tendency to systematically marginalise the mainstream and mainstream the marginal. The prevailing rationale shaping society's dominant information infrastructures is guided by market principles on almost all levels. As this increasingly applies to all types of information and forms of knowledge, it has far-reaching implications for how information is produced, judged, and vetted in the first place. Political economist William Davies (2018) makes the connection to neoliberal economic theorist and Noble prize winner (1974) Friedrich Hayek who, in a move away from the enlightenment understanding of knowledge and expertise, suggested that the credibility and trustworthiness of knowledge should be tested against consumers, and not against any internal scientific criteria. In such a perspective, Davies sums up, "[i]deas and knowledge should only be deemed trustworthy if they were tested in a competitive arena" (Davies, 2018, p. 163).

This view on how to establish what constitutes trustworthy knowledge, while at odds with the traditional values of civic debate and libraries (Tanner and Andersen, 2018), chimes well with how the algorithms of, for instance, social media platforms, search engines, recommender systems or rating sites work.

To simplify somewhat, the leading principle for visibility and reach of social media, recommender systems, and search engines is popularity. Further dimensions are involved, yet since monetisation through both data extraction and the placing of adverts depends on achieving high levels of exposure and interaction, it makes sense to assign weight to popularity. While visibility does not necessarily directly translate into trustworthiness, as its equivalent, the intimate association between the two factors still establishes what may be called a *trustworthiness chimaera*. This trustworthiness chimaera underlies a number of contradictions in media and information literacy expressions. Specifically, corroboration of information by establishing whether it is widely spread or just reported by one source is one of the basic recommendations for how to establish the credibility of a statement. Yet, if visibility is primarily and intentionally created for other reasons, the validity of the strategy of corroborating information by establishing how widely spread a claim is, if not entirely invalidated, at least compromised.

Visibility in social media is contingent on interactions and or engagements. Albeit slightly differently, this principle also applies to search engines. In a comparison between public agency websites and websites that repeatedly spread misinformation, the latter were shown to attract several times as many interactions as those of the WHO, the European Centre for Disease Control (ECDC) and the American Center for Disease Control (CDC) (Avaaz, 2020). Using the language of epidemiology, the same study identifies 42 "superspreaders" of misinformation on Facebook. It appears that misinformation and conspiracy theories are generally better suited to the creation of interactions, or at least they are more effectively produced and adapted for the purpose of creating interaction. Read with Hayek, as Davies does in his analysis, these can be said to fare better at the *market of ideas*. Yet, as Davies also remarks, there are ramifications to such an understanding, since here "markets are not so much tools for producing facts but for gauging our feelings" (Davies, 2018, p. 167). The emotionalisation of information, which we identify as an important facet of the crisis of information, needs to be understood through this idea of markets as shaping the value of information and knowledge, positioning them against each other. The means for gauging facts, trustworthiness, and credibility – which is precisely what media and information literacy is usually regarded as – are increasingly put to work on a terrain of feelings and, we should add, of ambiguities. In the course, they are being rendered increasingly ineffective and dysfunctional. This is intensified by what sociologist Noortje Marres (2018, p. 433) calls "a crisis of public evidence" and the "truth-less" (p. 435) character of social media, which produce knowledge primarily for data engineers to optimise the various models needed to monetise content and users of these platforms. Thus, she points out, "[d]igitization is challenging not just the status of facts in public discourse, it is undermining institutional architectures that ground accountability in empirical evidence across societal domains" (Marres, 2018, p. 343).

Erosion of trust

The ongoing fragmentation, individualisation, and emotionalisation of information in society need to be understood through a further development constitutive of the crisis of information, namely the erosion of the collective basis for trust. Indeed, their significance becomes even more tangible, when seen through the prism of trust or lack thereof. In the literature and social commentary more broadly, it has become commonplace to diagnose a decrease in trust in traditional knowledge institutions and intermediaries (Kavanagh and Rich, 2018). This is backed up by various national and transnational statistical reports, measuring the populations of different countries and regions concerning their trust in a selection of societal institutions, including the police, media, lawmakers and politicians, banks, healthcare providers, the military, universities, researchers, and so on. Generally, in these surveys, the level of measurable trust in institutions is shown to be in decline in most of the world, with implications across all domains, from business to banking, healthcare, and rule of law. The *Edelman Trust Barometer* introduce for example its 2021 report with:

> After a year of unprecedented disaster and turbulence – the Covid-19 pandemic and economic crisis, the global outcry over systemic racism and political instability – the 2021 Edelman Trust Barometer reveals an epidemic of misinformation and widespread mistrust of societal institutions and leaders around the world. Adding to this is a failing trust ecosystem unable to confront the rampant infodemic, leaving the four institutions – business, government, NGOs, and media – in an environment of information bankruptcy and a mandate to rebuild trust and chart a new path forward.
>
> *Edelman, 2021*

Despite this trend, there is great variation across and between different groups and countries. Since trust in institutions or processes and the way in which trust is manifested varies, the decrease in trust will also vary; not least in its effects. That said, the domain of knowledge is folded into other areas, and it is one that is constituted through trust at the most fundamental level. As trust is involved in processes of knowledge-making and vetting of information, knowledge cannot exist without it.

Trust, according to historian of science Steven Shapin (1994, p. xxv) can be conceptualised as the moral relation that the possibility of knowledge and knowing presupposes. Trust is thus, as he phrases it, central to "the building and maintaining of social order", and also to "building and maintaining cognitive order" (ibid.). Without trust, society is impossible. In a society, we need to – at least to some extent – rely on the testimony of others. "Knowledge is a collective good", writes Shapin (ibid.) in the same text, which makes its existence impossible without a general level of trust. The crisis of information is a crisis of this collective trust, of its actual manifestation, which of course is always imperfect, biased and contingent, and in constant need of re-examination, but, more importantly, of the very idea of its possibility and moral necessity.

How is media and information literacy imagined to have this unique power in responding to the crisis of information? Is media and information literacy even possible in an age of largely invisible algorithms and increasingly invisible information systems? These two questions are the points of departure for the journey this book embarks on. Posing them throws into sharp relief several paradoxes that are built into common understandings of media and information literacy and whose identification, in turn, helps to shed light on how the informational volatility that is characteristic of contemporary society and which we have come to call the crisis of information, is constituted. This serves as a basis for an examination of media and information literacy itself, assumptions about it, and for reflection on how the crisis of information is constituted through one of its most prominent and perhaps most widely agreed-upon solutions.

Media and information literacy

So far, we have talked about media and information literacy as a compound comprising two parts. Yet, while media literacy is generally well established and known outside its field of origin, this is not to the same extent the case for information literacy – a term that goes back to the 1960s and 1970s (Tuominen et al., 2005). Neither the problems information literacy orients itself towards nor the concept as such have reached the same level of prominence as media literacy has outside its own disciplinary and professional field. Therefore, when media and information literacy appears as a joint concept, the media part tends to dominate in both policy (Berger, 2019, p. 25) and research (Livingstone et al., 2008). This book foregrounds the rich and important tradition of information literacy research and the professional practices tied up in the concept, in order to address this imbalance. This, we argue, adds a necessary dimension to media and information literacy that is central to an understanding of the materiality of society's information infrastructure and the ways in which its control is challenged. That said, while our disciplinary origin gives priority to information literacy, we put it in relation to media literacy research and research on related concepts, such as digital literacy or data literacy.

To some extent, media and information literacy research can be understood in the context of literacy research without a prefix. While we recognise that this glosses over a number of complex issues, it helps to think of literacy research as very roughly divided into two theoretical groups (Street, 1984). On the one hand, there are those where literacy is considered as an independent, often measurable competence or skill that leads to social progress, and on the other hand, approaches that understand literacy (or rather literacies) as embedded in the myriads of practices making up everyday life. Leading theoretician of new literacy studies Brian Street (1984) famously describes these two ways of approaching literacy as the *autonomous* and the *sociocultural* traditions. We return to this discussion in Chapter 3, but for now, let us take an initial positioning in relation to these two traditions. In the broadest sense, in terms of Street's distinction, we place ourselves in the sociocultural tradition. Media and information literacy is much more than acquiring proficiency in the use of certain technologies, as many of the examples and arguments we will address later in this book will show.

The relationship between media and information literacy and progress is complicated, to say the least, which we discuss in more detail in the following chapters. Yet, at the policy level, media and information literacy is often seen as a tool for a mostly linear form of imagined progress, as in the autonomous approach. In fact, the internet as such, and later especially social media, were seen as drivers of democratisation at one point. More recently, search engines, social media, recommender systems, and other similar platform services, which make up a large part of our current information infrastructure, are instead increasingly seen as a major threat to democracy. We would therefore like to emphasise once more that the crisis of information must be seen in the context of other intertwined crises, including environmental, social and political crises.

In a narrower sense, we are informed by a sociomaterial understanding of media and information literacy that foregrounds the inseparable intertwining of the social, the discursive and the material (Barad, 2003, 2007; Orlikowski and Scott, 2015). This means that media and information literacy in its various forms cannot be understood as standing outside infrastructural arrangements, but is integrated into them. Media and information literacy, in other words, is materially and discursively intrinsic to our information infrastructure, but so are the major corporate internet platforms, the public sector, governments or international organisations and their sometimes conflicting and sometimes overlapping interests. Furthermore, we consider literacies in the plural and recognise the need for literacies to be contextually and situationally understood in relation to people's habitual doings and ways of being in and through society. For sure, the emergence of literacies must be related to norms and power structures in relation to how information is sought, valued, used, created, and communicated differently in different practices and how media is assigned meaning. Nevertheless, and we return to this discussion throughout, a situated understanding of media and information literacy entails several challenges, in terms of the conditions for stabilising public knowledge, that need to be acknowledged.

Since we are interested in deepening the understanding of media and information literacy by strengthening the position of information literacy in the composite, we need to provide some guideposts as to what this entails. Defining information literacy at this point would go against the intention to map and understand paradoxes in how it is constructed, used, and assigned meaning. Instead, we start by providing an outline of the purpose of information literacy in the most general of terms. Its purpose can broadly be described as supporting people's knowledge, competencies and resources in order to enable their proficient engagement with information, including finding, evaluating, producing, and communicating situated information in context-appropriate ways. In the educational sciences, literacy is a conceptual entity and as such, it is often delimited with appropriate qualifiers to establish a theoretical perspective. Information literacy on the other hand (and the same goes for media literacy) only specifies an entity, e.g. media or information, but also data, digital, or artificial intelligence (AI), for literacy to latch onto. This way theoretical and also professional discussions are obscured, or at least they are moved into the background. In Chapter 3, we attempt to make some of those theoretical discussions visible in order to examine how they might inform an understanding of media and information literacy operational for contemporary digital culture.

The specific contribution we claim information literacy research makes to media and information literacy can be understood through its origin in library and information science and specifically the field of librarianship. Through this, information literacy brings with it a focus on information infrastructures that differs from media literacy, and also from the educational sciences. In information literacy, at least as a professional practice, materialities of information, which libraries, after all, deal with, are foundational to the notion. The organisation and enabling of access to knowledge in its material form are, if we boil it down, the most basic responsibilities of libraries and other memory institutions. Thus, information literacy, in our understanding, derives from a notion of information, as epistemologically, ontologically, and axiologically constituted in and through different infrastructural arrangements. It can thus be argued that information in information literacy, since it is concerned with knowledge as it is materially arranged across and through society and its institutions, is fundamentally and literally – but of course not necessarily theoretically – sociomaterial. That being said, it is clear that this interest in the materiality of information infrastructures, much of which stems from professional practice, is by no means present in all information literacy research. Nonetheless, it is primarily this strand of information literacy that we present in the following and which we also develop further.

Of course, media literacy also takes materiality into account, but while information literacy is oriented towards the infrastructure of information, media literacy focuses on the media themselves - production, circulation, access and meaning - often from a critical perspective. Information literacy research can constitute an analytical glue for understanding how media and user data circulate in a culture whose sociality is increasingly shaped by algorithmic, mostly commercial information systems. Media literacy research, on the other hand, has the potential to contribute by strengthening critical awareness in the tradition of information literacy. The rise of media literacy as curriculum content began in the late 1970s (Bulger and Davison, 2018). This can be compared to a similar development in information literacy in the late 1990s, when libraries and library organisations began to develop information literacy programmes and set standards (Tuominen et al., 2005). Prior to this, although the term information literacy can be traced back to the 1960s and gained wider recognition in the 1980s, conceptual and instructional development was limited (ibid.).

This book does not intend to cover the emergence or the whole breadth of either media literacy or information literacy. This is, of course, a limitation of the book, but a limitation of our own choosing. So much is written under the conceptual umbrella of information literacy, media literacy, and other similar notions. Instead, we focus on how it is imagined that media and information literacy can respond to the crisis of information in a digital culture permeated by largely invisible algorithms and information systems. Such an interest implies a focus on searching information and the evaluation of information and information sources.

The change from the early systems of writing that can be traced back about 6,000 years to today's digitally infused world has been profound (Barton and Hamilton, 1999). Over the centuries writing technologies have changed and so has our understanding of what it means to be and to become literate. At the most basic level, the absence of literacy, illiteracy, indicates someone in need of learning something. In recent times, there has been a tendency to define a domain for this by prefixing literacy with a word such as media, information, data, digital, to name but a few. The myriad types of literacies constituting different aspects of contemporary life have been described and classified many times (Bawden, 2008). Yet, in many contexts, they appear to be used interchangeably. UNESCO's 2021 MIL Curriculum and Competency Framework, for example, media and information literacy comprises media literacy, information literacy and also digital literacy (Grizzle et al., 2021, p. 8). Yet, even though media literacy, information literacy and also digital literacy have different roots and are associated with different professional as well as academic communities, they are often used to describe the same phenomena and are presented as responses to roughly the same concerns. More recently, we can also see a growing interest in data literacy and, even more specifically, algorithmic or algorithm literacy and AI literacy. In fact, the various concepts compete with each other for policy space, media attention and promotion in the political landscape, and not least for visibility in the educational sector. What unites the various types of literacies floating around in different domains is their shared reference to coding and decoding symbolic representations, including of course, but also beyond, writing systems and the written word. While this depiction is undeniably oversimplified, it helps to bring one of the major difficulties of the concept to the fore. Who decides what should be learned and for what reason? What are the important skills, competencies, and resources that make a person literate in a given domain?

When former welfare societies, as many European nations were, and their institutions retreat or are made to withdraw, private solutions step into the vacated spaces. The education and training of people to act as consumers in this newly established market can be seen as compensating for the absent state. In this case, literacies become instrumental to meet the needs of the market, often in relation to a personal deficiency that can be addressed through the education and training of individuals. People need to be *digitally* literate to be able to choose an internet provider or a phone company. They need to be *financially* literate to plan investments for their retirement. They need to be *health* literate to choose the right solution for their health needs and reduce the costs to the public health sector, *media* literate to understand the power relations in the media sector, and *information* literate to avoid falling for conspiracy theories and religious or political extremism. One way to understand this development is through the notion of *responsibilisation*, a broader trend in society that is often described as a process that can be seen as closely linked to neoliberal or late-liberal political discourse (Juhila and Raitakari, 2016). We return to this concept and how media and information literacy can be understood through the lens it offers in Chapter 2.

In recent decades, media and information literacy – often referred to as MIL – as an approach to enabling what can loosely be called critical engagement with media and information in digital settings has been promoted by public authorities, by international bodies such as the European Union, UNESCO and The International Federation of Library Associations and Institutions (IFLA), and in many countries also by professional groups including teachers, librarians, and journalists. This is done in relation to a very different information infrastructure than the ones that existed when the compound's two parts were first devised. Acute awareness of the entwinement of social and material, including political, economic, and technical aspects of society's algorithmic information infrastructure, is beginning to shape not just research on, but also policy-level and certainly professional engagement with, media and information literacy. Yet, while all this might sound self-evident, its manifestations, assumptions, and thus its normative effects are far from uncomplicated. Rather, the manifestations, assumptions, and normative effects of media and information literacy are imbued with several paradoxes, which need to be considered in close relation to the crisis of information.

Paradoxes

A leading principle of this book is the notion that any understanding of media and information literacy must be developed in relation to contestations over knowledge and ignorance, and over information access and control. Different national and international actors, governmental and non-governmental alike, various professional organisations and also commercial players posit media and information literacy and similar approaches as responses to the situation by enabling people to assess the credibility and trustworthiness of different claims. Yet, the case for media and information literacy is made in contradictory ways advancing different goals or based on different and sometimes problematic assumptions about the opportunities for critical engagement within society's commercial, algorithmic information infrastructure. These tensions can be made tangible by teasing out contradictory expressions and opposing claims about the central premises of media and information literacy and by positioning those as paradoxes. We believe that framing the various contradictions and self-contradictions forming around media and information literacy as paradoxes that need to be understood rather than resolved helps to unpack the crisis of information by foregrounding some of the different interests involved in attempting to solve it. Whether it is information literacy, media literacy, digital literacy, or some other similar literacy, there is much hope that it has the potential to contain the worst upshots of the crisis of information. Moreover, it is part of the grand narrative of individual choice and personal responsibility that characterises contemporary societies, as they are seen as consisting of rational actors acting in their own best interests. In some ways, this is a convenient idea, as it does not challenge the capitalist premises of the information society, as state regulations of the large and near-monopolistic international corporations such as Google, Apple, Facebook, Amazon (GAFA) and their numerous platforms would (Buckingham, 2019).

Yet, while it is a way that is easy to talk about and to agree on, implementing it is far from straightforward. How do you *make* people, the entire population, media and information literate? How do you even agree on what it should entail? As this book circles back to throughout, media and information literacy and its conceptual siblings can be many different things depending on who is doing the talking. It can be a basis for lifelong learning in capitalist society and thus a premise for a competent, flexible, and employable workforce in a rapidly changing work life. With such focus, media and information literacy primarily concerns competencies and skills. However, media and information literacy can also be devised as the basis for a democratic society in which all citizens can participate (Carlsson, 2019). Such an interpretation of media and information literacy broadens the focus to include power-sensitive perspectives on information and media and the understanding that enabling awareness and critical questioning is more important than acquiring technical skills.

Democracy is the stated rationale for much of the practice, policy, and to some extent, research in media and information literacy. Yet, many times the tying together of media and information literacy with democracy appears as little more than a dutiful nod and lacks a deeper understanding of the ways in which democracy is far from a singular, straightforward idea, or even stable across time. This demands some clarification of our own position. At a general level, we hold to a broad understanding of deliberative democracy which foregrounds the importance of debate, participation, and communication for the formation of opinions, values, and decision-making. We seek to carefully balance a consensualist position with a pluralist one (Martí, 2017). On the one hand, we accept that access to reliable and trustworthy information in society is premised on a consensus on certain procedures and mechanisms in relation to the institutions involved in knowledge production and that this ultimately forms a basis of deliberative democracy. On the other hand, we also take our cue from the critique of the ideal of consensualist deliberative democracy, such as those voiced by Chantal Mouffe (Mouffe, 2000). Specifically, we subscribe to the notion that pluralism is better suited to foreground the at times incommensurable moral values of political positions (see also Rivano Eckerdal, 2017; Farkas and Schou, 2019). Thus, the notion of the rational citizen and the ideal of neutrality, both emblematic of enlightened liberalism and central to some consensualist approaches are problematised throughout the book. The criticism does not refer to their specific values, but to the unsubstantiated position assigned to them in justifying certain expressions of media and information literacy. In particular, their manifestation in the material-discursive arrangements and the socio-economic climate, in which democratic ideals are embedded, increasingly appear untenable and provide the undertone for at least some of the paradoxical relationships that shape media and information literacy.

The differing and at time conflicting views on the goals of media and information literacy are not just abstract constructs. Rather, we believe that they are performatively engaged in the way media and information literacy plays out in society and are thus implicated in shaping the crisis of information. This understanding differs from the way media and information literacy is usually viewed, namely as a means for individuals to navigate this crisis or for society to manage and contain it.

Of course, navigating and managing the crisis of information are important and worthwhile goals. However, we argue that media and information literacy is also – and profoundly – caught up in the emergence and development of the crisis itself. The implications of assuming such a perspective cannot be overstated, since it affects where literacies can be imagined to intervene, and consequently what interventions can achieve. Given that more and more of the information we encounter is pre-selected through invisible algorithms based on constantly changing rules, and information systems are increasingly vanishing into the background of everyday life, seeing opportunities for media and information literacy to latch onto in the first place is a major challenge. We propose an examination of ruptures and contradictions as a productive way to spot these. To return to the most basic questions we are grappling with in this book: How is it imagined that media and information literacy can play a role in addressing the crisis of information? How is media and information literacy possible in an age of increasingly ubiquitous information systems based on invisible algorithms, and premised on data extraction and market logic? While it is not our aim to provide a conclusive answer to these questions, there is still value in asking them. They help us to formulate a series of analytical questions to chart the various contradictions at play and by outlining the main fault lines, we hope to highlight possibilities for intervention.

We zoom in on five zones constituted by sets of contradictions: (i) responsibility; (ii) normativity; (iii) temporality; (iv) trust; and (v) neutrality. We interrogate those as folded into the platformised, algorithmic information infrastructure, and its specific affordances for information control and information access. A *responsibility paradox* puts the spotlight on how responsibility is located in relation to media and information literacy, and thus agency, to individual citizens, and their way of handling the volatility of information. We argue that a schism exists between information consumers and rational citizens, two discursively conflicting ideals as to how responsibility should be enacted in media and information literacy. A *normativity paradox* reveals a conflict between theoretical notions, drawing on the importance of practice or context, of media and information literacy that underlines a plurality of media and information literacies and a normative understanding in which media and information literacy is supposed to advance democratic participation in society. A *temporal paradox* concerns how media and information literacy functions as a site for anticipation in the sense that being media and information literate involves anticipating future information flows at the same time as training for media and information literacy often concerns timeworn technologies, just as research on media and information literacy most often has a retrospect methodological focus on what has happened. A *trust paradox* of media and information literacy takes aim at the fact that media and information literacy for empowering peoples' awareness to some extent carries with it a certain, necessary mistrust. You are supposed to question what you read, what you hear and what you see, but this questioning also runs the risk of becoming cynical and nihilistic, to the point of undermining the establishment of a position from which contradicting knowledge claims can be judged. Finally, a *neutrality paradox* deepens the trust paradox and focuses on the problematic assumption that media and information literacy has an inherent, unbiased, empowering effect that is assumed to work in the interest of democracy and participation. In fact, media and information literacy can be used for purposes that are exactly the opposite of the goals of many media and information literacy initiatives: namely, to sow doubt and destabilise the sites and mechanisms of democratic accountability.

Facing up to the multiple contradictions inherent in the notion of media and information literacy opens up a way to explore society's crisis of information, and vice versa. This, we argue, is a prerequisite for operationalising critical engagements with information, knowledge and ultimately society at large and for opening up spaces to act within the confines of a platformised, commercial information infrastructure, and importantly also for moving towards transforming these.

A note on methods and material

Our aim is to advance the analytical discussion of media and information literacy research by interweaving theoretical and conceptual reflections with discussions of a diverse empirical material. To support this aim, we draw on an empirical material created principally within the research project *Algorithms and Literacies: Young People's Understanding and Society's Expectations* (funded by the Swedish Research Council, 2017–03631). As the project title suggests, we not only explored young peoples' understanding of the issue, but also how certain societal expectations and interests are invested in advancing particular conceptions of media and information literacies.

During spring of 2019, we spoke with more than 60 young people in their late teens (17–19) in pair interviews (Polak and Green, 2016; for details, see Haider and Sundin, 2020, 2021). Most interviews, which followed a flexible, semi-structured guide, took place in Sweden, but a small number were also carried out in Denmark. There are methodological challenges involved in initiating and sustaining conversations with people about something that is invisible to all involved, such as the concept of algorithms which was a main topic in the interviews, and which mostly lack a vocabulary for discussion. We tried to navigate this challenge by talking mostly about the effects of algorithms in social media, search engines and recommender services, rather than algorithms per se. The project generated many hours of conversations with and between young people about their experiences, understandings, and expectations of interacting with algorithms in different services and platforms. In particular Chapters 2 and 4 draw on and explore this material.

The pair interviews supported our aim of studying young peoples' understanding of algorithms and their effects. Yet, a different type of material was needed to explore society's expectations. For this purpose, we aimed to create a diverse material, that allowed us firstly to employ an explorative approach, and secondly to couch the personal accounts gathered in the interviews in the wider narrative of the unfolding crisis of information. During 2019, 2020, and parts of 2021, we compiled and analysed data collected from Twitter, by means of searches in Google Search, Google Trends, and YouTube, and examples from national and international media, curricula and policy reports, to understand how media and information literacy is talked about, and by whom. Some of this material has a Swedish context, while other material is from other national settings, or presents a more international outlook. Many of the examples drawn on are from US or UK online and legacy media and policy documents, as well from a range of mainly Northern European countries and selected multi-national organisations. A limited data set retrieved from Twitter provides a starting point for our exploration of the role of critical evaluation of information in Swedish Society. It was compiled using a Swedish search term and quantitatively analysed with the freely available tool *Voyant*. Likewise, searches in Google Trends, on Google Search and YouTube were undertaken using Swedish search terms during 2020 and 2021. Consequently, the material generated by following links from these searches is also in Swedish. When quoted or in other ways represented, this material was translated into English by the authors. The material that very specifically concerns the situation in Sweden forms the empirical basis for Chapter 6, which explores the political polarisation forming perceptions and expressions of media and information literacy through the case of Sweden. We produced screenshots of search results, YouTube and Facebook posts, and of Google Trends data. The latter was also downloaded in spreadsheet form. For ethical reasons, no comments from ordinary social media users are quoted directly in the book and no names or aliases are provided. In addition, we use a gender-neutral language, including singular 'they', when referring to our participants.

In addition, yet to a lesser extent, the book draws on empirical material generated in two related research projects. Firstly, the project *Search Criticism and the Critical Assessment of Information in Compulsory School* (funded by The Swedish Internet Foundation, conducted together with Hanna Carlsson) explored how media and, particularly, information literacy is taught and assessed. It included a survey that was answered by 231 pupils in level 9 (age 15) from five secondary schools (for details, see Carlsson and Sundin, 2018) as well as 19 semi-structured interviews with teachers and librarians from the same schools in Southern Sweden. This is predominantly drawn on in Chapter 5. This project was carried out 2017 in collaboration between Hanna Carlsson and Olof Sundin.

Secondly, the project *Algorithm Awareness between Generations* (funded by the National Library of Sweden, conducted together with Lisa Olsson Dahlquist) had a similar focus to *Algorithms and Literacies: Young People's Understanding and Society's Expectations*. Yet here, interviews were conducted with members of 14 different families; in total, 40 people aged 10 to 70 (for details, see Dahlquist and Sundin, 2020). The families were selected using a snowball approach. The family interviews took place in the families' homes in Southern Sweden during the autumn of 2019 and the winter of 2020. This way, the project includes a focus on generational differences that came up in the dynamics of family interviews. This project was carried out in collaboration between Lisa Olsson Dahlquist and Olof Sundin. We draw on these interviews in Chapter 4.

The interviews from the three projects were all recorded and transcribed. The interviews were conducted mainly in Swedish, but also in English and Danish.

Where necessary, quotes were translated from the original language into English by the authors. In the case of quotations, the transcriptions were in some cases slightly converted from spoken to written language.

Outline of the book

Researching media and information literacy from a critical perspective comes with certain challenges. The area is made up of contradictions, competing interests, and paradoxes. We strive to be critical, but never cynical. We want to challenge some assumptions that are taken for granted in the area, to unpack and put into perspective some of the paradoxes it is founded on. Yet our intention is for this to constructively contribute to addressing the very real challenges that society faces and that citizens need to navigate. That is, with our book we want to develop media and information literacy, as a field of academic exploration, a policy area, and – in the long run – a professional practice. At the core of the book are the five paradoxes carved out and discussed in Chapters 2 to 6: the responsibility paradox; the temporal paradox; the normativity paradox; the trust paradox; the neutrality paradox. The final chapter brings these paradoxes together and thus offers a brief exploration of society's crisis of information through the prism of media and information literacy understood as a contested area.

In **Chapter 2**, we examine where the responsibility for ensuring a stable reference point in public knowledge lies. Media and information literacy usually focuses on the individual and the role of individual responsibility. In this chapter, we ask what media and information literacy might look like with an interest in social aspects. The chapter starts with a discussion of various aspects of media and information literacy in algorithmic culture, drawing on a discussion of algorithm awareness. We argue that a schism exists between rational information consumers and citizens, two discursively opposing ideas about how responsibility should be exercised in media and information literacy. In addition to media and information literacy, a number of other responses to the crisis of information and the instability of public knowledge are proposed. We briefly review three responses that are also offered: Fact-checking, regulation of platforms, and public support for content production (e.g., public services) and dissemination (e.g., libraries). Examples from a variety of international media and policy reports are brought together with interview material from our research to show how the agency is distributed across the information infrastructure with implications for where responsibility is located, and how that responsibility is exercised. We maintain that media and information literacy, such as digital literacy or fact-checking, when used to critically assess the credibility of sources, chimes poorly with the ongoing fragmentation and emotionalisation of public knowledge. This mismatch is grounded in how these approaches tend to be based on the assumption that they are applied by rational citizens who share a common interest in establishing the truth about an issue. The chapter concludes by capturing the resulting tensions in the form of a *responsibility paradox*.

In **Chapter 3**, we show how media and information literacy is oriented towards different aspects: the content of a message, its source, the technical infrastructure involved in its creation and circulation, the specific situation or social practice in which it is embedded, and its possible effects. Where the need for media and information literacy is situated has implications for what it is capable of achieving and its limitations. At the core of the chapter lies a discussion of the tensions arising from different, unspoken, and sometimes normative assumptions of media and information literacy goals or their conceptual framing. We provide a theoretical understanding of media and information literacy while reflecting on how different actors in society engage with it in different ways. Research on media and information literacy often promotes a contextual understanding and views literacy as situated and embedded in specific social practises. In contrast, when media and information literacy is promoted by professional groups – such as library associations – or international organisations – such as UNESCO – it tends to be treated in a more normative way as a precondition for democracy. We argue, being able to act in media and information literate ways and successfully make use of the information infrastructure to advance particular interests is not just a matter for democratic forces in society. The often-normative goal of promoting democratic participation seems to be at odds with situational notions of a plurality of media and information literacies, where the meaning of competence is context dependent. We draw on the concept of infrastructural meaning-making to discuss the intermingling of content and infrastructure and the significance of understanding the material-discursive relations at play, particularly in a situation where trust in public knowledge is in question. The various tensions that emerge throughout the chapter are summed up in the chapter's conclusion under the term *normativity paradox*.

There is a disconnect between understanding media and information literacy as responding to existing information sources in order to evaluate them, and of people's enactments of media and information literacy in relation to social practices involving digital intermediaries that have consequences for their future information encounters and those of others. In **Chapter 4**, we argue that media and information literacy needs to be both future-oriented and historically aware; however, the latter aspect is usually assigned more significance. In this chapter, we describe media and information literacy as a moving target that connects to different time scales. In particular, we highlight a negative dynamic that arises from the fact that media and information literacy education and policymaking today often focus on the mastery of digital skills that are frequently already outdated in relation to the technology available at the time. This is necessitated by the prevailing paradigm of technological progress, continuous acceleration, and economic growth, characterised most pertinently perhaps by the phenomenon of planned obsolescence. This dynamic is also reflected in how different generations are pitted against each other in different ways, whether due to deficits in skills, access, or needs. Conceptualising media and information literacy as anticipatory practice helps us to articulate how acting media and information literate also involves anticipating future information flows and understanding ways in which present and past intra-actions shape future information. The main points of the chapter are summarised and described in terms of a *temporal paradox*.

In **Chapter 5**, we begin with a brief examination of the various ways in which media and information literacy and related concepts have been incorporated into the curricula and educational practises of various countries, as well as by PISA, an international programme for assessing pupils' media and information literacy skills and knowledge. In particular, we zoom in on curricula and standards from USA, England, and Sweden – countries with different approaches to media and information literacy. Referring to earlier chapters, we discuss what kinds of media and information literacy are taught and measured in schools. We then highlight various difficulties that arise. Particular attention is given to the notion of trust and how trust relates to questioning and doubt. We argue for the need to distinguish between constructive mistrust and destructive distrust and point out the risks that intermixing mistrust and distrust in relation to educational goals carries with it. We employ the notion of performative probing to describe a practice of situated meaning-making through critical engagement with media and information as situated and productive of trust rather than merely reactive. The chapter consolidates the various contradictions by discussing what the authors call a *trust paradox*.

In **Chapter 6**, we turn to Sweden as a case study that shows us how media and information literacy is performatively enlisted not only in determining what counts as credible and trustworthy knowledge, but also in manufacturing doubt. In Sweden, critical evaluation of information and information sources, a cornerstone of media and information literacy, is assigned a prominent role in the fight against misinformation and disinformation. Swedish has its own word for this – källkritik [source criticism]. It is taught in school, endorsed on television, promoted by government agencies and libraries, and satirised and mocked in social media. Although this level of attention is unique to Sweden, the trend can be seen in other countries as well. However, the Swedish preoccupation with a single term rather than a multitude of different expressions, as is the case in many other languages, is a particularly useful case that functions as a magnifying glass. This is reinforced by Sweden's exposed position as a projection screen for different, often conflicting, political ideas. In this chapter, we show how the concept of source criticism brings together very different actors, from policymakers to educators, librarians and politicians, and how it is increasingly used as a rhetorical device to criticise opponents. We draw on a combination of quantitative and qualitative analyses of Twitter feeds, media material, and Google search results, including topic maps and hashtag networks. We maintain that certain expressions of media and information literacy have deliberatively been reverse engineered, and repurposed, contributing to the destabilisation of trust in public knowledge. Media and information literacy and information control are always political. The chapter concludes by presenting the neutrality paradox to grasp the various tensions brought into relief.

By relating the five paradoxes carved out in the previous chapters, we open **Chapter 7** with a brief exploration of society's crisis of information through the prism of media and information literacy, understood as a contested area.

Responsibility, normativity, temporality, trust, and neutrality are presented as folded into the platformised, algorithmic information infrastructure and its specific means of information control and access. Against this backdrop, we reflect on how expressions of media and information literacies, as critical engagements with information, can include awareness of their own contradictions and normative assumptions and still be possible and productive. Critical engagements with information, we argue, need to be affirmative of the ways in which performativity and anticipatory action work together in various material-discursive assemblages that are ultimately political. Facing up to this opens up opportunities for action within the platform-based information infrastructure, as well as possibilities for bringing about change.

References

Arendt, H. (2000[1967]). Truth and politics. In *The Portable Hannah Arendt* (pp. 545–575). Penguin Books.

Avaaz (2020). *Facebook's Algorithm: A Major Threat to Public Health*. https://avaazimages.avaaz.org/facebook_threat_health.pdf [2021-08-23]

Barad, K. (2003). Posthumanist performativity: Toward an understanding of how matter comes to matter. *Signs: Journal of Women in Culture and Society*, *28*(3), 801–831. doi: 10.1086/345321

Barad, K. (2007). *Meeting the Universe Halfway: Quantum Physic and the Entanglement of Matter and Meaning*. Duke University Press.

Barton, D. & Hamilton, M. (1999). Social and cognitive factors in the historical elaboration of writing. In A. Lock & C. Charles (Eds.), *Handbook of Human Symbolic Evolution* (pp. 793–858). Blackwell Publishing.

Bawden, D. (2008). Origins and concepts of digital literacy. In C. Lankshear & M. Knobel (Eds.), *Digital Literacies: Concepts, Policies and Practices* (pp. 17–32). Peter Lang.

Bawden, D., & Robinson, L. (2020). Information overload: An introduction. In *Oxford Research Encyclopedia of Politics*. Oxford University Press. doi: 10.1093/acrefore/9780190228637.013.1360

Beer, D. (2017). The social power of algorithms. *Information, Communication & Society*, *20*(1), 1–13. doi:10.1080/1369118X.2016.1216147

Berger, G. (2019). Whither MIL: Thoughts for the road ahead. In U. Carlsson (Ed.), *Understanding Media and Information Literacy (MIL) in the Digital Age: A Question of Democracy* (pp. 25–35). Department of Journalism, Media and Communication (JMG), University of Gothenburg.

Buckingham, D. (2019). *The Media Education Manifesto*. Polity Press.

Bulger, M., & Davison, P. (2018). The promises, challenges, and futures of media literacy. *Journal of Media Literacy Education*, *10*(1), 1–21.

Carlsson, H., & Sundin, O. (2018). *Sök- och källkritik i grundskolan: En forskningsrapport*. Department of Arts and Cultural Sciences, Lund University.

Carlsson, U. (2019). MIL in the cause of social justice and democratic rule. In U. Carlsson (Ed.), *Understanding Media and Information Literacy (MIL) in the Digital Age: A Question of Democracy* (pp. 11–24). Department of Journalism, Media and Communication (JMG), University of Gothenburg.

Dale, D., & Subramaniam, T. (29-5-2020). Fact check: Breaking down Trump's 654 false claims over 14 weeks during the coronavirus pandemic. *CNN*. https://edition.cnn.com/2020/05/29/politics/fact-check-trump-coronavirus-pandemic-dishonesty/index.html

Davies, W. (2018). *Nervous States: How Feeling Took Over the World*. Jonathan Cape.

Edelman (2021). *Edelman Trust Barometer 2021*. https://www.edelman.com/trust/2021-trust-barometer [2021-07-18]

Farkas, J., & Schou, J. (2018). Fake news as a floating signifier: Hegemony, antagonism and the politics of falsehood. *Javnost – The Public, 25*(3), 298–314. doi: 10.1080/13183222.2018.1463047

Farkas, J., & Schou, J. (2019). *Post-Truth, Fake News and Democracy: Mapping the Politics of Falsehood*. Routledge.

Grizzle, A., Wilson, C., Tuazon, R., Cheung, C. K., Lau, J., Fischer, R., Gordon, D., Akyempong, K., Singh, J., Carr, P. R., Stewart, K., Tayie, S., Suraj, O., Jaakkola, M., Thésée, G., & Gulston, C. (2021). *Think Critically, Click Wisely! Media and Information Literate Citizens*. 2nd ed. of the UNESCO Model Media and Information Literacy Curriculum for Educators and Learners. UNESCO.

Haider, J., & Sundin, O. (2020). Information literacy challenges in digital culture: Conflicting engagements of trust and doubt. *Information, Communication & Society*. doi:10.1080/1369 118X.2020.1851389

Haider, J., & Sundin, O. (2021). Information literacy as a site for anticipation: Temporal tactics for infrastructural meaning-making and algo-rhythm awareness. *Journal of Documentation*. doi:10.1108/JD-11-2020-0204

Islam, M. S., Sarkar, T., Khan, S. H., Kamal, A. H. M., Hasan, S. M., Kabir, A., … & Seale, H. (2020). COVID-19–related infodemic and its impact on public health: A global social media analysis. *The American Journal of Tropical Medicine and Hygiene, 103*(4), 1621–1629. doi:10.4269/ajtmh.20-0812

Juhila, K., & Raitakari, S. (2016). Responsibilisation in governmentality literature. In K. Juhila, S. Raitakari, & C. Hall (Eds.), *Responsibilisation at the Margins of Welfare Services* (pp. 11–34). Routledge. doi:10.4324/9781315681757

Kavanagh, J., & Rich, M. D. (2018). *Truth Decay: An initial Exploration of the Diminishing Role of Facts and Analysis in American Public Life*. Rand Corporation. doi:10.7249/RR2314

Livingstone, S., van Couvering, E., & Thumin, N. (2008). Converging traditions of research on media and information literacies. In J. Coiro, M. Knobel, C. Lankshear, & D. J. Leu (Eds.), *Handbook of Research on New Literacies* (pp. 103–132). Lawrence Erlbaum Associates.

Lloyd, A. (2019). Chasing Frankenstein's monster: Information literacy in the black box society. *Journal of Documentation, 75*(6), 1475–1485. doi:10.1108/JD-02-2019-0035

Marres, N. (2018). Why we can't have our facts back. *Engaging Science, Technology, and Society, 4*, 423–443. doi:10.17351/ests2018.188

Martí, J. L. (2017). Pluralism and consensus in deliberative democracy. *Critical Review of International Social and Political Philosophy, 20*(5), 556–579. doi: 10.1080/13698230.2017.1328089

Mouffe, C. (2000). *The Democratic Paradox*. Verso.

Dahlquist, O., & Sundin, O. (2020). *Algoritmmedvetenhet i mötet mellan generationer: En forskningsrapport inom ramen för Digitalt först med användaren i focus*. Department of Arts and Cultural Sciences, Lund University.

Orlikowski, W. J., & Scott, S. V. (2015). Exploring material-discursive practices. *Journal of Management Studies, 52*(5), 697–705. doi:10.1111/joms.12114

Polak, L., & Green, J. (2016). Using joint interviews to add analytic value. *Qualitative Health Research, 26*(12), 1638–1648. doi:10.1177/1049732315580103

Rivano Eckerdal, J. (2017). Libraries, democracy, information literacy, and citizenship: An agonistic reading of central library and information studies' concepts. *Journal of Documentation, 73*(5), 1010–1033. doi: 10.1108/JD-12-2016-0152

Rogers, R. (2021). Marginalizing the mainstream: How social media privileges political information. *Frontiers in Big Data, 4*, 689036. doi:10.3389/fdata.2021.689036

Shapin, S. (1994). *A Social History of Truth*. Chicago University Press.

Simon, F. M., & Camargo, C. Q. (2021). Autopsy of a metaphor: The origins, use and blind spots of the 'infodemic'. *New Media & Society*. doi:10.1177/14614448211031908

Society of Professional Journalist (n.d.). *Code of Ethics*. https://www.spj.org/pdf/spj-code-of-ethics.pdf [23-8-2021]

Street, B.V. (1984). *Literacy in Theory and Practice*. Cambridge University Press.

Striphas, T. (2015). Algorithmic culture. *European Journal of Cultural Studies*, *18*(4–5), 395–412. doi:10.1177/1367549415577392

Tanner, N., & Andersen, G. (2018). Contextualizing the "marketplace of ideas" in libraries. *Journal of Radical Librarianship*, *4*, 53–73.

Tuominen, K., Savolainen, R., & Talja, S. (2005). Information literacy as a sociotechnical practice. *The Library Quarterly*, *75*(3), 329–345.

WHO (2020). *Novel Coronavirus (2019-nCoV): Situation Report – 13*. https://www.who.int/docs/default-source/coronaviruse/situation-reports/20200202-sitrep-13-ncov-v3.pdf [9-9-2021]

Wikipedia (9-9-2021). *COVID-19 Misinformation*. https://en.wikipedia.org/w/index.php?title=COVID-19_misinformation&oldid=1043246164 [9-9-2021]

2
RESPONSIBILITY AND THE CRISIS OF INFORMATION

In Umberto Eco's early 1980s novel, The Name of the Rose, old Jorge of Burgos, a fictional fourteenth-century monk, takes his duty to protect readers from harmful, corrupting content very seriously. He goes to great lengths in his quest to protect his fellow monks in a Benedictine monastery from what he considers dangerous books. Not enough that the library itself is set up like a labyrinth with shelves, aisles and rooms arranged like a map of the world, the librarians have developed a classification system that makes locating anything near impossible for anyone except themselves. The library's most secret room – finis Africae – is protected in a way that only solving a riddle can gain you access. Yet even if visitors succeed in solving the riddle, that might not be the end of their problems in accessing the books they want. The hero of the novel, William of Baskerville, along with a young Benedictine novice, uses the library in his search for evidence to solve a murder. He solves the mystery and finds out that the old monk in charge of the library has put deadly poison – arsenic – onto the pages of what he considers the most dangerous book in the collection – Aristotle's Second Book of Poetics. In Eco's novel, when readers lick their fingers while leafing through it, they ingest the poison, and almost immediately die an agonising death.

In reality, librarians are not in the business of killing their patrons to protect them or society from dangerous books. Yet, the history of libraries and of the library profession is also one of information control and thus of negotiating responsibility with other actors for enacting it. The development of national libraries in the 17th and 18th century was not only, or even primarily, a means for supporting the freedom of speech or circulation of literature to the wider society. Rather, the so-called legal deposit, which aims at collecting all that is published within a country, was initially contrived as a way to also control what was published and by whom, ultimately to create a basis for censorship (Crews, 1988). While the aim of collection

DOI: 10.4324/9781003163237-2

building is of course no longer to provide a basis for state censorship, the conflict between *access* and *control* that it ties into is formative of the institution and the profession. Not unlike public service media, who usually need to balance providing and producing educational content with entertainment and restrict potentially harmful content, libraries need to unite two often conflicting goals, that of providing access and that of safeguarding patrons through controlling access. How to strike a balance between providing access to high quality and diverse literature and information, being inclusive of different groups and communities, and at the same time acting as gatekeepers is a constant discussion in the field (e.g. Pawley, 2003).

In many countries, facilitating information literacy or media and information literacy falls within the purview of libraries, even if the public discourse does not always recognises the role libraries and librarians can have (Tallerås and Sköld, 2020). IFLA, the International Federation of Library Associations, is heavily invested in the concept, with action plans, a section dedicated to information literacy, workshops and events, and publications. It acts in a manner akin to a clearing house, compiling mentions that official authorities or international organisations make on the role of libraries in media and information literacy. The same is the case for national library associations, and many national libraries have launched public-facing online guides with educational resources on media and information literacy. The objective of educating patrons, or citizens more broadly, to develop skills, competencies and resources to act in ways that enable them to assess the credibility or suitability of mediated information, is rooted in the same professional ethos as other information control measures. But the responsibility shifts from providing quality books to providing tools for citizens to steer clear of harmful information, from making decisions on behalf of people to enabling them to arrive at similar decisions by themselves.

This transfer of responsibility is part of a larger trend in society that is often described as *responsibilisation*. Responsibilisation is a process that can be considered as tightly connected to neoliberal or late liberal political discourse (e.g. Juhila and Raitakari, 2016), whereby citizens are tasked with taking on responsibilities previously assigned to public institutions. The term originates in the notion of governmentality, as proposed by Michel Foucault (1991). Through the lens of governmentality, the responsible citizen, or consumer, can be fathomed as internalising society's rules for conduct thus enacting self-control (Miller and Rose, 2008). In addition to the state controlling its population directly through a network of institutions (e.g. public agencies, libraries, schools, police), subjects also and increasingly govern themselves enacting the same rules through internalised forms of "self-control". In this sense, media and information literacy education can be regarded as a self-control mechanism or, cast in the terminology of governmentality, as a means of disciplining the responsible citizen and increasingly the responsible consumer (see also Forsman, 2018, 2020). At the same time, as processes of responsibilisation rearrange citizen-state relations, the information infrastructure is ever more corporatised, reorganising societies on further levels. This calls for a nuancing of the understanding of media and information literacy through the prism of responsibilisation to consider how the governing of the self also extends to internalisation of corporate rules, algorithmic decisions, and the demands of the market. Thus, an important question with regard to media and information literacy as means for addressing the crisis of information through information control is, where is responsibility placed for responding to the volatility of information in society and how is responsibility envisioned and expressed in media and information literacy initiatives?

Protection or empowerment: Information consumer, employable worker, or citizen?

This chapter concerns the place of responsibility for containing the crisis of information; in particular, it serves to comprehend how shifting the location of responsibility affects the conditions for media and information literacy. This concern is intimately tied to the purpose of media and information literacy. Is it needed for empowered citizens to participate in democracy or for information consumers to make rational choices in a free market of ideas? Obviously, this question is polarising, and in fact it is intentionally polemic. Still, posing it points to a series of conflicts embedded in encouraging media and information literacy. These conflicts have to do with the goal that media and literacy is meant to attain and where responsibility for realising this goal is located. Much of the discourse shaping media and information literacy emphasises the rational choices individuals should make when they select and evaluate information. Yet, when examining different understandings of the purpose and meaning of media and information literacy more closely, varying ideas of responsibility shine through.

As a policy issue, media and information literacy frequently concerns the protection of individuals from harmful information. This way it ties into society's dominant norms and values, while also connecting to other forms of information control, including state censorship, legally enforced or industry regulated age restrictions for certain content, various intellectual property rights and specifically copyright, and also to banned books that have been and still are locked away in libraries or archives in creatively labelled cupboards. That said, the argument we want to make is not that media and information literacy is the same as or that it is internalised censorship; that would be far too simple and severely underestimate the importance of the democratic and social justice movements that likewise have contributed to its formation. Not least, it is also connected to freedom of speech and freedom of information laws, as well as to ideals of citizen participation and empowerment. In this sense, media and information literacy implies a balance between the different sides of information control, which regulates the relations between the state and citizens, as well as of a set of private entities such as publishers, film producers, or newspapers and other media. Yet, the current transfer of control over information from public institutions to corporate platforms and their increasing infrastructuralisation represents a fundamental shift in the constitution of these relations and, in particular, in the role of platforms in establishing trust (van Dijck, 2021). This shift profoundly unsettles the conditions for deliberation, for instance, in terms of how information control should be enacted, how it should be distributed across different actors, which norms and values it should enact, and how or when it must be considered futile and unjust. In other words, the ramifications for media and information literacy are vast.

Yet, the specific version of media and information literacy that often surfaces in policy contexts and official statements fails to account for this shift. Instead, information control tends to be couched in an understanding of democratisation as responsibilisation in a largely instrumental sense. Media literacy researcher David Buckingham (2009, p. 16) astutely observes:

> Of course, this comes packaged as a democratic move – a move away from protectionism and towards empowerment. But it is also an individualising move: it seems to be based on a view of media literacy as a personal attribute, rather than as a social practice.
>
> *(Buckingham, 2009)*

The rhetoric Buckingham refers to is linked to consumerism rather than to democracy and, as Buckingham continues: "It has become the duty of all good consumers – and, when it comes to children, of all good parents — to regulate their own media uses" (ibid., 17). In a similar vein, media researcher Mikael Forsman (2018) discusses the increasing use of the concept of digital competence. He makes visible how digital competence connotes "an educational system penetrated by corporate interests and neoliberal governance" instead of a media literacy tradition that puts emphasise on Bildung and citizenship (ibid., 28).

This tendency is exemplified in the work of an organisation such as the European Union network *Better Internet for Kids*. This network aims to coordinate the policy implementation of the Commission's strategy under the same name across all member states and to provide knowledge resources for that purpose:

> The Digital Agenda for Europe aims to have every European digital. Children have particular needs and vulnerabilities on the internet; however, the internet also provides a place of opportunities for children to access knowledge, to communicate, to develop their skills and to improve their job perspectives and employability.
>
> *(Better Internet for kids, n.d.)*

Two elements frame this aim: firstly, the protection of minors from harmful content, and secondly, their training for the job market. In the strategy, talk is of digital and media literacy or of media literacy and critical thinking. The entire strategy is infused in a language advancing an instrumental view of literacies as means for children to protect themselves from harmful content or privacy violations. This is further motivated by industry needs, on the one hand of skilled future employees, and on the other of markets. The intention seems to be to advance a form of self-regulation that enables control over content, employability, and consumption.

Digital and media literacy acts as a mechanism to place responsibility with the individual child and, to some extent, with parents (European Commission, 2012).

An interesting connection can be made between this specific version of media and information literacy, or digital literacy, and the system of auditing films and television productions; in particular, age ratings. These ratings were also often established with a view to protect children and youths, and to shield them from encountering harmful content. In some national contexts, this connection is kept alive by institutional mergers, such as with OfCom in the UK, or through institutional continuity. The latter can be found in particular where film rating used to be a task carried out by state authorities rather than through industry self-regulation. Interesting cases are the Nordic countries, Sweden, Norway, Denmark, and Finland. In Sweden, the precursor to the Swedish Media Council was responsible for the rating of films until 2011. Now, the Swedish Media Council has taken the lead among Swedish public authorities in promoting media and information literacy. The goal of protecting citizens is the same, but the methods have changed from controlling access to content to educating citizens to control themselves. There is a similar connection in the other Nordic countries at the Norwegian Media Authority, the Danish Media Council, and the Finnish National Audiovisual Institute (KAVI). They all share the responsibility for protecting their countries' citizens, and they are all nodes in the European network of Safer Internet Centres (SICs), which is part of the Safer Internet for Kids strategy mentioned earlier.

Today, most film auditing and rating in Europe is informed by the same classification system. The Kijkwijser classification is maintained by the Netherlands Institute for the Classification of Audiovisual Media (NICAM), whose recommendations also cover ratings for series, television programmes, smart phone applications, and video and computer games that are used in many countries across Europe. However, while there is some continuity in terms of who is addressed and what type of media content is regulated, there is a clear shift in the underlying logic between state regulation and industry self-regulation. The goal of industry self-regulation is not only to keep state regulation at bay, but also to satisfy its customers, in many cases parents. Similarly, media and information literacy, or digital literacy, in this understanding, is a mechanism that facilitates citizen self-regulation to recognise harmful or otherwise problematic content. Yet, as soon as it is seen as a commodity that for instance increases employability, as in the example above, it also puts the person or their guardian in the position of a customer vis-à-vis the provider of said commodity.

Individual responsibility and automated intention

The terms "media literacy" and "information literacy" designate what is learned and taught *about* media and information, and how to deal with them. The objective of learning differs significantly both within and between the traditions of media literacy and information literacy. However, they share a focus on the individual learner, a person learning to deal with media and information in ways that are considered literate. Being literate implies various types of competencies and critical under-standing, and also having access to the resources to display or enact them. Learning does not only happen in goal-oriented activities within the frameworks provided by dedicated learning institutions, such as schools and, to some extent, libraries, but also outside those settings in everyday life or at work. Yet, often, research regarding media and information literacy focuses on precisely these formal educational set-tings. There are often strong and direct ties between research and how educational policies advancing media and information literacy are formulated. This close con-nection between research and policymaking forms a normative agenda based on shared ideas of an ideal society to strive towards. This agenda acts as the starting point for what types of literacy are seen as *necessary* and what they *should* contain (Erstad and Amdam, 2013). In itself, this does not have to be problematic. However, failing to make the underlying normative assumptions visible is fraught with risks. David Buckingham (2009, p. 13–17) draws our attention to challenges that might arise from media literacy research and policymaking coming too close to each other. Specifically, he identifies a risk of it turning into a question of "selling media lit-eracy on the back of a whole series of other desirable commodities" (ibid., 4), nec-essary for successful participation in society. The same risk exists also for media and information literacy. Here normative ideas of an ideal society might be advanced through implicit assumptions about the goal of media and information literacy without making them explicit.

Since media and information literacy is often conceptualised as everyone's indi-vidual responsibility, the step from identifying *desirable commodities* to making people accountable for gaining those is a short one. The ramifications of placing the *primary* responsibility for, for example, dealing with false or ambiguous claims – here under-stood as epistemic content – about complex issues, for instance, health concerns, sci-entific debates, technology, or historical events, disproportionately with individuals are vast. These stretch beyond the specific epistemic content in question and extend to the very edifice upholding knowledge institutions in society and ultimately they affect society's shared sense of truth. A shared sense of truth, however, requires soci-etal trust, especially institutional trust, at least as an anticipated ideal. The conditions for this, in turn, are increasingly destabilised by, among other things, the inbuilt logic of our platformised, corporate information infrastructure that almost invari-ably foments the fragmentation and individualision of knowledge, and also of values.

Returning themes in almost all contexts where media and information literacy circulates are notions like mis- and dis-information. These, and especially their per-ceived proliferation and circulation, have become the epithet for the crisis of infor-mation. Enabling people to identify those types of false claims is often the expressed aim of initiatives endorsing and promoting media and information literacy educa-tions. The difference between those differently prefixed forms of information is the intention behind the claims (e.g. Søe, 2018). *Misinformation* refers to false information that is passed on without the intention of spreading lies. *Disinformation*, on the other hand, denotes false information that is spread purposely, and the person passing it on is aware of it being false. In addition, the notion of malinformation has emerged to signify a further type of false information (Wardle and Derakhshan, 2017). Here, the information is correct in itself, yet it is taken out of context and given new meaning in a way that makes it intentionally misleading and potentially harmful. It is most likely misinformation when you see how a relative on Facebook shares a YouTube clip about the health benefits of drinking colloidal silver, urine, or bleach. However, the person or organisation who has created that film in the first place *might* have done so fully aware that it propagates a false claim, and they might have produced and uploaded it sow doubt and create uncertainty; i.e. in this case, the same content would be called disinformation. It is the reason behind producing, sharing, and distributing a certain type of informational content that makes it either misinformation or disinformation. Thus, the very same film circulating on a specific social media platform can be both misinformation and disinformation, depending on who is sharing it, and when, where, and in which context or situation.

These are interesting nuances and it is obvious that paying attention to these more or less subtle differences is required in order to understand the crisis of information. That said, what this discussion also shows is that the distinctions between mis-, dis- and other forms of prefixed information, however fine-grained and consistent in themselves, are fraught with problems when it comes to media and information literacy (see also Cooke, 2017). The intention that justifies attaching a certain prefix to the word information is not normally available for the creation of meaning for those who encounter it. It therefore cannot be reliably invoked to determine what kind of information something should be classified as, certainly not when the terrain is shifting and constantly evolving, as is the case with the current media and information landscape. Furthermore, it should be noted that disinformation cannot be reduced to a perfidious sender and an unsuspecting audience. The spread of disinformation on social media depends on people's active participation; it is enabled or even dictated by the way many of these platforms are designed (Starbird et al., 2019). The profound significance of these systems' architecture is also why there are differences regarding the scale and exact manifestation of the problem depending on which platform we are talking about (Theocharis et al., 2021). In addition, what is the intention of a bot, of an algorithm, of a computer program? Their purpose, we can call it *automated intention*, might be to maximise data extraction by exploiting engagements, while the information they circulate for this purpose is just corollary without any intention beyond that. At best it is collateral entertainment, at worst collateral damage. Yet all these are involved in the circulation of information and in mis-, dis-, mal-, or accurate information being amalgamated in the actual content that people create, encounter, and engage with, and where the border between one and the other should be drawn is all but distinct.

Critical evaluation of the information infrastructure?

It is nearly impossible to establish the parameters of individual responsibility for determining the reliability or trustworthiness of information in digital cultures characterised by an increasingly invisible, data-driven, and privately owned algorithmic information infrastructure. The functioning of algorithmic information intermediaries and curators – which include ever more machine learning and artificial intelligence (AI) elements – is implicated in what content people come across, what information they encounter, when they encounter it, or how it is presented. Does the responsibility of individuals to critically assess information and its provenance, as it is advanced in many dominant notions of media and information literacy, also include an obligation to consider the workings of the information intermediaries and their automated intentions, including various algorithms and mechanisms for data extraction?

Let us consider the example of search engines, which have become intrinsic elements in everyday life and of the various practices it comprises. The search engine suggests search terms; the results are ordered in specific ways, next to adverts or fact boxes, the geographic position of the searcher affects what the result will be. In addition, all this constantly changes, and depends on which device and software are used and so on. With social media, it is even more challenging. The decision to follow, like, share, comment on – or whatever else a specific service affords – something irreversibly affects what you and others will encounter, including not least which terms you might want to submit to a search engine. Yet often, there are no direct clues as to how this actually works. In addition, these platforms – social media, search engines, recommender systems – are interconnected. Activities on one have implications for information encounters on another. The profound interconnectedness includes other people's information encounters and extends to the informational texture of issues in society. It becomes apparent how difficult it is to distinguish between the decisions people make and those the engine makes in dialogue with other systems. This has vast implications for how individual responsibility can be imagined and enacted within these infrastructural arrangements and for how it is related to other actors' duties, along with their interests and agendas.

Most of us know very little about the workings of the various algorithmic systems surrounding us. Nevertheless, when we pay attention, we can notice their effects. Often consciously seeing them is triggered by changes which directly include the user experience or functionality of a service. To borrow language from communication researchers Stine Lomborg and Patrick Heiberg Kapsch's (2020, p. 8), "algorithms do become visible as they provoke, disturb, or surprise the user". Social media platforms and search engines continually change and evolve. Sometimes the changes introduced are noticeable in ways that also attract attention in the media or are accompanied by user-organised campaigns. It is not uncommon for specific algorithm changes to reach the news and be reported alongside other important events. A prominent example can be found in Instagram changing its algorithms in 2016 as it moved away from a chronological feed to achieve a more personalised one. This change led to users organising themselves in a campaign called #RIPINSTAGRAM to announce their dissatisfaction with this new ordering of images in their feeds. In Sweden, for instance, this specific update was reported on in the news programme of the country's public service children's channel (SVT, 17-3-2016), acknowledging just how central commercial social media are to children's everyday lives. The UK tabloids reported on the change, with the *Daily Mail* describing Instagram as being under fire (MacDonald, 2016), and *The Mirror* reporting on the fury of Instagram users (Hamill, 2016). By now, examples like this have begun to accumulate. The level, style, and focus of reporting fluctuates. It can be found in the business or current events sections as much as in the children's segments or consumer reports. Yet, at the same time as social media and, albeit to a lesser degree, search engines have reached such a level of notoriety that the news includes reports on their algorithms being updated, their actual workings continue to melt into the background and are increasingly difficult to notice. Identifying these seemingly contradictory developments helps us better understand how responsibility for information control is primarily assigned at a superficial level to those available for intervention rather than those who actually control information.

Understanding how algorithms of social media and search engines actually operate has proven to be difficult (Lewandowski et al., 2018). Peoples' individual or collective reactions to changes in the workings of algorithms are not necessarily based on a correct understanding of how algorithms work. Yet, while it might be grounded in folk theories and rumours (Dogruel, 2021) rather than inaccurate knowledge (see also Eslami et al., 2016), it is not inconsequential. People have notions about the constitution of society's information infrastructure and also about how algorithms are involved. These notions are deeply rooted in the experiences and practices of everyday life and have implications for how people understand algorithm-based systems and how they imagine them to work (Bucher, 2017, 2018). People do not just perceive them, they are "doing algorithms", to borrow language from Lomborg and Kapsch (2020, p. 11). They sense them in positive and in negative ways and enter what can be described as performative relations with algorithmic information systems, consciously feeding or refusing them data in line with certain ideas of how to optimise their performance (ibid.) or to resist algorithmic power (Velkova and Kaun, 2021). People create meaning from infrastructural arrangements of which they are themselves co-constitutive. What we call infrastructural meaning-making (Haider and Sundin, 2019) involves dimensions of understanding, awareness, and competencies and, as we will see in the next section, also has a strong affective dimension. These are inextricably embedded in the practices engendering it, as well as in their sociomaterial conditions, including their value systems and economic rationale.

Different expressions of responsibility

Let us bring in some voices from our research. In pair interviews with adolescents in their late teens, we discussed, among other things, their evaluation of information and information sources (see also Haider and Sundin, 2020, 2022). It was not only the information (understood as content) or the sources as such they assessed, but also – albeit they did not use the term – the algorithms that had led them to the sources, and further, their agency in relation to those. The spectrum was broad, and the way responsibility was located varied considerably, often in relation to what *being critical* was imagined to imply. The following exchange illustrates the complicated terrain that a particular understanding of being critical leads into:

RESEARCHER: *So, what do you think critical evaluation of sources means?*
INTERVIEWEE 2: *Well, I would say it means that you are critical of sources, whether or not they are credible.*
INTERVIEWEE 1: *Yes, that you sort of question them, whether there's a reason why they're not true, sort of thing.*

Here, being critical is the opposite of trusting. The assumed starting point is the falsehood of a claim, doubting its truthfulness. Responsibility means to ask the guiding question, which invariably becomes: Why is it untrue? Another interview participants attributed agency to the method for critical evaluation itself and suggested: "Critical evaluation of sources is like a huge filter really, it filters out incorrect information". Yet another person expressed the following:

> Using an intellectual lens, questioning things. Questioning information and questioning information in the form of "Okay, how much more of this thing is there – who is saying it?" So, you put all the information you get into a larger perspective – and into a larger context. This is my take on critical evaluation of sources.

This is a considerably more nuanced approach that also allows for contextualisation. The span created between these two positions – on the one hand an instrumental view of the method of critical evaluation of information that performs virtually by itself, on the other hand a relational approach creating space for situated human agency – helps to frame a larger discussion interrogating the locating of responsibility.

Some of the positions that we were able to identify in our interview material functioned as ideals to strive after, while others served as scarecrows and were either used to depict other positions or to distance oneself from. In particular, the notion that the system, including the technical system such as search engines or social media, delivers information that is basically credible and trustworthy and that it therefore needs no further evaluation, functioned in this way. What does this mean for how responsibility is envisioned? For the purpose of understanding this, we first need to consider ways in which individual agency is expressed and how it is constituted in relating differently to trust. Trust and thus also mis- and distrust exist through other people, through institutions, and increasingly through algorithmic systems. This has implications for the conditions that enable and situate the responsibility for engaging with information. While exact correspondence between what people say they do and what they actually do is rare, the material created in our pair interviews still makes visible the different ideals that exist for how to evaluate information. Attending to how the association between trust, agency and algorithmic information systems is assembled differently supports the construction of different positions of critical evaluation of information. The way people gather around those ideals helps to elucidate the complex relations at play.

In schematic terms, three positions relating to the critical evaluation of information can be distinguished and placed on a continuum. At one end, the *non-evaluator* or naïve evaluator never questions anything and directly or indirectly puts high trust in both the sources and the algorithms' ability to provide the best possible information. The non-evaluator hardly exists in reality, and is not assumed to do so by our participants, but is often used as a negative example to distance oneself from. After all, in an interview about critical evaluation of information, no one wants to present themselves as not being critical at all. That said, neglecting to consider the role of algorithms, data, or more broadly, the rationale guiding corporate platforms, is common. Specifically, peoples' belief in the ability of Google to provide the best links on any given topic tends to be high (Hargittai et al., 2010; Sundin and Carlsson, 2016). In the middle of our schematic continuum, the *pragmatic evaluator* displays self-confidence and the ability to balance distrust and trust, considering the constitutive role of algorithmic information systems. This pragmatic evaluator takes what can be described as a realistic approach, endorsing the fact that in everyday life a certain trust in people, institutions, texts, and so on is inevitable. While some of those actors are justifiably considered more trustworthy than others, trust is never perceived as fixed, but as having to be established, re-established, and to be met by accountability. Finally, at the other end of the continuum, the *sceptical evaluator* claims to never trust anything without personal experience. This includes in particular public authorities and their systems for knowledge production. Once again, this position is in effect untenable and does not exist in real life. Yet, in contrast to the position of the non-evaluator, which is always presented as undesirable, the figure of the sceptical evaluator, though frequently inclined to cynicism, is by many positioned as an ideal to aspire to. Accordingly, the interview participants, who described themselves in terms that can be situated close to what we term the sceptical evaluator often regarded themselves as the true critics, who did not put much trust in institutions, media houses, science, or public service. Yet even here, in a combination of high agency and low trust, this is not fully extended to the technical side of the information infrastructure itself.

Invariably, in almost all interviews, the conversation turned to conspiracy theories, as they exist on social media and specifically on YouTube. At the time, the flat earth conspiracy theory was widely discussed. Films circulated on YouTube, and Swedish public service television had broadcast a documentary about the movement convening around the theory that earth is in fact flat and there is a conspiracy going on to keep this secret from the population. One interview participant illustrates the position of a sceptical evaluator in a characteristic way:

> I'm always critical of everything because I've never been in space myself and seen that the earth is round. So, it might sound like I believe in that theory now, but I don't. But I still think there's a slight risk that this is the case. You can never know for sure.

Nearly all interview participants were drawn to conspiracy theories, but most were interested in them as entertainment. That said, a minority did believe in some conspiracy theories, or at least they did not want to refute them entirely, as the person quoted above. These people often described themselves as particularly critical since they would always go against the tide and did not automatically accept the established version of things. Nothing can or should be taken for granted: "[b]ecause conspiracy theories are a kind of source criticism, if you think about it", one of our participants suggested. If being critical is the aim – for instance of evaluating the information you encounter – and critical is taken to mean to doubt and contest, then not trusting scientific institutions or the school system is necessarily construed as more critical, not less.

The pragmatic evaluator is also an idealised and idealising position, albeit in a very different way. It is probably best described as the ideal the educational system wants to advance, a well-educated, self-confident person, knowing what and how to trust and gauging information against well-established and societally accepted value systems and norms, always considerate of their own role in searching, selecting, assessing, and so on. It is too stereotypical to be useful in real life, yet once again it is formative in the sense that it is upheld as an ideal to strive for. Articulating the ideal of a pragmatic evaluator throws into relief just how deeply imbued conceptualisations of media and information literacy are by the social, cultural, economic and of course political system from which they emerge, and in fact, to which they are also said to contribute. When to trust and when to doubt, how to contest accepted claims, what to challenge or what to assent, can never be established in non-concrete ways regardless of the specific situation. As one of our interviewees so pertinently maintained:

> Let's put it this way, had we been in North Korea, for example, it would be a given that we questioned everything the authorities told us, but they don't think the same way at all. We, therefore, cannot be sure either that our authorities always, well, value the truth.

Responsibility is located on shifting terrain and it gains meaning by being moored, to use a metaphor – to individual agency, to the information infrastructure, and to the political make-up and organisation of society. The question arises as to what role of media and information literacy initiatives can still play at all in such a situation of dwindling trust.

Other responses to the crisis of information

Until this point, this chapter has concentrated on how individual responsibility emerges as a key feature in most understandings of media and information literacy. This is particularly the case when it appears in policy texts, but also, to a considerable degree, in the media, and in public discourse more generally. If we agree that media and information literacy tends to be advanced as a response to societal challenges to information control and that those challenges have intensified in the face of a ubiquitous corporate information infrastructure, the question is how do other dominant responses to these same challenges locate responsibility? In what follows, we consider three further responses that are often presented as broadly addressing the same set of problems as media and information literacy, namely: controlled production and circulation of vetted content, self-regulation of platforms, and fact-checking. The list is not intended to be comprehensive. Most glaringly, we neglect to discuss the important roles of legal regulation and international treaties. The point is here not to deep-dive into each of those responses, but to use them to understand the problem space media and information literacy is part of. It also constitutes an attempt at delimiting the crisis of information by zooming in on how different solutions proposed by different actors and in various roles locate responsibility for addressing the volatility of information.

Content production and dissemination of vetted knowledge

A solution that seems to promote an almost contrary approach to media and information literacy can be found in the production of content and the dissemination of verified knowledge. If availability of and access to trustworthy public knowledge constitutes part of a valid answer to the current crisis of information, then production, and specifically dissemination of this type of content is crucial; so the reasoning goes. After all, in order to counter fragmentation, individualisation, emotionalisation, and the erosion of public trust, content that warrants high trustworthiness must not only be produced, but also made available. In simple terms, other responses to the crisis – media and information literacy, fact-checking, regulations and self-regulations – depend on the presence of trustworthy content in the first place. Public funding plays an important part, such as through the funding of schools, universities, libraries, research institutes, public authorities, or public service media. Also, various commercial actors such as news media or publishing houses, production companies and similar assume crucial roles. That said, whatever economic, political, or scientific reason underlies the creation of knowledge and production of content, they are increasingly mixed up in a rationale informed by algorithmically driven corporate information platforms, albeit of course in different and distinct ways.

As illustrated by health information, such as in a pandemic, typically public health authorities are responsible for providing information about political decisions and reaching out with guidance to the general public and to specific groups. How do you reach out to the general public with information that might be vital, but not commonly entertaining, scandalous, or even unusual, when the platforms for communication largely work on the premises of popularity? A movie on YouTube with a medical practitioner instructing viewers on how to wash their hands or how to use a face mask is almost certain to generate less interaction than a captivating conspiracy theory. Of course, the latter might also be – as we have noted above – watched purely for entertainment. Still, this example illustrates a dilemma for content producers, also including scholars and universities, who, in their outreach activities, are increasingly made to rely piecemeal on these and similar platforms, either directly or through science journalism, news media or public relations.

One attempt to create a website for the dissemination of verified content is the *Verified* project, funded by the United Nations together with commercial partners. *Verified* aims to disseminate trustworthy knowledge about COVID-19 through social media. The intended reach is global and they "produce content based on the latest information and guidance from the United Nations, the World Health Organization and other UN agencies" (Verified, n.d.). The content is intentionally designed to be easily shared, taking advantage of the networked information environment and logic of social media: "By promoting and sharing Verified's messages, people are playing a crucial role in spreading reliable information about COVID-19 to their friends, families, and social networks, with the goal of saving lives and countering misinformation" (ibid.). The production and sharing of information become activities linked to the agency of the platforms – incorporating their rules for creating visibility – on which the information is shared.

A number of years ago, we carried out ethnographic fieldwork in the offices of two Scandinavian commercial encyclopaedias, both with pre-internet histories. Specifically, we followed their editorial work, which includes the production of content, and also increasingly making this content visible and accessible in an algorithmically curated information infrastructure (Haider and Sundin, 2013; Sundin and Haider, 2013). Compared to just a couple of decades earlier, the editorial work had undergone profound changes. Adapting the encyclopaedic content and metadata to the rules established by Google was now a question of economic survival. In an interview in a newspaper, a web analyst (in itself an entirely new position at an encyclopaedia) working at one of the editorial offices we followed expressed it in the following way:

> Store Norske Leksikon [a Norwegian commercial encyclopaedia] was a party without guests. That is, they had few hits on Google. It doesn't help if you have the best articles, or the best music at the party, if no one shows up.
> *(Bøe, 2011, translated to English by the authors.)*

The traditional encyclopaedia, one of Western society's most traditional publication genres, the epitome of enlightenment ideals, has come to depend on functioning according to algorithmic rules of multi-sided, corporate platforms, optimised for the exploitation of open data created by their toughest competitor, Wikipedia.

News media too are heavily dependent on social media and search engines. There is a difference between public service news media and commercial news media, in terms of funding, yet both need to be seen and to be accessible on the same commercial platforms, which are beyond their control. Despite the fact that they can be more independent of certain commercial platforms than, for example, news media, libraries too exist increasingly in relation to the logics of commercial platforms. These include not only recommender services for streaming books, films, or music, but also scholarly communication platforms, such as ResearchGate,

Google Scholar, or the various all-encompassing solutions by commercial research infrastructure providers such as Elsevier. Furthermore, library users are getting more and more used to the workings of the various commercial platforms, and expect library systems to work in similar ways. At the same time, they can also constitute an essential counterweight to commercial platforms and base their selection and presentation on other principles than commercial ones. In schools, the curriculum as such is established by public authorities, normally at a national level. Still, pupils often find information through Google and occasionally other search engines. Once again, this draws the rationale informing those corporate platforms into the ways in which information is used, assessed, and even created in the educational system. We will return to this in more detail in Chapter 5.

For sure, this particular approach to information and media control, which above we only touch upon in a few examples, is definitely not new. In fact, the attempt to control what is produced, published, and communicated, is the traditional way of exercising power, not only by incentivising, funding, or creating conditions for free and basic research, but also through censorship or political steering. Moreover, it is a means of enacting responsibility. Yet, the way formal content production and dissemination of vetted knowledge happens on new grounds that are laid out along rules established by corporate information platforms adds a new dimension. The conditions for accountability are mediated by commercial infrastructures. Still, the various algorithmic arrangements and data exploitation strategies involved are not passive, and neither are the people on the platforms. Rather, as the example of *Verified* throws into sharp relief, the latter are often encouraged to adapt themselves and their practices to the logic of these platforms. In this way, responsibility is partially delegated to the various platforms and services. Instructional strategies, on the other hand, aim to get people to behave responsibly and to counteract the effects of algorithms that are designed to fragment knowledge and to bring the outrageous to the surface.

Self-regulation of platforms

In their role as providing platforms and de-facto news editors, social media companies have enormous power over what their users can publish, what they will see, and even who are allowed to be users. One way of controlling the visibility of specific information is to alter the algorithms of platforms and search engines. Yet, search engines and social media companies also employ humans for content moderation and curation (Rogers, 2021). In his book *Custodians of the Internet*, communications scholar Tarleton Gillespie (2018) sheds light on their guidelines and shows how social media moderate sexual content, hate speech, harassment, self-harm, illegal activities, and so forth. Information studies researcher Sarah T. Roberts (2018) highlights the inhumane conditions and intense psychological and emotional pressure under which human content moderators work to rid the feed of sometimes extremely violent and offensive content. They are made to execute formulaic algorithms that follow a protocol, but the psychological toll on the person who actually has to watch and listen to the content is often indescribable.

After the 2016 US presidential election, Facebook was particularly heavily criticised for acting as a hotbed for political lies and, perhaps even more seriously, foreign disinformation campaigns orchestrated to influence the result of the election. As a response, Facebook employed thousands of new content moderators, but to what effect? Gillespie (2020, p. 330) reminds us: "There are some kinds of problems that simply cannot be cleaned up, because they are systemic, because the platform and the entire information ecosystem play into their circulation, because they reflect the very nature of the platform itself". He goes as far as describing this type of disinformation as "parasitic", which he defines as:

> those contributions that are aware of the workings of the platform, and are designed with that awareness in mind — constructed to appear "genuine"— but they take advantage of the circulation, legitimacy, and context the medium offers to do something beyond (or even counter) its apparently genuine aims.
>
> *(Gillespie, 2020, p. 331)*

In elections and referendums since 2016, there has been a fear in governments of foreign – but also domestic – influence operations, taking advantage of the way social media works. In Germany, then Chancellor Angela Merkel remarked in 2016, "[t]he big internet platforms, via their algorithms, have become an eye of a needle, which diverse media must pass through to reach users" (BBC 28-10-, 2016). Needless to say, politicians and political parties also have to go through the same eye of a needle. In the US, Google CEO Sundar Pichai was summoned before Congress to explain why searches for 'idiot' yielded images of Trump (Robertsson, 2018). In 2021, the then US President Joe Biden tersely replied "They are killing people" to a journalist who asked his opinion on Facebook's role in spreading health-related misinformation (Luciano and Segers, 2021).

According to the New York Times (Rose and Dance, 2020), citing an internal Facebook report, the company identifies users who comment and read news more than others as "Power News Consumers" and "Power News Discussers". The article also refers to Facebook's "news ecosystem quality" (NEQ) score. The calculated score ranks news outlets according to how much Facebook users trust them. In the first weeks of the COVID-19 pandemic, for example, Facebook ensured that "Power News Consumers" and "Power News Discussers" encountered news from sources higher up in the NEQ score, thus temporarily assuming social responsibility. Facebook and Twitter also invested resources in fact-checking during the 2020 US presidential election. Another New York Times article (Roose et al., 2020) reports that Facebook increased the influence of the NEQ score in the algorithm that determines what users see in their feeds just days after the November 2020 presidential election. However, according to the same article, the change resulted in less user interaction on average and was soon reversed. The economic model of social media, especially Facebook, and search engines is based on user engagement and data extraction. This almost inevitably means that the financial returns from outrageous content and high user satisfaction are higher than those from content moderation and social responsibility.

In Chapter 1, we briefly mention a report published by the non–profit organisation Avaaz concerning the spread of health misinformation. In it they call for Facebook to "[d]etox the algorithm by downgrading misinformation posts and systematic misinformation actors" (Avaaz, 2020, p. 1). While demands like this have been voiced for a long time by different actors, they have become increasingly common during the time of the COVID-19 pandemic. The fundamental conflict between society's need for reliable information infrastructures and the business model of multi-sided platforms has become increasingly apparent during the COVID-19 pandemic, leading to an explosion of references to an 'infodemic', metaphorically likening the spreading of misinformation to the spreading of a virus. For instance, Health GeoLab Collaborative has, with support from among others, including WHO, set up a *Covid Infodemics Observatory* with an *Infodemic Risk Index*, not unlike the many indexes detailing the spread of the virus, counting deaths, or measuring uptake of vaccinations (covid19obs, n.d.). The interface allows one to compare countries based on Twitter statistics with categories such as human or bots, reliable news, or unreliable news.

The large number of conspiracy theories circulating, and the extreme challenges brought about by the pandemic forced the major internet giants to act, or perhaps, rather to give, the impression of doing so – at least in some parts of the world and in certain languages, and again specific to the topic at hand, without addressing broader concerns about how platforms operate and exploit users as data producers. Thus, Google introduced warning texts and fact boxes to accompany search results for COVID-19. YouTube published a May, 2020 COVID-19 Medical Misinformation Policy announcing that, "YouTube doesn't allow content that spreads medical misinformation that contradicts local health authorities' or the World Health Organisation's (WHO) medical information about COVID-19" (YouTube 20-5-2020). Twitter has published a policy which, among other things, states that dangerous content may be removed, accounts may be suspended, and warnings may be placed "in situations where the risks of harm associated with a Tweet are less severe but where people may still be confused or misled" (Roth and Pickles, 2020). As a result, during 2020, tweets by US president Donald Trump were first assigned a warning flag, then his account was closed, temporarily at first, and finally he was permanently suspended from the platform in response to his tweeting about the storming of the White House in January 2021. Meta Platforms (formerly known as Facebook), which incorporates Instagram, Messenger, and WhatsApp, declared: "Ever since the World Health Organization (WHO) declared COVID-19 a global public health emergency, we've been working to connect people to accurate information and taking aggressive steps to stop misinformation and harmful content from spreading" (Clegg, 2020).

The above examples of how social media platforms and search engines try to give the impression that they are taking social responsibility for possible consequences that links, posts and tweets might have on people's health or the outcome of elections imply a very different approach to the crisis of information – namely, controlling content and its circulation, rather than putting most of the responsibility on the user. As with media and information literacy, but in a different way, the regulation and self-regulation of platforms is about power and control over information access. This approach to the crisis of information has certain advantages, but also disadvantages. And clearly, it provides us with another strong argument for the need to extend media and information literacy to infrastructural meaning-making. We have argued elsewhere for the need to consider the emergence and shaping of "societal relevance" by examining, for example, how search engines adopt social responsibility in the design of their results pages (Sundin et al., 2021). Similarly, Richard Rogers (2021), but broadening the perspective to also discuss social media, describes how both social media platforms and search engines act upon "editorial epistemologies". He suggests developing a "platform criticism" to better understand how the editorial principles of different platforms affect the kind of information we come across.

The many examples in this section show, first, how deeply rooted the connection between search engine results social media, and social and personal information control is, and second, how deeply intertwined the various actors involved are. Nevertheless, in such situations there is a tendency to attribute responsibility to the algorithms involved, to the non-human actor, to a failure of protocol. Most often this is done in what might be called a whack-a-mole approach. Problematic issues – for instance anti-vaccine, antisemitic, racist, or sexist content – are highlighted by the media or by users or both. Only when these cause potentially damaging problems for the brand of the respective platform are they addressed one by one, always with the aim of avoiding regulation and never calling into question the underlying logic and specific commercial rationale of the respective platform.

Fact-checking

In 2020, an article on CNN.com claims that the network debunked 654 false claims about COVID-19 over the course of 14 weeks (Dale and Subramaniam, 2020-5-29). They refer to their *Fact First* database, which is described as: "CNN holds elected officials and candidates accountable by pointing out what's true and what's not" (CNN Facts First, n.d.). You can either follow the links to one of the six main categories, of which coronavirus is one, or use the website's search engine. If you type the word "masks" into the search box, one of the "fact checks" in the results concerns Anthony Fauci's stance on wearing a face mask as protection from the disease. Dr. Fauci was, at the time of writing, a leading member of the US Task Force on COVID-19, and was in many ways the public face of the scientific response to the pandemic. The results page of *Facts First* is divided into the three headings: *claim*, *conclusion* and *evidence*:

> CLAIM
> In a heated exchange with former Vice President Joe Biden, President Donald Trump said that Dr. Anthony Fauci changed his mind about the impact of wearing masks.

CONCLUSION

This needs context. Fauci, the Director of the National Institute of Allergy and Infectious Diseases, did change his mind about masks, but the need to wear one is not an ongoing debate, as Trump implied.

EVIDENCE

Last week, Fauci told CNN's Chief Medical Correspondent Dr. Sanjay Gupta during a CITIZEN by CNN Conference that his evolving advice about masks is a "classic example" of how guidance can change as additional scientific evidence emerges. The pandemic, he said, is an "evolving situation."

CNN Facts First, n.d.

As can be seen, fact-checking depends on the empirical testing of a specific factual claim backed up with sources and evidence. Fact-checking is most effective in cases where clear answers exist: true or false, yes or no. Yet, when a statement is ambiguous and defies such clear demarcations, fact-checking might have unintended effects, a point we will return to in due course.

In 2015, The International Fact-Checking Network (IFCN) was established at the Poynter Institute for Media Studies. At the time of writing, the IFCN has almost 100 signatories from six continents (Poynter, n.d.). Those are vetted against a code of principles by external reviewers in a two-step process. Their applications and reviews of those are openly available. The IFCN's code of principles emphasises non-partisanship and transparency concerning funding, sources, methodology, and corrections of mistakes. Fact-checking plays an essential role in journalism, and news companies have engaged in it for a long time. Accordingly, many of the verified signatories of the IFCN are traditional media organisations and national press agencies. However, since around 2000, there has been a growing trend with independent organisations carrying out fact-checking (Graves and Amazeen, 2019). Fact-checking organisations have grown in both numbers and importance, along with the spread of social media and other new ways of publishing, sharing, and circulating information. UK based organisation *Full Fact* describes on their website the background of their service in the following way:

> Bad information ruins lives. It harms our communities, by spreading hate through misleading claims. It hurts our democracy, by damaging trust in politicians and political processes. It leads to bad decisions, by disrupting public debate on the issues that most affect us, including climate change and public spending
>
> *(Babakar, 2016)*

Fact-checking normally attributes the responsibility for information control to professional fact-checkers, mostly journalists, but occasionally also librarians, instead of individual citizens. When Twitter launched its crowdsourced fact-checking project *Birdwatch*, it was precisely the challenge it posed to the professional status and expertise associated with fact-checking that led to criticism (Poynter 21-2-2021). Outsourcing fact-checking to users, albeit registered ones, and an algorithm, ranking the helpfulness of those users' notes, is an interesting approach to addressing misinformation on the platform at scale. However, it also shows how entrenched polarisation is in the edifice of the platform itself, with a substantial share of fact-checking notes being found to be clearly biased or even partisan (Pröllochs, 2021).

Fact-checking always needs to be related to a discussion from which position facts are checked. The majority of verified signatories to the IFCN are from North America and Europe; the English language dominates. The dominant social media platforms themselves prioritise the USA both in their automated detection, and also in how they work with third-party providers for fact-checking. The ramifications of this indifference to other positions and conditions are potentially worsening the situation for already disadvantaged groups and democracy movements in different parts of the world. For instance, Alexander Onukwue, 2020, writer for *Techabale*, a pan-African online publication on technology and innovation, suggests that "[b]y having an American-first focus on their misinformation detection, Facebook and Twitter might fail to take the peculiar needs of African democracies into account". He describes how fact-checking can be misappropriated to work as a tool for the oppression of oppositional voices and democratic forces rather than for advancing transparency or good governance and how the social media companies' approach to fact-checking, as it is informed by the US political and media system, is implicit in this. Onukwue's report concerns Nigeria, but his analysis certainly also applies to other countries, also outside Africa.

The notion of *fact* provides an air of objectivity, suggesting a statement can be either right, which makes it a fact, or wrong, which means it is not a fact. While this is of course applicable in many situations, it also has its drawbacks. Fact-checking sites often address this difficulty by using a scale or similar visual aid with a pointer marking out a position between two extremes, frequently by using traffic light colours, green on the one side and red on the other. These are often workable solutions for specific statements which blend degrees of truthfulness. Still, there are several more profound concerns associated with fact-checking that have to do with some of the underlying assumptions informing the practice. One such resides with the lack of cultural contextualisation and the underlying neglect of non-Western political or cultural conditions. We touched upon this above regarding the US-centric approach to fact-checking that is particularly noticeable in social media.

This leads to a further concern, namely how fact-checking might further the ongoing fragmentation and decontextualisation of knowledge and information. By carving out individual statements or even a "checkable part of any sentence" (Babakar, 2016), fact-checking risks treating factual statements as pieces of facts, removed from their context. Sociologist Noortje Marres argues that fact-checking, as it attempts to draw clear lines between facts and non-facts, between good information and potentially dangerous information, and between valid and non-valid statements, practises a "politics of demarcation", which

secures respect for factual knowledge through the validation and de-valida-
tion of statements, and these selective operations upon content produce a
normative distinction between "good" sources capable of producing valid
statements and those that don't, between "good" users capable of discerning
valid statements and those who aren't.

(Marres, 2018, p. 428f)

Despite apparent important differences between media and information literacy
and professional, but also automated, and even crowdsourced, fact-checking, simi-
larities also exist. In Marres' (2018) understanding, the epistemology underlying
fact-checking that aims for demarcations between "good" and "bad" corresponds
with the one fundamental to media and information literacy. There, the distinction
is between "good" and "bad" users, based on explicit norms of what a "good" user
should be like.

Marres' analysis adds an important dimension to comprehending not just how
fact-checking works as a solution to a specific problem with information control,
but also as potentially fuelling the conditions that form the basis of the problem in
the first place. At the same time, pointing this out does not imply that fact-checking,
like other means of information control and regulation, is entirely futile. On the
contrary, at this point it is indispensable. Yet, it is also crucial to address how these
politics of demarcation might undermine the very concept of fact – as a delimited,
provable truth-bearing unit – that our society has come to rely on. This might
occur in at least three ways: First, by disqualifying everything that is not a fact in
the narrow sense as its opposite. Second, by flagging fact-checked misinformation
as false, unflagged content might inversely appear to be reliable and truthful (see
also Pröllochs, 2021), and third, as indicated, by further fuelling the conditions that
enable the increasing volatility and fragmenting of information in the first place.

Conclusion: the responsibility paradox

In this chapter we zoomed in on the location of responsibility for challenging the
crisis of information and for securing a stable reference point in common public
knowledge. More precisely, we enquired after the location of responsibility placed
for responding to the volatility of information in society. We started out by situating media and information literacy in a tradition of regulating society's cultural
production and controlling access to it. This includes collection building in libraries,
editorial control exercised by the media, and traditional encyclopaedias' selection of
entries, age classification for media content, and also censorship. These methods for
regulating access are directly related to the figure of the responsible individual controlling themselves, making sure to avoid inappropriate material in the first place.

Yet, this line of reasoning is increasingly complicated by a schism between two
different ideals. Increasingly, *the informed citizen* is, while not necessarily replaced,
imagined as *a rational consumer* of information. These discursively conflicting arche-
types regarding the purpose of media and information literacy have implications

for how and where responsibility for the stability of public knowledge is allocated. While the rational consumer ideal locates the main responsibility to the individual, concerning the individual's information selection and consumption, the responsibility of the informed citizen or member of society is collective and concerns an individual's relation to society. These two ways of assigning and justifying responsibility are informed by entirely different rationales, something which in itself is not necessarily problematic. Yet, rifts emerge when these two ideals come together and the informed citizen, who is assumed to participate in society according to the rules of deliberative democracy, is cast as a rational consumer exercising their freedom of choice to support their individual interests. Information literacy, like media literacy and digital literacy, when used for the purpose of evaluating the credibility of information sources, chimes poorly with the ongoing individualisation, fragmentation, and emotionalisation of information and the proliferation of strategically circulated mis- and malinformation. This mismatch is grounded in the way in which these approaches often tend to be based on an assumption that they will be expressed or enacted by rational citizens who share a common interest in establishing the truth about an issue.

Another conflicting arrangement further complicates this contradictory positioning. Exploring the place of responsibility by asking how it arises at the intersection of agency and trust brings to light additional tensions. While what we call the *pragmatic evaluator* seeks to balance trust and questioning, the stereotypical *sceptical evaluator* rejects the possibility of trust as a prerequisite for knowledge and in this way advances distrust and suspicion as dominant motivations. The tension here is not so much whether responsibility is directed towards collective understanding or individual choice at the level of usefulness. Rather, the tension concerns the conception of knowledge itself. These two ideals, in terms of what media and information literacy entails, are based on different conceptual understandings of what this literacy concerns. Is it media or information understood as knowledge in its material form, created by mechanisms that can be used as proxies for judging its trustworthiness, or is it knowledge that each person must reproduce through observation and experience?

Let us end this chapter by returning to Umberto Eco's *The Name of the Rose* (1983) and compare the information infrastructure as a labyrinth that media and information literacy can never fully or definitively solve. The narrator, the young Benedictine novice, recounts the following exchange between him and William of Baskerville: "'To find the way out of a labyrinth,' William recited, 'there is only one means'," (ibid., 178). William then explains to the young novice what that means is. The novice then asks,

> How do you know that? Are you an expert on labyrinths?
> No, I am citing an ancient text I once read.
> And by observing this rule you get out?
> Almost never, as far as I know. But we will try it all the same'
>
> *(ibid., 176)*

Responsible citizen and information consumer, pragmatic and sceptical evaluator, are all ideals, or normative positions, that are grounded not least in how and where responsibility for information control is located. This includes different understandings of what it is that a media and information literate person is considered to be responsible for: democratic deliberation or individual choice; societal trust or experiential truth. All are increasingly bound by a corporate information infrastructure that implements mechanisms for information control and regulation, recasting them to support profit-maximising, primarily through data extraction. These mechanisms are ever more automated and rendered invisible in various algorithmic arrangements. The notion of responsibility for either democratic deliberation or consumer choice, as well as the intricate balancing of trust and agency increasingly exists only in relation to or even within this pervasive platformised information infrastructure. This justifies talk of a responsibility paradox, that is, the basic idea of individual responsibility as it informs media and information literacy in most policy texts, instructional guides, and people's own understanding is countered by the infrastructural conditions through which it is enacted. The conditions for information control, for the volatility of information, for regulation of access and ultimately for trust and the stability of public knowledge are set by and large by private entities. In their dealings with information as a commodity subject to algorithmic selection and optimisation, these platforms have exhibited monopolising tendencies. Means for civic participation are extremely limited as is accountability to democratic institutions and societal control is predominantly carried out through courts. Responsibility is located with the individual, the person acting in various media and information literate ways. Yet, accountability is left floating. This leads to the paradoxical situation whereby while people are responsible for governing their own conduct regarding information control, they have no way of demanding to be involved in any of the mechanisms that govern the circulation of information in the first place.

References

Avaaz (2020). *Facebook's Algorithm: A Major Threat to Public Health*. https://avaazimages.avaaz. org/facebook_threat_health.pdf [23-8-2021]

Babakar, M. (17-11-2016). *Full Fact: Automated Fact Fecking*. https://fullfact.org/blog/2016/ nov/automated-factchecking-hub/ [9-7-2021]

BBC (28-10-2016). Angela Merkel wants Facebook and Google's secrets revealed. *BBC*. https://www.bbc.com/news/technology-37798762 [24-8-2021]

Better Internet for kids (n.d.) *Better Internet for Kids*. https://www.betterinternetforkids.eu/ en-GB/policy/better-internet [24-8-2021]

Bøe, A. (9-11-2011). Web encyclopaedia uses blogs as bait [Nettliksikon bruker blogger som lokkemat]. *VG*.

Bucher, T. (2017). The algorithmic imaginary: Exploring the ordinary affects of Facebook algorithms. *Information, Communication & Society*, 20(1), 30–44. doi:10.1080/13691 18X.2016.1154086

Bucher, T. (2018). *If… then: Algorithmic Power and Politics*. Oxford University Press.

Buckingham, D. (2009). The future of media literacy in the digital age: Some challenges for policy and practice. In EuroMeduc (ed.), *Media Literacy in Europe. Controversies, Challenges and Perspectives* (pp. 13–24). EuroMeduc.

Clegg, N. (25-3-2020). *Combating COVID-19 Misinformation Across our Apps.* https://about.fb.com/news/2020/03/combating-covid-19-misinformation/ [10-9-2021]

CNN Facts First (n.d.). *Facts First.* https://edition.cnn.com/factsfirst/politics [24-8-2021]

Cooke, N. A. (2017). Posttruth, truthiness, and alternative facts: Information behavior and critical information consumption for a new age. *The Library Quarterly,* 87(3), 211–221.

Covid19obs (n.d.) *Covid19 Infodemics Observatory.* https://covid19obs.fbk.eu/ [10-9-2021]

Crews, K. D. (1988). Legal deposit in four countries: Laws and library services. *Law Library Journal,* 80(4), 551–576.

Dale, D. & Subramaniam, T. (29-5-2020). Fact check: Breaking down Trump's 654 false claims over 14 weeks during the coronavirus pandemic. *Facts First.* https://edition.cnn.com/2020/05/29/politics/fact-check-trump-coronavirus-pandemic-dishonesty/index.html [24-08-2021]

Dogruel, L. (2021) Folk theories of algorithmic operations during Internet use: A mixed methods study. *The Information Society,* 37(5), 287–298. doi:10.1080/01972243.2021.1949768

Eco, U. (1983). *The Name of the Rose.* Harcourt.

Erstad, O., & Amdam, S. (2013). From protection to public participation: A review of research literature on media literacy. *Javnost – The Public,* 20(2), 83–98. doi:10.1080/13183222.2013.11009115

Eslami, M., Karahalios, K., Sandvig, C., Vaccaro, K., Rickman, A., Hamilton, K., & Kirlik, A. (2016). First I "like" it, then I hide it: Folk theories of social feeds. In *Proceedings of the 2016 CHI conference on human factors in computing systems* (pp. 2371–2382). doi:10.1145/2858036.2858494

European Commission (2012). *European Strategy for a Better Internet for Children.* Communication from the commission to the European parliament, the council, the European economic and social committee and the committee of the regions. https://eur-lex.europa.eu/legal-content/EN/TXT/HTML/?uri=CELEX:52012DC0196&from=EN [18-7-2021]

Forsman, M. (2018). Digital competence and the future media citizen: A preliminary conceptual analysis. *The Journal of Media Literacy,* 65(1–2), 24–29.

Forsman, M. (2020). Media literacy and the emerging media citizen in the nordic media welfare state. *Nordic Journal of Media Studies,* 2(1), 59–70. 10.2478/njms-2020-0006

Foucault, M. (1991). *The Foucault Effect: Studies in Governmentality.* University of Chicago Press.

Gillespie, T. (2018). *Custodians of the Internet: Platforms, Content Moderation, and the Hidden Decisions that Shape Social Media.* Yale University Press.

Gillespie, T. (2020). Platforms throw content moderation at every problem. In M. Zimdars & K. McLeod (Eds.), *Fake News: Understanding Media and Misinformation in the Digital Age* (pp. 329–340). The MIT Press.

Graves, L., & Amazeen, M.A. (2019). Fact-checking as idea and practice in journalism. In *Oxford Research Encyclopedia of Communication.* doi:10.1093/acrefore/9780190228613.013.808

Haider, J. & Sundin, O. (2013). The networked life of professional encyclopaedias: Quantification, tradition, and trustworthiness. *First Monday,* 18, (6). https://firstmonday.org/ojs/index.php/fm/article/download/4383/3686 [24-08-2021] doi: 10.5210/fm.v18i6.4383

Haider, J., & Sundin, O. (2019). *Invisible Search and Online Search Engines: The Ubiquity of Search in Everyday Life.* Routledge.

Haider, J., & Sundin, O. (2020). Information literacy challenges in digital culture: Conflicting engagements of trust and doubt. *Information, Communication & Society.* doi:10.1080/1369118X.2020.1851389

Haider, J., & Sundin, O. (2021). Information literacy as a site for anticipation: Temporal tactics for infrastructural meaning-making and algo-rhythm awareness. *Journal of Documentation*.

Haider, J. & Sundin, O. (2022). Information literacy as a site for anticipation: temporal tactics for infrastructural meaning-making and algo-rhythm awareness. *Journal of Documentation*, 78(1) 129–143. https://doi.org/10.1108/JD-11-2020-0204

Hamill, J. (16-6-2016). Instagram is about to become a lot like Facebook and everyone's FURIOUS about the changes. *The Mirror*. https://www.mirror.co.uk/tech/instagram-become-lot-like-facebook-7565030 [16-6-2016]

Hargittai, E., Fullerton, L., Menchen-Trevino, E., & Thomas, K.Y. (2010). Trust online: Young adults' evaluation of web content. *International Journal of Communication*, 4, 468–494.

Juhila, K., & Raitakari, S. (2016). Responsibilisation in governmentality literature. In K. Juhila, S. Raitakari, & C. Hall (Eds.), *Responsibilisation at the Margins of Welfare Services* (pp. 11–34). Routledge. doi:10.4324/9781315681757

Lewandowski, D., Kerkmann, F., Rümmele, S., & Sünkler, S. (2018). An empirical investigation on search engine ad disclosure. *Journal of the Association for Information Science and Technology*, 69(3), 420–437. doi:10.1002/asi.23963

Lomborg, S., & Kapsch, P. H. (2020). Decoding algorithms. *Media, Culture & Society*, 42(5), 745–761. doi:10.1177/0163443719855301.

Luciano, L. & Segers, G. (21-7-2021). Biden accuses social media platforms of "killing people" with spread of COVID misinformation. *CBC*. https://www.cbsnews.com/news/biden-facebook-social-media-covid-19-killing-people/ [24-8-2021]

MacDonald, C. (3-6-2016). Instagram under fire as it rolls out controversial new algorithmic feed – and says it will be permanent. *Daily Mail*. https://www.dailymail.co.uk/sciencetech/article-3624611/Instagram-fire-rolls-controversial-new-algorithmic-feed-says-permanent.html [6-10-2021]

Marres, N. (2018). Why we can't have our facts back. *Engaging Science, Technology, and Society*, 4, 423–443. doi:10.17351/ests2018.188

Miller, P., & Rose, N. (2008). *Governing the Present: Administering Economic, Social and Personal Life*. Polity.

Onukwue, A. (22-10-2020). How Facebook and Twitter act-check information in Africa. *Techabal*. https://techcabal.com/2020/10/22/the-backend-facebook-twitter-factcheck-africa/ [24-8-2021]

Pawley, C. (2003). Information literacy: A contradictory coupling. *The Library Quarterly*, 73(4), 422–452.

Poynter (21-2-2021). *Fact-checkers Express Initial Skepticism About Twitter's 'Birdwatch'*. https://www.poynter.org/fact-checking/2021/fact-checkers-express-initial-skepticism-about-twitters-birdwatch/ [30-7-2021]

Poynter (n.d.). *Verified Signatories of the IFCN Code of Principles*. https://www.ifcncodeofprinciples.poynter.org/signatories [20-7-2021]

Pröllochs, N. (2021). *Community-Based Fact-Checking on Twitter's Birdwatch Platform: Version 2*. https://arxiv.org/abs/2104.07175v2

Roberts, S.T. (2018). Digital detritus: 'Error' and the logic of opacity in social media content moderation. *First Monday*, 23(3). doi:10.5210/fm.v23i3.8283

Robertsson, A. (11-12-2018). Sundar Pichai had to explain to Congress why Googling 'idiot' turns up pictures of Trump. *The Verge*. https://www.theverge.com/2018/12/11/18136114/trump-idiot-image-search-result-sundar-pichai-google-congress-testimony [24-08-2021]

Rogers, R. (2021). Marginalizing the mainstream: How social media privileges political information. *Frontiers in Big Data*, 4, 53. doi:10.3389/fdata.2021.689036

Roose, K., Isaac, M., & Frenkel, S. (24-11-2020). Facebook struggles to balance civility and growth. *New York Times.* Updated January 7, 2021. https://www.nytimes.com/2020/11/24/technology/facebook-election-misinformation.html [10-9-2021]

Rose, K., & Dance, G. (24-3-2020). The coronavirus revives Facebook as a news powerhouse. *The New York Times.* https://www.nytimes.com/2020/03/23/technology/coronavirus-facebook-news.html [10-9-2021]

Roth, Y., & Pickles, N. (11-5-2020). *Updating our Approach to Misleading Information.* https://blog.twitter.com/en_us/topics/product/2020/updating-our-approach-to-misleading-information [24-8-2021]

Søe, S. O. (2018). Algorithmic detection of misinformation and disinformation: Gricean perspectives. *Journal of Documentation,* 74(2), 309–332. doi:10.1108/JD-05-2017-0075

Starbird, K., Arif, A., & Wilson, T. (2019). Disinformation as collaborative work: Surfacing the participatory nature of strategic information operations. *Proceedings of the ACM on Human-Computer Interaction,* 3(127), 1–26. doi:10.1145/3359229

Sundin, O., & Carlsson, H. (2016). Outsourcing trust to the information infrastructure in schools: How search engines order knowledge in education practices. *Journal of Documentation,* 72(6), 990–1007. doi:10.1108/JD-12-2015-0148

Sundin, O., & Haider, J. (2013). Professional Digital Encyclopaedias as Socio-Technical Systems. *Paper presented at International Conference on Conceptions of Library and information Science, 2013-Royal School of Library and Information Science,* Copenhagen University, Copenhagen, Denmark. https://portal.research.lu.se/portal/files/6353825/4002744.pdf [24-8-2021]

Sundin, O., Lewandowski, D., & Haider, J. (2021). Whose relevance? Web search engines as multisided relevance machines. *Journal of the Association for Information Science and Technology.* doi: 10.1002/asi.24570

SVT (17-3-2016). Lilla aktuellt [The Children's News]. The Swedish public service television.

Tallerås, K., & Sköld, O. (2020). What they talk about when they talk about the need for critical evaluation of information sources: An analysis of Norwegian and Swedish news articles mentioning 'source criticism'. In A. Sundqvist, G. Berget, J. Nolin & K. I. Skjerdingstad (Eds.), *Sustainable Digital Communities: 15th International Conference, iConference 2020 Boras, Sweden, March 23–26, 2020, Proceedings* (pp. 380–388). Springer. doi:10.1007/978-3-030-43687-2_30

Theocharis, Y., Cardenal, A., Jin, S., Aalberg, T., Hopmann, D. N., Strömbäck, J., Castro, L., Esser, F., Van Aelst, P., de Vreese, C., Corbu, N., Koc-Michalska, K., Matthes, J., Schemer, C., Sheafer, T., Splendore, S., Stanyer, J., Stępińska, A., & Štětka, V. (2021). Does the platform matter? Social media and COVID-19 conspiracy theory beliefs in 17 countries. *New Media & Society.* doi:10.1177/14614448211045666

van Dijck, J. (2021). Governing trust in European platform societies: Introduction to the special issue. *European Journal of Communication,* 36(4), 323–333. doi:10.1177/02673231211028378

Velkova, J., & Kaun, A. (2021). Algorithmic resistance: Media practices and the politics of repair. *Information, Communication & Society,* 24(4), 523–540. doi:10.1080/1369118X.2019.1657162

Verified (n.d.). *Our Mission.* https://shareverified.com/about/ [24-8-2021]

Wardle, C. & Derakhshan, H. (2017). *Information Disorder: Toward an Interdisciplinary Framework for Research and Policymaking.* Council of Europe report DGI(2017)09. Cancel of Europe.

YouTube (20-5-2020). *COVID-19 Medical Misinformation Policy.* https://support.google.com/youtube/answer/9891785?hl=en

3
SITUATING MEDIA AND INFORMATION LITERACY

One of the authors vaguely remembers a peculiar event taking place in a Swedish university town in the early 1990s. The evening's main attraction was an invited scholar, who had memorised the *Iliad* in its entirety in old Greek (or was it the *Odyssey*?). In front a small audience, on a stage, the scholar's recollection abilities were put to the test. The evening's host asked him to *read* a particular song and verse from his memory, and he started to recite as demanded. It was remarkable. The audience applauded. At the same time, the situation felt highly outdated and very strange. Why memorise a whole book in a language that no one except a few scholars use anymore? Why make a show of it? In an oral culture, or when printing material was absent or unaffordable, the capacity to memorise large swathes of text is understandable; in fact, it can be considered central to media and information literacy. Ancient Scandinavian sagas were memorised and passed on in a predominantly oral culture. But in the late twentieth century, this was not the case, and certainly not for the *Iliad*. Several decades later, as we recount this event, the situation appears even more awkward in its resemblance to TV game shows, and almost abusive of the scholar whose old-fashioned eccentricity is put on display in this way. Yet, it reminds us that literacies are as fluid as the medium they are tied to and the society they are part of. Another more recent and less peculiar example throws a similar point into relief. In a focus group concerned with the use of search engines, one participant, a young person, shared a story about how they were approached by a tourist asking for directions. The tourist had a paper map and wanted them to point out the way on it. Yet, our research participant found that they could not actually read it. they had become so used to Google maps, they said, that a printed map was "Greek" to them explicitly using the Shakespearean idiom. In the earlier example, the ability to memorise epic poems from ancient Greece was considered an admirable skill in a small community of academics. In the latter case, *Greek* is idiomatically reduced to a metaphor describing something incomprehensible and archaic.

DOI: 10.4324/9781003163237-3

If we agree that these are stories about media and information literacy, what can we learn from them? Both indicate how norms of what constitutes media and information literacy are not fixed. Instead, it is quite apparent that these norms are situational, context-dependent, change over time, and, importantly, also in relation to materialities. The scholar reciting the *Iliad* by heart in the 1990s enacted media and information literacy in a glaringly outdated way. Indeed, it can barely be considered to be an enactment of media and information literacy in a contemporary setting, other than as a demonstration of what it would have looked like in antiquity and the middle-ages in Europe. Still, the anachronism of the situation helps to accentuate just how central materiality is and to what degree social expectations and norms are an intrinsic part of the relation between materiality and the media and information literacy practices that are or which are considered reasonable. The young person's failure to use a paper map, something that just a few years before her experience was the norm, helps to emphasise this point even more clearly. They cannot help the tourist because they cannot find the moving dot on the paper map that in a smartphone map connects the symbolic to the physical space. The change brought about by the shift from paper to the interface of a smartphone is substantial. It alters the composition of the practices involved in the encounter between her and the tourist asking for directions. Both maps are more or less the same in terms of epistemic content, but the material properties, technologies, and functionalities are profoundly different. In fact, they differ to such an extent that the person cannot use her expertise in using the digital map to read the paper map, at least not in a way that is appropriate for the situation.

Theoretical notions of media and information literacy

As a research object, media and information literacy presents us with several dilemmas when it comes to how different disciplinary and theoretical approaches congregate around it. Based on different theoretical traditions and epistemological standpoints, researchers from different disciplines work side by side rather than together. Media and information literacy is an object of study, but increasingly it also forms a conceptual umbrella that unites otherwise disparate research. Behaviourism, cognitivism, constructivism, various flavours of sociocultural approaches, discourse analysis, practice theory, media studies, library and information studies, the educational sciences, psychology, sociology, and many more approaches and disciplines converge around the topic. There exist many attempts at mapping the theoretical field or at least segments of it (e.g. Sundin, 2008; Limberg et al., 2012; Erstad and Amdam, 2013; Johansson and Limberg, 2017). These attempts reveal conflicting, almost contradictory, theoretical approaches, with cognitive approaches coexisting with critical approaches. It is not our intention to present a comprehensive classification or mapping of the field. Instead, to set out our approach, we paint in broad strokes the multifaceted research context to which it contributes, highlighting several tensions along the way.

To a degree, the roots of the theoretical and epistemological diversity in contemporary media and information literacy research can be traced back to its origins in literacy research more generally. One type of literacy research starts from "cognitive effects" (Barton and Hamilton, 1999, p. 804) and investigates how literacy in society is associated with "'progress', 'civilisation', individual liberty and social mobility" (Street, 1984, p. 2). Such a starting point foregrounds attention to the mental processes involved in learning to read and write, including the challenges specific deficits, such as dyslexia or attention disorders, might bring to the development of these literacies. Literacy is referred to as an ability that is expressed in various cognitive skills necessary for reading, writing, and arithmetic. These skills can be subject to measurement. For example, UNESCO's Literacy Assessment and Monitoring Programme (LAMP) measures "reading of continuous texts (prose), reading of non-continuous texts (document) and numeracy skills" (UNESCO, 2017). This notion of literacy as a measurable individual attribute also has a strong, mostly implicit, presence in media and information literacy research, and it is easy to see why. After all, cognitive processes must be involved when we read, write, or communicate through other symbolic systems and clearly, this has implications for how humans exist in the world.

Interest in cognitive abilities typically starts from a demarcated object of investigation, defined as a particular type of literacy, and then proceeds to study how this unfolds. In contrast, a sociocultural framing starts from various cultural practices and processes of meaning-making and then conceptualises some of those as literacies in the specific context and situation in which they occur and which they also contribute to creating. This type of literacy research often takes an ethnographic approach, studying literacy practices in various cultures, current as well as historical (e.g. Scribner and Cole, 1981; Street, 1984). While the first type of literacy research has no trouble in being normative, defining what literacy *should* entail on a universal level, sociocultural approaches consider this possibility in more complex ways. As noted in Chapter 1, literacy researcher Brian Street (1984) distinguished two types of research traditions in literacy research: the *autonomous model* and the *ideological model* of literacy. The autonomous model regards literacy as individual cognitive skills, independent of social circumstances. The ideological model, on the other hand, considers literacy as bound to the material culture in which it is practiced. Certainly, dividing the very complex and multifaceted field that is media and information literacy research into two large opposing clusters of theoretical directions does not come close to painting a complete picture, and by magnifying the most basic distinguishing traits, nuance is missed. Nevertheless, there is a reason for doing this. It helps to highlight just how deeply entrenched the differences between the two most dominant clusters of media and information literacy research are. One primary source of tensions regarding how media and information literacy is perceived, specifically in and through public debates in connection to policymaking, might lie not so much with the existence of these dissimilarities, but with how they are overlooked.

With the above distinction in mind, we can see how the promotion of literacy by international organisations, as a universal precondition for democracy and progress, is elicited from an autonomous model of literacy. In fact, as literacy researcher Mary Hamilton (2016, p. 6) argues, while the ideological model of literacy is today the dominant one in research, "the autonomous view has retained its power within much policy and assessment". This, we suggest, is also the case for media and information literacy. In 2019, for instance, UNESCO published an anthology (to which we also contributed a chapter) under the title *Understanding Media and Information Literacy (MIL): A Question of Democracy* (Carlsson, 2019). If people are not sufficiently media and information literate, it is often said, the very foundation for progress and democracy is unstable. One of the authors, Guy Berger, the director for Freedom of Expression and Media Development (UNESCO), introduces his chapter with, "Media and Information Literacy (MIL) is one step amongst many that humanity enjoined to take if we hope to edge the world closer to sustained development" (Berger, 2019, p. 25). Similarly, in the foreword to the 2021 UNESCO report *Think Critically, Click Wisely! Media and Information Literate Citizens*, Audrey Azoulay, Director General of UNESCO, emphasises the progressive role of media and information literacy: "The future of democratic societies and our response to all manner of global challenges will depend in part on ensuring every citizen can 'Think Critically and Click Wisely'. It will depend on ensuring media and information literacy for all" (Grizzle et al., 2021, p. v). Underlying this understanding of media and information literacy is the assumption that strengthening a population's media and information literacy will inevitably lead to development and democracy in some form (see also Pilerot and Lindberg, 2011). It assumes that the link between media and information literacy as a predefined entity, social progress, defined as the pursuit of democracy, and economic development is causal and reciprocal. In many ways, this reasoning is strategic, as it justifies spending resources on further education, which is of course a legitimate goal. It is therefore also found in the rhetoric of many national library organisations and publications from the professional field of librarianship. In this sense, there is a divide between the policy production of national and international organisations and professional literature on the one hand, and the academic field interested in sociocultural aspects of media and information literacy on the other.

Within a narrative informed by an ideological model, as linguist David Barton and adult educational researcher Mary Hamilton (1999, p. 809) suggest, "[t]here appears to be no necessary relationship between literacy and democratic political participation". Indeed, the assumption that democracy and economic progress, by necessity, flow from a literate population does not hold up. To elucidate this specific point, Barton and Hamilton cite a relevant historical example, namely the case of seventeenth-century Sweden (see also Johansson, 1977). As far back as the mid-seventeenth century, the Swedish population was characterised by a widespread ability to read, something highly unusual outside the societal elite of the period. Yet, at the same time, protestant Sweden was one of the poorest countries in Europe. What's more, despite its unusually long history of literacy, Sweden did not, in fact, introduce general suffrage for both men and women until 1919, and the first sub-sequent elections were held in 1921. This was later, and certainly not earlier, than other similar countries whose population developed the same level of literacy con-siderably later. Swedish historian Egil Johansson (1977) shows how literacy in the Swedish example was identified as the ability to read, while a general literacy level that also included writing came centuries later. And it was not reading any kind of text, but religious texts. Johansson (1977) relates the development of this functional literacy to religion – of course in relation to the availability of affordable printed texts, rather than other factors – including the development of a national, publicly funded school system for all. Protestantism's desire for ordinary people to read the Bible and other sacred texts on their own, and in their vernacular created a strong imperative for teaching everyone to read. Accordingly, literacy – narrowly defined as the ability to read a limited number of religious texts – was for a long time much higher in Sweden compared to mainly Catholic and Orthodox countries.

The rest of this chapter primarily zooms in on information literacy, while it considers media literacy only cursorily. Information literacy research has often had a skill-based approach, focusing on learning certain technologies, particularly for searching out information, rather than being grounded in theory. Many researchers have repeatedly put forward this critique, constructing a divide between technical and theoretical aspects. This critique is not easy to shake off, and many times it has undeniably been valid, but what if there is good theoretical reason for an interest in technical aspects? The chapter centres around tensions arising from different, unspoken, and sometimes normative assumptions of information literacy goals and of their conceptual framing. We couch our discussion of the ensuing contradictions in an exploration of material aspects of media and information literacy, orienting the discussion towards the following questions: *What do the tensions between different information literacy goals look like?* And: *How can these conflicting goals come to terms with each other?*

Goals of media and information literacy

A significant difference in approaching information literacy, one which can very easily be traced back to the distinction we introduced above between an ideologi-cal and an autonomous framing, concerns whether information literacy is taken as a starting point or as the result of an investigation. Library and information studies researchers Anna Lundh, Louise Limberg and Annemaree Lloyd (2013) conclude from an analysis of research articles on information literacy that, "[o]n the one hand, in the articles where the concept is predefined, information literacy is considered as something that exists as a set of skills and abilities". Accordingly, it is not only policy documents or professional literature on information literacy with normative con-tent. Normativity is also present in the academic literature on the topic. The authors continue: "On the other hand, in the studies where information literacy is post-defined, or not clearly defined, the concept of information literacy is approached as a theoretical construct" (ibid. 2013). Either you start with a set of skills and abilities at hand and investigate if people or a group of people have these skills and under-standings, or you explore the ways information is enacted in a context, practice, or similar and describe and analyse information literacy on the basis of these. The first approach, identified by Lundh and colleagues (2013) as *the evaluative approach*, often includes a strongly normative element, in the sense that the starting point is also the ideal to reach. The second approach – *the explorative approach* – does not usually advance an explicit normative goal to be reached. Yet, as we will get back to below, it could, in fact, include normative ambitions.

A normative standpoint

Large swaths of the otherwise heterogeneous field of information literacy are infused with implicit and explicit norms from which people can be categorised and described as more or less literate. The normative standpoint, stemming from the autonomous model of literacy, has been heavily criticised for "creating an oppressive great divide between those who are seen to be literate and those who are not" (Hamilton, 2016, p. 5). An explicitly normative approach to information literacy often involves a list of criteria, based on which someone can be evaluated as information literate or not. An important organisation for identifying clear standards for information literacy is the USA Association for College and Research Libraries (ACRL). Earlier versions of ACRL's information literacy standards have been a target for much criticism. In their current version from 2016 version, they have deliberately dropped the concept of standard, and instead propose a framework "based on a cluster of interconnected core concepts, with flexible options for implementation, rather than on a set of standards or learning outcomes, or any prescriptive enumeration of skills" (ibid.). The current version contains six so-called "frames", presented in alphabetic order: (1) Authority Is Constructed and Contextual (2) Information Creation as a Process (3) Information Has Value (4) Research as Inquiry (5) Scholarship as Conversation (6) Searching as Strategic Exploration. Each frame centres around a core concept, which is associated with two types of learning goals conceptualised as sets of dis-positions and sets of knowledge practices. The framework presents a dynamic and highly nuanced approach to the complexities, power structures and assumptions in which information literacy is embedded. The definition offered reflects this open-ness to ambiguity. It is as follows:

> Information literacy is the set of integrated abilities encompassing the reflec-tive discovery of information, the understanding of how information is pro-duced and valued, and the use of information in creating new knowledge and participating ethically in communities of learning.
>
> *(ACRL, 2016, p. 8)*

It is important to note that this is by no means a handbook for students, but for those involved in teaching information literacy or designing educational resources and doing so at an academic level. Many of the issues we raise in this book in the form of paradoxes seem to underlie the framework as it is highly characterised by attempts to balance different needs, agendas, interests, conditions, ethical positions, or ways of asserting expertise.

Another type of normative goal for media and information literacy can be identi-fied in school curricula, as we discuss more thoroughly in Chapter 5. After all, infor-mation literacy-related learning goals are what pupils – as well as researchers – have to relate to. These goals are often presented as advancing transferable skills. Usually, they are embedded in other subjects, such as history, civics, or the national language, rather than as media and information literacy as a subject in its own right. Standards and learning outcomes formulated in curricula are tools for the professional work of teachers and librarians. They exist and make sense mostly in relation to this specific professional expertise. The evaluation of pupils, students, or other groups in society as living up to standards, can then be undertaken more or less formally by teachers, librarians as well as researchers. A normative understanding of information literacy in school settings, therefore, not only comes as no surprise, but is also a precondition for how it can enter the bureaucratic structures governing the sector.

Information literacy standards and lists often contain steps that a person needs to take to be considered acting in information literate ways. This is particularly so when focusing on the evaluation of information and its credibility. A model that has been influential, in the USA, but also in other places, is called the CRAAP model (Currency, Relevancy, Accuracy, Authority, Purpose). It adheres to a form of 'check-list' approach, that has repeatedly been accused of neglecting to consider the need for a contextual understanding (e.g. Meola, 2004). Another, newer model, called the SIFT model (Stop, Investigate, Find, Trace), was developed specifically in response to this criticism. It is considerably more nuanced, and, as information literacy researcher Alaina C. Bull and her colleagues (2021) suggest, it is designed to "help people recontextualise information through placing a particular work and its claims within the larger realm of content about a topic" (Bull et al. 2021). The SIFT model values information as a relational quality between documents rather than an internal quality of a document. In this way, the SIFT model is said to be better adapted to the conditions of digital culture. There also exist models or comparable generalisations, derived from the study of how people actually search for informa-tion in educational settings or situations (e.g. Kuhlthau, 1991; Limberg, 1999). These models have emerged from empirical research and as such are strictly speaking closer to an explorative approach to information literacy. At the same time, they form the basis for much of the information literacy teaching, which aims to prepare students for their information searching.

If we want to propose media and information literacy as part of a response to the unfolding crisis of information, there must be some normative elements involved. Thus, the crucial question we need to address is how to avoid a simplistic checklist approach and at the same time not stop at analyses of information literacy practices as they occur. This is particularly important when referring to information literacy outside the educational sector, in the various domains and situations making up the messiness and politics of everyday life. Another concern regards how to adopt and endorse normative standpoints while acknowledging and dismissing the colonial and racist views concerning what qualifies as information and what constitutes desirable forms of information literacy that have informed many previous attempts (Hudson, 2012; Pilerot and Lindberg, 2011; see also Hamilton, 2016, p. 5). The volatility of information that characterises much of contemporary society, our relations with each other, with institutions, professionals, experts, and authorities, has made the need for literacies that specifically concern the networked, corporate infrastructure for media and information obvious. Yet how do we know what we should know to qualify as media and information literate in everyday life, and who decides that? We will get back to this question later on, in particular in Chapters 5 and 6.

Situatedness

Sociocultural media and information literacy research regards media and information literacy as situated and as embedded in the routines of specific social practices. In their seminal work, Sylvia Scribner and Michael Cole (1981, p. 236) discuss how to "approach literacy as a set of socially organised practices which make use of a symbol system and a technology for producing and disseminating it". In this understanding, literacy is an integrated part of a sociomaterial practice, and different practices imply different literacies. The quote also points to a broader understanding of literacy than mastering a writing system. From the position of a situated standpoint, there is no such thing as *one* de-contextualised and generalised information literacy. A practice-oriented view of information literacies, in the plural, has developed since around 2005. It is consistent with a range of theories of importance to education and learning, such as the theory of community of practice (Lave and Wenger, 1991) and other practice theoretical perspectives that have explored different expressions of literacy (e.g. Scribner and Cole, 1981; Street, 1984; Lankshear and Knobel, 2008). Learning information literacy is, in this tradition, a question of learning norms, doings, and values of information literacy within a particular practice or context (e.g. Lloyd, 2005; Tuominen et al., 2005; Elmborg, 2006; Veinot, 2007; Pilerot, 2014; Schreiber, 2014). On one hand, the enlightenment ideal that libraries and much information literacy work are built upon encompasses the notion that improved access to information leads to a better society. Yet, it is not any kind of information, but information produced by a cultural and academic elite in society. From a normative perspective on information literacy, this is usually taken for granted. In contrast, researching information literacies by paying attention to how they are situated takes a starting point in the local practices of variously defined groups – such as students, firefighters, immigrants, vault inspectors, or parents – necessarily talks of a plurality of literacies.

Library and information studies researcher Christine Pawley (2003) formulates what can be seen as a credo, not for all, but for a lot of situated information literacy research – an expressed interest in groups that are excluded from what is considered the elite: information literacy, she writes, "need[s] to go beyond the top-down Enlightenment model in which books and journals were necessarily produced by an educated few" (p. 448). Two decades ago, she described the role of information literacy to help users from other groups to make sense of what has been translated and made abstract through the many systems and practices of classification, indexing, cataloguing, and so forth. These traditional library practices of organising necessarily remove information from its original context. In the age of search engines and social media, we have seen an entirely new type of automated knowledge organisation. Nevertheless, the underlying principle of separating content from information describing that content is similar. Where a catalogue entry points to a book on a shelf somewhere in a library, the search results, after querying the index, point to specific websites. Pawley (2003, p. 448) continues, "we need to be both explicit about the moral and political commitment to flattening rather than reinforcing current information and literacy hierarchies". It is hard to disagree. Yet, what happens when *elitism* is challenged by *populism*? What might the flattening of information literacy hierarchies result in when the most vocal opposition to supposed elites comes from groups that uphold and spread conspiracy theories advancing extremist, often far right-wing, ideals and systematically and strategically redefine who counts as a member of the elite in the first place?

When advocated by professional groups – such as library associations – or promoted by international organisations – such as UNESCO or the OECD – media and information literacy is considered a precondition for democracy, while democracy, often and most certainly intentionally left undefined, is vaguely portrayed as flowing from increased literacy amongst the population. However, being able to act in media and information literate ways and to successfully make use of the information infrastructure in promoting particular interests is not only a matter for democratic forces in society. We saw that earlier in the chapter in the historical case of the spread of literacy in Sweden during the seventeenth century, and we see that today. In fact, in many cases, current anti-democratic voices demonstrate a high level of media and information literacy and infrastructural meaning-making. For instance, one characteristic of far right groups in contemporary societies in the so-called Western world, often called the alt-right, is their awareness of how algorithmic systems like search engines and social media function, something which they put to use in strategic and often impactful ways (Maly, 2019). The same is true for groups intentionally and strategically planting misinformation (Nazar and Pieters, 2021) or Islamic State terrorists when they recruited young disciples to their organisation (Liang, 2015), amongst others. Sharing conspiracy theories on social media or judging an extremist website as trustworthy makes perfect sense within the community of origin. What constitutes trustworthy sources varies, as does what counts as "hostile media" (Perloff, 2015). A far-right community will have a different position on this than a radical left or neoliberal community, as will religious fundamentalists or secular groups. Accordingly, they implement different values in their media and information literacy practices and come to different conclusions, regardless of whether they agree on the accuracy of a particular factual claim.

To sum up, the relationship between literacy and progress, literacy and democracy, or literacy and increased equality or social justice more broadly, does not materialise by itself. This might be a very obvious point to make, but it is not trivial. The connection needs to be established as a normative goal. This implies that any moral and political values within media and information literacy need to be made visible for what they are, ideals to strive for, and not, as is often the case, as a corollary.

Where does this leave us? If the notion of literacy – either information or media or both – does not point at something shared, it runs the risk of becoming void of meaning. A slightly polemic point: if literacies are conceptualised as so profoundly entwined into practices and situations that they dissolve in them, why do we need the concept of literacy at all? This is not a new observation but relates to points about the demarcations of literacy already made by others in discussions of new literacies, multimodal literacies, and sociocultural literacy approaches in general (for an overview, see Mills, 2016). As sociologist of education Basil Bernstein (2000, p. 178) highlights, what to include and exclude from qualifying as literacy relates to power issues and quite concretely to status and resources within the educational system. That said, rather than within the educational sciences, the roots of media literacy and information literacy lie within media studies and library and information studies, respectively. Hence, while some of the debate that has been going on in the educational sciences spills over into how media and information literacy has been studied and, in fact also encouraged, there also exist different traditions with tensions of their own that have formed the theoretical and pragmatic underpinnings of media and information literacy. We relate to the broad concept of media and information literacy, but we recognise the overlap between different traditions that come with the concept.

A critical standpoint

Our book leans towards the ideological model of literacy by seeking to carefully relate media and information literacy to its cultural and material manifestations in different practices and situations. At the same time, we want to avoid what we regard as a potential pitfall of the ideological model. Stating that media and information literacy often differs between different settings is not the same as saying that all types of literacy are equally valuable or that the goal of all research should be exploratory only. In this sense, we have a normative agenda. We are not satisfied with merely showing how media and information literacy manifests itself differently in different settings. Instead, we want to provide critical tools so that some media and information literacies prevail over others. Such an ambition is indeed at odds with some research on information literacy formulated within a loosely defined sociocultural tradition. Moreover, as we argue in Chapter 7 in particular, such a normative agenda implies a critical stance towards neutrality as a self-evident leitmotif for media and information literacy as well as for public institutions such as public service television or public libraries.

One line of work within information literacy research has put the word 'critical' before the term information literacy. This writing frequently takes its cue from Paolo Freire's critical pedagogy, which relates education and literacy to power, social justice, and equity (Luke, 2014). Critical information literacy research often focuses on higher education and librarians' educational functions. In his review article, Eamon Tewell describes critical information literacy as engaged with "[t]he power structures underpinning information's production and dissemination" (Tewell, 2015, p. 24). It is implicit that a neoliberal economic system generates the power structures at play here. Critical information literacy research shares much of the critique that a situated understanding of information literacy has formulated against a skills approach, but it clearly emphasises its critical role (Nicholson, 2016). Library and information studies researcher James Elmborg (2006, p. 193) describes the goal of critical information literacy as "[d]eveloping [students'] critical consciousness". A key concept in such a critical understanding is *transformation*. The research interest is not to explicate literacy differences in various social practices, but to provide resources for how people can be empowered through literacy in order to contribute to transformation and social change (e.g. Kapitzke, 2003). The transformative power of information literacy, the resources for bringing about change, are then tied to the normative goal of advancing social justice and equity rather than just transformation in general. Library and information studies researchers Veronica Johansson and Louise Limberg (2017) show how the traditions of critical literacy and information literacy can be combined. They particularly stress the agency of users in what they refer to as "[s]ituated enactments of critical literacy (critical literacies)".

The same concerns we expressed earlier regarding the foundational work of Christine Pawley (2003) become also apparent here. When Pawley and Elmborg articulated their analyses, most people probably took for granted that social critique was about a critique of capitalism and neoliberalism in the name of social justice and equity. Today, some of the loudest voices of social critique come from the far right, their goals are in stark contrast to those oriented towards social justice that was implicit in critical information literacy. The intention to be critical of current "power structures underpinning information's production and dissemination", as Pawley expresses it, is shared by communities with widely different political orientations and whose norms and values are largely incompatible. This is not a particularly spectacular observation. Still, foregrounding the existence of this conflict might help in understanding some of the more unlikely associations that have emerged or that are being intentionally created to repurpose resources for critical information literacy for the spreading of misinformation and the ongoing erosion of trust in public knowledge. We will get back to and exemplify this many times in the book, particularly in Chapter 6, where we explore the case of Sweden.

Materialities of information literacy

The history of reading and writing is a history of technology. Materialities have changed, as have information technologies. Just considering information organisation and information retrieval conjures up a parade of tools, methods, and institutions built on the materiality of print. These include bibliographies, classification systems, cataloguing, indexing techniques and, of course, archives and libraries. More recently, in the wake of the digital transformation, networked databases, metadata, information retrieval algorithms, and so forth, have become ubiquitous. Information literacy refers not only to the user of these or the quality of a particular information source, but also to the information infrastructure and thus to its conditions and affordances, such as those of social media platforms, discussion forums, or search engines. Information literacy research has included materiality as part of its research agenda. In particular, the work of information studies scholar Annemaree Lloyd has contributed to advance our understanding of how bodies and experiences with them constitute a crucial part of our information landscapes (Lloyd, 2005; Lloyd, 2010; Lloyd, 2014; see also Hicks and Lloyd, 2016). This approach to information literacy, informed by practice theory, provides an opportunity to explicitly analyse the materiality of the medium and the information infrastructure. But before we elaborate theoretically on the concept of information infrastructure and explore how it can be understood from a sociomaterial perspective, we need to reflect on the distinction between content and source.

Content of message or source of information?

If we remember the interview participant quoted in Chapter 2, a young adult, about 18 years old, who describes the rationale behind the reasoning that nothing can be taken for granted. Arguing from a position that assumes everything should be questioned, they explain:

> I'm always critical of everything because I've never been in space myself and seen that the earth is round. So, it might sound like I believe in that theory now, but I don't. But I still think there's a slight risk that this is the case. You can never know for sure.

We return to this specific type of scepticism throughout the book, approaching it with different questions. Here, the quote helps to illustrate the difference between evaluating a certain content versus evaluating the source of this content. The young person argues that they have never been in a position to confirm with their own eyes that the earth is indeed a globe. Therefore, they cannot be sure about it. The teenager's position on evaluating information concerns evaluating the content, no matter where the content is published (source). That is a type of scepticism that leaves us with doubt concerning most topics in life. Each day, we are dependent on a substantial number of information sources that we need to trust in order to navigate life. We need to trust the timetable app for public transport, if such an app exists where we live, we need to trust the cashier at the local shop, we need to trust the thermometer when we are ill, we need to trust the news we watch, and we need to trust Google to provide us with appropriate results when we search for information. The last example specifically also makes it apparent that, depending on the situation and the source, we do not trust blindly, but we have at least some trust in the sources of information. If our standard news programme or newspaper reports on a war going on somewhere, that is probably true, even if we might question their analyses of the conflict or why they choose to report on a war in this specific region, but not on one happening in another part of the world. Most people do not generally question the existence of the war as such, just because they have not been to the site of conflict and experienced it themselves. Likewise, if the public health agency declares a vaccine against a disease safe and effective, most of us trust it to be safe and effective and will get vaccinated if this is advised.

Cognitive scientist Gloria Origgi writes: "Trusting others is one of the most common epistemic practices to make sense of the world around us" (Origgi, 2008, p. 35). We do not always trust all of these sources, and our trust varies due to many circumstances, but if we never trust, we will struggle. Social computing researcher Dario Taraborelli (2008, p. 195) refers to the notion of epistemic deference, by which he means "the ability to trust external sources of information to form new beliefs". He advocates focusing more on predictive judgement than on evaluative judgement. An evaluative judgement about the credibility of information concerns the content. In contrast, a predictive judgement refers to judgements made based on information that describes a source. Information describing a source could be referred to as metadata or simply information describing the information, which might include reviews, ratings, recommendations, and so on. While the distinction between evaluating content and evaluating a source is not always razor-sharp, it is an important one. Sometimes it is possible to ascertain the content of a message directly. For example, if someone says it is freezing outside, we can often verify that claim by checking the thermometer or simply sticking our nose through the door. However, if we read somewhere that the same freezing temperature is proof that the climate crisis is not happening, or even that it is a hoax, the circumstances for evaluating the information are fundamentally different. In the absence of relevant research training and access to the data and resources to set up a scientific study to investigate the link between this particular weather event and climate change, we have to rely on others. We have to ask ourselves how credible is the source compared to other sources in the domain, such as other publications, environmental scientists, or public authorities? The empirical basis, in other words, must be science itself, and the observation, based on a shared experience, that science is demonstrably effective as a knowledge-producing institution. This includes the realisation that scientific knowledge is not constituted by objective and stable truth claims, but emerges from consensus between groups of experts, and that diversity within these groups makes the consensus more reliable and stable (Oreskes, 2019).

Yet, in the broader general discussion, this difference is often blurred. The late information scholar Patrick Wilson refers to information sources as second-hand knowledge: "All I know of the world beyond the narrow range of my own personal experience is what others have told me. It is all hearsay" (Wilson, 1983, p. 13). And he continues, "[b]ut I do not count all hearsay as equally reliable. Some people know what they are talking about, others do not. Those who do are my cognitive authorities" (ibid.). By talking of "cognitive authorities", Wilson stresses that it is often the *source* of information rather than the *content* as such that we assess. He outlines three tests that are usually put to a source: what we know about the content creator, the publishing (or similar) history of the source, and the intrinsic plausibility (Wilson, 1983, p. 24–25). The creator can, for example, be an author, an organisation, or an institute. The publishing history could be based on previous experiences with a specific journal, platform, encyclopaedia, or whichever publication form and genre is at issue. *Intrinsic plausibility* designates people's inclination to trust information that is in line with what they already know of a topic. The three tests that Wilson proposes highlight several recurring challenges with evaluating sources and make apparent how these challenges get more and more pronounced in face of what we discuss in terms of a crisis of information. Wilson's reasoning, of course, comes from a pre-digital era, and there is a rich tradition of studying the cognitive heuristics people rely on when evaluating online information, where an extreme number of potential sources on a given topic is often overwhelming. Communication researchers (Miriam J. Metzger et al., 2010, p. 425; see also Metzger and Flanagin, 2013), for example, identify "five heuristics commonly used by participants when evaluating credibility: reputation, endorsement, consistency, expectancy violation, and persuasive intent". These cognitive heuristics show the continuous importance of sources in people's evaluation, with some heuristics gaining in importance. The *consistency* heuristic, for example, depends on digital tools for "cross-validation" (Metzger et al., 2010, p. 428). The concepts of intrinsic plausibility and expectancy violation can both be related to what is often called the *hostile media effect* in media studies (Perloff, 2015). That is, people's inclination to be more or less positive about a particular source of information depends to a large degree on their group identity.

Nevertheless, at this point, we can already stress that the growing fragmentation, individualisation, and emotionalisation of information, poses a challenge to attempts at leveraging people's critical media and information literacies to address problems arising from the circulation of mis- and disinformation. Cognitive authority is a useful concept for many analytical purposes, but as a normative concept it is in itself increasingly unstable and fragmented, and moreover potentially fragmenting. To make a case in point, to their followers, many influencers and similar content producers on social media have acquired all the traits of cognitive authorities or they might work to attain those (see also Multas and Hirvonen, 2021). The three tests – open for partisan application as afforded by the logic of social media itself – could even be put to work to confirm that. Wilson's writing on cognitive authority stems from the early 1980s. It lacks an explicit interest in materiality and how information sources are always embedded in and part of the information infrastructures of the time. In the next section, we elaborate more in-depth on the materialities of information literacy and the concept of infrastructural meaning-making.

Infrastructural meaning-making

The materiality involved in communicating codified information has implications for what is regarded as literacy in the first place. With information literacy in focus, it is not just the text, the image, video, or sound recording as such that is in mind, but the many types of technologies for organising and retrieving those and other documents and their various uses and meanings in society. This amalgamation of technologies and our use of them make up, we suggest, our *information infrastructure*. What we watch, read, and listen to is to a large extent based on the premises of the working of the information infrastructure. Major challenges for media and information literacy arise from the increasingly digital information infrastructure, rather than from information sources or content in isolation. Without including an understanding of contemporary information infrastructure, media and information literacy remains at the surface. This does not refer to technical abilities – such as software skills or knowing how to handle specific digital platforms and services. Rather, it concerns an overarching understanding of the infrastructure's make-up, always in flux, local and monolithic, personalised and conformity-inducing.

We must consider the social and the technical as profoundly integrated into each other when conceptualising information literacy. With some exceptions (e.g. Bruce, 1997; Tuominen et al., 2005; Pilerot, 2016; Andersson, 2017; Cooke, 2017; Haider and Sundin, 2019), such an understanding has not been commonly adopted in information literacy research. Nevertheless, relating communication technology to changes in society has a long tradition in literacy research more broadly (e.g. Eisenstein, 1979), albeit sometimes attracting criticism for advancing a technological-determinist view of literacy. Literacy practices are not simply caused by, but are also co-constituted through technology, and technology exists through literacy. Learning how to read and write, evaluating the quality, even the locating of books or the importance of, for example, memorising, as the illustrative example introducing this chapter highlighted, differed when publications were few and unaffordable and inaccessible for most. When reference is made to technology in media and information literacy research, this often concerns practical applications, but its role is seldom theoretically grounded. Yet, databases, social media, search engines, and other information systems are complicit in the shaping of information and its current crisis, thus an understanding of the infrastructural conditions for information should be explicitly included in conceptions of media and information literacy. Infrastructural meaning-making enables a power-sensitive, material-discursive understanding of how people, sources, and content converge and are shaped in practices that are part of infrastructural arrangements. These arrangements increasingly include algorithmic information systems whose design is informed by a corporate rationale with specific socio-political and economic interests.

Drawing on infrastructure studies as developed by science and technology researchers Susan Leigh Star together Geoffrey Bowker and Karen Ruhleder (e.g. Star and Ruhleder, 1996; Bowker and Star, 1999; Star, 1999), infrastructural meaning-making, thus, is a concept and an approach that attempts to counter the current fragmentation and individualisation of information. The concept of infrastructure highlights how technologies that seem to lie in the background of everyday life, often without us thinking about them, are better understood as entangled across it in constitutive and performative ways. The concept also underlines how technologies are far from passive but "emerge[s] for people in practice" (Star and Ruhleder

[2015]1996, p. 379). The notion of infrastructural meaning-making supports the analysis of information infrastructures that come into play in various social practices and of how these co-constitute the practices in question (Haider and Sundin, 2019, p. 102). It shows how agency is not limited to humans but extends to information systems, their data, algorithms, and design principles (see also Head et al., 2020). It also combines an interest in how people find information with how information finds people through algorithms of social media, search engines, and other similar and emerging platforms (see also Bull et al., 2021).

Both the user and the source of information found through a search engine or social media are *made* in specific practices, as are the information systems themselves. Such an approach, as it is inspired by the agential realism of Karen Barad (2003; 2007), considers people and matter as constitutively entangled through material-discursive or sociomaterial practices. As Wanda Orlikowski and Susan Scott (2015, p. 700) note: "This material-discursive approach thus allows us to ask how specific materializations make a difference in the enactment of reality in practice." The phenomena that infrastructures constitute cannot be understood separate from their use, rather, to quote Barad: "It is through specific agential intra-actions that the boundaries and properties of the 'components' of phenomena become determinate and that particular embodied concepts become meaningful" (Barad, 2003, p. 815). Algorithms, various types of data, and digital traces constantly shape and are being shaped, and form society's information infrastructure. Like the scientific instruments that Barad (2003; 2007) highlights in her analyses, algorithms shape information in profound ways, at the same time as they are being re-made and rearranged when they are used. The digital information infrastructure permeates almost every aspect of everyday life, at the same time as it is rendered more and more invisible. To visualise and make people aware of how our doings are a part of this infrastructure simultaneously as it contributes to performing our understanding and doing in the world is an essential aspect of media and information literacy that is rarely discussed.

Let us revisit fact-checking, which we already discuss in Chapter 2. Sometimes, fact-checking is seen as the responsibility of the general public, who are cast as either consumers or responsible citizens. Then the challenges fact-checking faces are similar to the challenges that media and information literacy grapples with. Free access to, say, *Encyclopaedia Britannica* is simply not the answer for someone who distrusts vaccines, the election results, or the role of anthropogenic pollution in the climate crisis, neither is setting up a portal tracking and correcting misinformation about any of those topics. This is not to say that debunking false information by using correct information on which there is consensus has no function, or that promoting correct information about, for example, COVID-19 vaccines will inevitably backfire, as has been suggested (Swire-Thompson et al., 2020). Noortje Marres (2018, p. 430), describes how fact-checking builds on the *principle of demarcationism* that "does not directly address the role that digital media technology itself plays in undermining respect for knowledge in public discourse". Demarcation here refers to the distinct separation between true and false, and between literate and illiterate. As Marres (2018, p. 431) convincingly argues, such an understanding deflects "critical attention away from the technologies of source selection that regulate content circulation online". In other words, it misses the very reason why fact-checking has become so popular (and necessary) in the first place. That is, in order to consider how the creation and use of data is historically, politically, and socially contingent, it is necessary to reject the notion that data are facts that merely show how things really are (Gray et al., 2018). Similarly, without a situated understanding of the information infrastructure that takes into account the conditions of its socio-economic and cultural constitution, it is impossible to develop a media and information literacy that has the potential to address, or even just understand, the current crisis of information.

Conclusion: the normativity paradox

In this chapter, we attend to some of the tensions between different information literacy goals and enquire how these conflicting goals might be reconciled with each other. More precisely, this chapter primarily concerns the tradition of information literacy, its theoretical starting points, goals, and the importance of materiality. Yet, since similar challenges can also be found within research on media literacy, digital literacy as well as many other similar literacies, the general points we want to make also apply to media and information literacy more broadly. In fact, differences within each tradition in a narrow sense are sometimes far more significant than between traditions (e.g. Erstad and Amdam, 2013). Clearly, different research orients information literacy towards different aspects; the epistemic content of a message, its source, the technical infrastructure involved in its creation and circulation, the specific situation or social practice it is part of or its possible effects. We can appreciate that these aspects are not stable, either in themselves or in how they interlace. Instead, they are subject to change and negotiation and co-constitutive of each other.

Still, for various and often good reasons, in research as in education and policy-making, certain aspects are usually foregrounded. Where the need for information literacy is situated has implications for what it is seen as achieving and where its limits are to be found. A recurring motive for information literacy is the advancement of both human development and democracy; normative goals no doubt. The problem of normativity is a discussion that has run like a common thread through the different parts of the chapter. Above all, a normative information literacy discourse, produced and reproduced by national and international organisations and professionals, formulates what people should know in order for democracy to ensue, and from this for growth and development to flow. Also, in educational settings, the learning goals are relatively straightforward and distinct. Yet, how to establish and prescribe norms for the different domains of everyday life is extremely complex and of course potentially problematic.

The causal relation between media and information literacy and democracy is a rhetorical device whose material-discursive effects legitimise the institutions advancing it. We contend, that this makes political sense in that the policy effects of this not only advance definitional power but are also agenda-setting with material implications. In research of media and information literacy or even of literacy itself, such a causal relation fails to hold up within an ideological model or within an autonomous model of information literacy. The often-normative aim of advancing democratic participation appears to contradict situated notions of a plurality of information literacies where the meaning of literacy is contextually arrived at. At the same time, if we regard the crisis of information as a genuine challenge for society, potentially threatening humanities' ability to respond to life-threatening crises, such as the climate crisis, pandemics, or authoritarianism, there is a need to go beyond problematising normativity. Pawley (2003) considers information literacy as a *contradictory coupling*, bringing together conflicting ideals as to what the goal of the practice should be. Library and information studies researchers Ola Pilerot and Jenny Lindberg (2011, p. 357) identify the divergence of "the research strand and the policymaking strand within the IL narrative" as a fundamental problem with potentially profound consequences. Not least, the situatedness of media and information finds itself in stark contrast to the notion of literacy it is wedded to. This, in its claim to contribute to social coherence, necessarily needs to be carried by a normative current regarding the transformation that *becoming literate* is seen to support. This, we propose to call a normativity paradox. It arises from the paradox of (liberal) democracy itself (Mouffe, 2000), namely that certain normative assumptions must be presupposed in order for a plurality of positions, voices, and opinions to be possible. These include assumptions about the legitimacy of plurality itself and, of course, about the limits of plurality. As library and information studies researcher Johanna Rivano Eckerdal (2017, p. 1026) emphasises: "Information literacy is always a way to describe certain aspects, enactments, of that practice. It is normative as the description is brought up in relation to a specific set of norms. Someone makes the description."

The normative understanding linked to an autonomous theoretical model dominates the way information literacy is often advanced by UNESCO, IFLA, national library organisations, and professional actors, but also some of the researched-based literature. At the same time, the most relevant research is currently carried out within a situational understanding of information literacy that often regards any kind of evaluative understanding as a fault. Thus, what is at issue is how to integrate, or cross-connect, normative and situational approaches in ways that take advantage of the contradictions. Once more, we need to return to the issue of trust. To trust or not to trust a specific source of information is, in many cases, a question of identity rather than of an information deficit. This is often reinforced by the so-called *hostile media effect*, that is the partisan perception of bias in media coverage and its appeal to group identity (Perloff, 2015) and the ways in which search engines, not least, can be used to strengthen confirmation bias and information-based group affiliation (Tripodi, 2018). In this sense, the many critical studies, informed not least by practice or sociocultural theory, but also by discourse theory, are right. Identifying how information is a profoundly entrenched part of a community's identity and its practices rather than something external whose absence can be measured and easily amended, is a fundamental contribution from this line of research.

At this point, for media and information literacy to be able to engage with the volatility of information, attention should also be paid to understanding where openings for meaningful crossing-over between communities exist in domains of societal significance and where collective agreement and solutions at a structural level can be found. Understanding the precarious situation trust finds itself in as a currency in society's corporate information networks is, we suggest, one way for media and information literacy research to contribute to this. This might mean reframing normativity, not merely as a position to identify, describe, and problematise, but as a productive means for advancing shared standpoints that enable collective meaning-making.

References

ACRL (2016). *Framework for Information Literacy for Higher Education.* Association of College and Research Libraries. https://www.ala.org/acrl/standards/ilframework [12-9-2021].

Andersson, C. (2017). "Google is not fun": An investigation of how Swedish teenagers frame online searching. *Journal of Documentation, 73*(6), 1244–1260. doi:10.1108/JD-03-2017-0048

Barad, K. (2003). Posthumanist performativity: Toward an understanding of how matter comes to matter. *Signs: Journal of Women in Culture and Society, 28*(3), 801–831. doi: 10.1086/345321

Barad, K. (2007). *Meeting the Universe Halfway: Quantum Physic and the Entanglement of Matter and Meaning.* Duke University Press.

Barton, D. & Hamilton, M. (1999). Social and cognitive factors in the historical elaboration of writing. In A. Lock & C. Charles (Eds.), *Handbook of Human Symbolic Evolution* (pp. 793–858). Blackwell Publishing.

Berger, G. (2019). Whither MIL: Thoughts for the road ahead. In U. Carlsson (Ed.), *Understanding Media and Information Literacy (MIL) in the Digital Age: A Question of Democracy* (pp. 25–35). Department of Journalism, Media and Communication (JMG), University of Gothenburg.

Bernstein, B. (2000). *Pedagogy, Symbolic Control, and Identity.* Rowman & Littlefield Publishers.

Bowker, G., & Star, S. L. (1999). *Sorting Things Out: Classification and its Consequences.* The MIT Press.

Bruce, B. C. (1997). Literacy technologies: What stance should we take? *Journal of Literacy Research, 29*(2), 289–309. doi:10.1080/10862969709547959

Bull, A., MacMillan, M., & Head, A. (21-7-2021). Dismantling the Evaluation Framework. *In the Library with the Lead Pipe.* https://www.inthelibrarywiththeleadpipe.org/2021/dismantling-evaluation/ [12-9-2012]

Carlsson, U. (Ed.) (2019). *Understanding Media and Information Literacy (MIL) in the Digital Age: A Question of Democracy.* Department of Journalism Media and Communication (JMG), University of Gothenburg.

Cooke, N. A. (2017). Posttruth, truthiness, and alternative facts: Information behavior and critical information consumption for a new age. *The Library Quarterly, 87*(3), 211–221.

Eisenstein, E. 1979. *The Printing Press as an Agent of Change.* Cambridge University Press.

Elmborg, J. (2006). Critical information literacy: Implications for instructional practice. *The Journal of Academic Librarianship, 32*(2), 192–199. doi:10.1016/j.acalib.2005.12.004

Erstad, O., & Amdam, S. (2013). From protection to public participation: A review of research literature on media literacy. *Javnost – The Public, 20*(2), 83–98. doi:10.1080/13183222.2013.11009115

Gray, J., Gerlitz, C., & Bounegru, L. (2018). Data infrastructure literacy. *Big Data & Society*, 5(2). doi:10.1177/2053951718786316

Grizzle, A., Wilson, C., Tuazon, R., Cheung, C. K., Lau, J., Fischer, R., Gordon, D., Akyempong, K., Singh, J., Carr, P. R., Stewart, K., Tayie, S., Suraj, O., Jaakkola, M., Thésée, G., & Gulston, C. (2021). *Think Critically, Click Wisely! Media and Information Literate Citizens*. 2nd ed. of the *UNESCO Model Media and Information Literacy Curriculum for Educators and Learners*. UNESCO.

Haider, J., & Sundin, O. (2019). *Invisible Search and Online Search Engines: The Ubiquity of Search in Everyday Life*. Routledge.

Hamilton, M. (2016). Imagining literacy: A sociomaterial approach. In K. Yasukawa & S. Black (Eds.), *Beyond Economic Interests* (pp. 1–17). SensePublishers.

Head, A. J., Fister, B., & MacMillan, M. (2020). *Information Literacy in the Age of Algorithms: Student Experiences with News and Information, and the Need for Change*. Project Information Literacy. https://projectinfolit.org/pubs/algorithm-study/pil_algorithm-study_2020-01-15.pdf [12-7-2012]

Hicks, A., & Lloyd, A. (2016). It takes a community to build a framework: Information literacy within intercultural settings. *Journal of Information Science*, 42(3), 334–343. doi:10.1177/0165551516630219

Hudson, D. (2012). Unpacking "Information Inequality": Toward a critical discourse of global Justice in library and information science/Pour exposer la question de «l'inégalité de l'information»: Vers un discours critique de la justice mondiale en sciences de l'information et bibliothéconomie. *Canadian Journal of Information and Library Science*, 36(3), 69–87.

Johansson, E. (1977). *The History of Literacy in Sweden: In Comparison with some other Countries*. Dissertation. Umeå University.

Johansson, V., & Limberg, L. (2017). Seeking critical literacies in information practices: Reconceptualising critical literacy as situated and tool-mediated enactments of meaning. *Information Research*, 22(1). http://InformationR.net/ir/22-1/colis/colis1611.html

Kapitzke, C. (2003). Information literacy: A positivist epistemology and a politics of outfor-mation. *Educational Theory*, 53(1), 37–53. doi:10.1111/j.1741-5446.2003.00037.x

Kuhlthau, C. C. (1991). Inside the search process: Information seeking from the user's perspective. *Journal of the American Society for Information Science*, 42(5), 361–371.

Lankshear, C., & Knobel, M. (2008). Introduction: Digital literacies – concepts, policies and practices. In C. Lankshear & M. Knobel (Eds.), *Digital Literacies: Concepts, Policies and Practices* (pp. 1–16). Peter Lang.

Lave, J., & Wenger, E. (1991). *Situated Learning: Legitimate Peripheral Participation*. Cambridge University Press.

Liang, C. S. (2015). Cyber Jihad: Understanding and countering Islamic State propaganda. *GSCP Policy Paper*, (2). https://www.giovaniemedia.ch/fileadmin/user_upload/3_Medienkompetenz/Gegennarrative/Cyber_Jihad_-_Understanding_and_Countering_Islamic_State_Propaganda.pdf [28-9-2021]

Limberg, L. (1999). Three conceptions of information seeking and use. In T. D. Wilson & D. K. Allen (Eds.), *Exploring the contexts of information behaviour. Proceedings of the Second international conference on research in Information Needs, seeking and use in different contexts. 13/15 August 1999. Sheffield, UK* (pp. 116–135). Taylor Graham.

Limberg, L., Sundin, O., & Talja, S. (2012). Three theoretical perspectives on information literacy. *Human IT: Journal for Information Technology Studies as a Human Science*, 11(2). https://humanit.hb.se/article/view/69/51 [12-9-2021]

Lloyd, A. (2005). Information literacy: Different contexts, different concepts, different truths? *Journal of Librarianship and Information Science*, 37(2), 82–88. doi:10.1177/0961000605055355

Lloyd, A. (2010). Framing information literacy as information practice: Site ontology and practice theory. *Journal of Documentation*, 66(2), 245–258. doi:10.1108/00220411011023643

Lloyd, A. (2014). Building information resilience: How do resettling refugees connect with health information in regional landscapes – implications for health literacy. *Australian Academic & Research Libraries*, 45(1), 48–66. doi:10.1080/00048623.2014.884916

Luke, A. (2014). Defining critical literacy. In J. Z. Pandya & J. Ávila (Eds.), *Moving Critical Literacies Forward: A New Look at Praxis across Contexts* (pp. 19–31). Routledge.

Lundh, A. H., Limberg, L. & Lloyd, A. (2013). Swapping settings: Researching information literacy in workplace and in educational contexts. *Information Research*, 18(3) paperC05. http://InformationR.net/ir/18-3/colis/paperC05.html [12-9-2021]

Maly, I. (2019). New right metapolitics and the algorithmic activism of Schild & Vrienden. *Social Media + Society*, 5(2), 1–15. doi:10.1177/2056305119856700

Marres, N. (2018). Why we can't have our facts back. *Engaging Science, Technology, and Society*, 4, 423–443. doi:10.17351/ests2018.188

Meola, M. (2004). Chucking the checklist: A contextual approach to teaching undergraduates Website evaluation. *Portal: Libraries and the Academy*, 4(3), 33–344. doi: 10.1353/pla.2004.0055

Metzger, M. J., & Flanagin, A. J. (2013). Credibility and trust of information in online environments: The use of cognitive heuristics. *Journal of Pragmatics*, 59, 210–220. doi:10.1016/j.pragma.2013.07.012

Metzger, M. J., Flanagin, A. J., & Medders, R. B. (2010). Social and heuristic approaches to credibility evaluation online. *Journal of Communication*, 60(3), 413–439. doi: 10.1111/j.1460-2466.2010.01488.x

Mills, K. A. (2016). *Literacy Theories for the Digital Age: Social, Critical, Multimodal, Spatial, Material and Sensory Lenses*. Multilingual Matters.

Mouffe, C. (2000). *The Democratic Paradox*. Verso.

Multas, A. M., & Hirvonen, N. (2021). "Let's keep this video as real as possible": Young video bloggers constructing cognitive authority through a health-related information creation process. *Journal of Documentation*. doi:10.1108/JD-02-2021-0027

Nazar, S., & Pieters, T. (2021). Plandemic revisited: A product of planned disinformation amplifying the COVID-19 "infodemic". *Frontiers in Public Health*, 9, 649930. doi: 10.3389/fpubh.2021.649930

Nicholson, K. P. (2016). "Taking back" information literacy: Time and the one-shot in the neoliberal university. In N. Pagowsky & K. McElroy (Eds.), *Critical Library Pedagogy Handbook (vol. 1)* (pp. 25–39). ACRL.

Oreskes, N. (2019). *Why Trust Science?* Princeton University Press.

Origgi, G. (2008). Trust, authority and epistemic responsibility. *Theoria. Revista de Teoría, Historia y Fundamentos de La Ciencia*, 23(1), 35–44.

Orlikowski, W. J., & Scott, S. V. (2015). Exploring material-discursive practices. *Journal of Management Studies*, 52(5), 697–705. doi:10.1111/joms.12114

Pawley, C. (2003). Information literacy: A contradictory coupling. *The Library Quarterly*, 73(4), 422–452.

Perloff, R. M. (2015). A three-decade retrospective on the hostile media effect. *Mass Communication and Society*, 18(6), 701–729. doi:10.1080/15205436.2015.1051234

Pilerot, O. (2014). Making design researchers' information sharing visible through material objects. *Journal of the Association for Information Science and Technology*, 65(10), 200–2016. doi:10.1002/asi.23108

Pilerot, O. (2016). A practice-based exploration of the enactment of information literacy among PhD students in an interdisciplinary research field. *Journal of Documentation*, 72(3), 414–434. doi:10.1108/JD-05-2015-0056

Pilerot, O., & Lindberg, J. (2011). The concept of information literacy in policy-making texts: An imperialistic project? *Library Trends*, 60(2), 338–360. doi:10.1353/lib.2011.0040

Rivano Eckerdal, J. (2017). Libraries, democracy, information literacy, and citizenship: An agonistic reading of central library and information studies' concepts. *Journal of Documentation*, 73(5), 1010–1033. doi: 10.1108/JD-12-2016-0152

Schreiber, T. (2014). Conceptualizing students' written assignments in the context of information literacy and Schatzki's practice theory. *Journal of Documentation*, 70(3), 346–363. doi: 10.1108/JD-01-2013-0002

Scribner, M., & Cole, M. (1981). *The Psychology of Literacy*. Harvard University Press.

Star, S. L. (1999). The ethnography of infrastructure. *American Behavioral Scientist*, 43(3), 377–391. doi: 10.1177/00027649921955326

Star, S. L., & Ruhleder, K. (1996). Steps toward an ecology of infrastructure: Design and access for large information spaces. *Information Systems Research*, 7(1), 111–134. doi: 10.1287/isre.7.1.111

Street, B. V. (1984). *Literacy in Theory and Practice*. Cambridge University Press.

Sundin, O. (2008). Negotiations on information-seeking expertise: A study of web-based tutorials for information literacy. *Journal of Documentation*, 64(1), 24–44. doi:10.1108/00220410810844141

Swire-Thompson, B., DeGutis, J., & Lazer, D. (2020). Searching for the backfire effect: Measurement and design considerations. *Journal of Applied Research in Memory and Cognition*, 9(3), 286–299. doi:10.1016/j.jarmac.2020.06.006

Taraborelli, D. (2008). How the web is changing the way we trust. In K. Waelbers, A. Briggle, & P. Breg (Eds.), *Current Issues in Computing and Philosophy* (pp. 194–204). IOS Press.

Tewell, E. (2015). A decade of critical information literacy: A review of the literature. *Communications in Information Literacy*, 9(1), 24–43. doi:10.15760/comminfolit.2015.9.1.174

Tripodi, F. (2018). Searching for alternative facts: Analyzing scriptural inference in conservative news practices. *Data and Society*. https://datasociety.net/library/searching-for-alternative-facts/ [24-8-2021]

Tuominen, K., Savolainen, R., & Talja, S. (2005). Information literacy as a sociotechnical practice. *The Library Quarterly*, 75(3), 329–345. doi:10.1086/497311

UNESCO (2017). *Implementation in Diverse Settings of the Literacy Assessment and Monitoring Programme (LAMP): Lessons for Sustainable Development Goal 4 (SDG 4)*. http://uis.unesco.org/sites/default/files/documents/implementation-diverse-settings-lamp-2017-en.pdf [30-7-2021]

Veinot, T. C. (2007). The eyes of the power company: Workplace information practices of a vault inspector. *The Library Quarterly*, 77(2), 157–179. doi:10.1086/517842

Wilson, P. (1983). *Second-Hand Knowledge: An Inquiry into Cognitive Authority*. Greenwood Press.

4
MEDIA AND INFORMATION LITERACY AS A SITE FOR ANTICIPATION

"I have manipulated my Instagram quite a bit. I started to like things that were good for me to see", a participant recounts in one of our pair interviews with older teenagers, and continues to explain: "I was trying to recover from an eating disorder a little bit, so I started to like things that were good for me to see, like animals". This way of reasoning and acting is, we found, surprisingly common. Many people appear to be quite conscious of their own role in navigating social media and the way in which their actions, choices, likes, clicks, mentions, comments and whichever form of interaction a platform affords are implicated in the information they will and will not come across. If we consider this way of relating to and acting within the information infrastructure as an expression of everyday life media and information literacy, then how can we understand it? The account describes a pronounced *temporal* orientation, where past experiences of acting within the platform are related to the future with potentially serious implications for the person's health and everyday life. The way of acting described is oriented towards foreseeing different algorithmic futures; futures involving information to avoid, to create, to put up with, or to ignore. More precisely, the specific future that Instagram is anticipated to deliver is considered undesirable. The young person foresees it as emotionally and physically harmful and intervenes to craft a different algorithmic informational future. The intervention described lies within the bounds of the platform service, Instagram in this case. It does not subvert it, but adheres to its rules. Nevertheless, rather than abdicating, the person describes how they act to make Instagram show pictures of animals, far removed from anything that might trigger thoughts or behaviours that are detrimental to the rehabilitation process. While this might seem quite trivial, it is far from simple, involving various intersecting temporalities and time regimes and the tying together of "algorithmic imaginaries" (Bucher, 2017) with predictive and anticipatory strategies.

DOI: 10.4324/9781003163237-4

Anticipation offers a conceptual way to coordinate different strategies to bring about and order diverging future orientations and to tie those to present hopes and speculation (Clarke, 2015). "Anticipation", write medical anthropologist Vincanne Adams, together with science and technology researchers Michelle Murphy and Adele E. Clarke (2009, p. 247), "is the palpable effect of the speculative future on the present". And they continue, "[a]s an affective state, anticipation is not merely a reaction, but a way of actively orienting oneself temporally. Anticipation is a regime of being in time in which one inhabits time as future". Anticipation has been described as a fundamental trait of the chronopolitics of modern and late-modern society (ibid.; Müller, 2014). However, it is also a fundamental element of predictive analytics, which forms the basis for the operation of many algorithmic information systems.

Paying attention to the specific form of future-orientation to which the notion of anticipation refers, as we have set out to do, has another advantage. Such a focus makes clear the extent to which media and information literacy is in fact shaped by an anticipatory orientation, and the extent to which these future orientations are mixed up in paradigms of growth, acceleration, and development. Two specific manifestations of this future orientation stand out. These are, first, the way in which media and information literacy, by virtue of its intimate relationship with technological development, is always already obsolete, or at least appears to be so, and must always be reinvented; and second, the way in which generational differences enter into its conception and thus also how it is performed. Both are inherently self-contradictory in that they advance goal-oriented narratives that always delay their own fulfilment.

The question that guides the rest of this chapter revolves around these temporally based contradictions and ways of reasoning and acting: *How is media and information literacy shaped by the temporal regime of predictive decision-making and anticipatory intervention and by the conflicting time scales of technological development, generational relations, and the paradigms of acceleration?* The question attempts to unite two interests, both of which are concerned with the discursive-material implications of the future-orientation inherent in media and information literacy. These are the specific ways in which infrastructural meaning-making occurs through anticipatory intervention and the variously expressed future orientation in understandings of media and information literacy.

Meaning-making through anticipatory intervention

What the person describes doing at the beginning of the chapter is more than foreseeing their own future interest in certain content or information. Rather, they predict the prediction that the system is likely to make, and then intervene to make it predict differently. Despite the ordinariness, some might even say banality that this brief account conveys, it does involve creative strategies and an interest in productive involvement in the infrastructure on part of the individual. And as suggested earlier, this way of reasoning was not uncommon among our participants in the pair interviews. To illustrate, another participant in our pair interviews recounts acting in the following way:

> There was a period when I had just gotten my salary, for instance, and then you often tend to look at more expensive clothes, because then you have money to spend, but then also my ads on Instagram were for more expensive clothes. So then when I didn't have the money anymore, I felt that I didn't want to see expensive clothes anymore, because then I would want those clothes even more and more. So I had to start searching again and change, I changed somewhat what I searched for. […] And now I see more, like, sports stuff, some ads, and such like.

This account resembles in many ways the one that introduced the chapter. Yet here, not the person's health, but their finances are at stake. This person too strategically anticipates the predictive analytics of the algorithm to deliver content that they expect to deem unsuitable. Therefore, they provide it with data that they foresee making the system change its predictions. This results, the person describes, in Instagram displaying different adverts to them, adverts that will not tempt them. Thus, the affective dimension of the regime of anticipation is further shaped by its intersecting with the temporal regime of working life, cyclically structured by repetitions and routines, here by reference to paydays. In both cases, anticipatory information control is a form of self-control. For this, acting in the specific, system-appropriate anticipatory way becomes a necessary intervention to prevent certain content from showing up. The option of no information does not exist. In the two cases described here, the interventions thus lead to harmful content in the feeds being replaced by harmless content. In other words, it is a strategy of information avoidance. Since the profound implications that increasingly opaque algorithmic information systems have on everyday life is often only noticed when dissonance occurs, sometimes giving rise to strategies to avoid or minimise it, this is quite common. But this need not be the only way of going about it. Similar anticipatory strategies are also used in affirmative ways that focus not on avoidance but on consciously shaping one's feed to display what is of interest. The following is an example of this:

> But if, for example, because sometimes on YouTube only the same things come up as recommended, and that is pretty boring. So, then I usually go and, either watch a new video or an old video from before, but one that is a completely different genre. If I then watch two, three of these in a row, it usually changes what is recommended.

Here, a young person recounts an intervention where the platform service, in this case YouTube, is provided with user data, in the form of engagements, with the expressed aim of shaping future recommendations of videos. This direct and deliberate intervention then enables YouTube to predict different content to be relevant and populate the feed (or recommended videos) with.

The same person concludes their account by explaining: "So that is a way in which I try to change that algorithm". In a strict sense, this is not what they do. They do not change the algorithm. On the contrary, they affirm it, play by its rules. They might even contribute to improving it (whatever that means). Nevertheless, it is an interesting statement, because it provides a glimpse into people's *algorithm awareness* (Gran et al., 2021), and more precisely, into how they imagine algorithms to operate. We already encountered some of these *algorithmic imaginaries* in Chapter 2. These are, in the words of media researcher Taina Bucher, "the way in which people imagine, perceive and experience algorithms and what these imaginations make possible" (Bucher, 2017, p. 31). How people conceptualise invisible algorithms and algorithmic systems, how they make sense of their effects, and how they consider themselves and their actions in relation to them, cannot be dealt with in terms of correct or incorrect. Rather, the different ways of imagining algorithms and algorithmic systems have implications for how they are used, interpreted, and understood.

In fact, participants in our pair interviews describe enacting algorithmic imaginaries in their depictions of how they relate to the algorithmic systems in question, mainstream social media platforms, and their predictive decision-making. Unavoidably, the meaning attributed to the content encountered, and also to the content that is deterred, implicates these conceptualisations. It could be argued that infrastructural meaning-making occurs by way of algorithmic imaginaries and increasingly involves variously layered anticipatory strategies. Consider the following account conveyed by another participant in one of our pair interviews. This time the information system in question is Google Search:

> For example, if I'm going to have a discussion with a friend, about something, then I google what I want to google, for example, "coffee causes cancer". Then I google "coffee causes cancer" and I get a lot of articles. Then he googles "coffee is good for your health", and then he also gets a lot of articles.

Not only does this person reflect on their employing the search engine as a tool for confirmation bias and the importance of choosing keywords, but they also talk about how they act based on an understanding of how the search engine's algorithms work. They describe how they create meaning from on the one hand the infrastructural conditions that their acting is part of and on the other hand from the specific social situation the search belongs to. This involves several intricately linked layers of anticipation and awareness. These go beyond awareness of what algorithms are, or what they might do, to include an understanding of the co-constitutive relation of social practices and infrastructures, acknowledging the distribution of agency across these sociomaterial arrangements. In addition, and this is what this chapter is about, such a stance entails an anticipatory dimension that shapes the way media and information are encountered and situates them in relation to both society and the individual. "The future is neither fully determined nor empty and open", notes the late sociologist John Urry (2016, p. 12), articulating precisely the location that anticipation inhabits at the intersection of personal and collective time regimes and the affective potential that this position gives rise to.

In our pair interviews, we came across numerous examples in which our participants describe how they make their own social media updates visible to others. They have certain ideas about what attracts attention and how to achieve engagement. This includes the realisation that the *when* is as important as the *what*. One participant explains, "[p]eople who wear revealing clothes usually get a lot of likes. And faces usually get a lot of likes too, and nature usually does not get that many likes." Another respondent who is very active on Instagram describes deleting a post with too few likes and re-posting it at a different time of day. The person explains, "One of my friends said to me, 'I see you posted the same picture three times today.' It's very embarrassing. But it's true." The assumption is that people and algorithms work hand in hand, as part of the same mechanism that creates both visibility and invisibility. Algorithm awareness here also means *algorhythm* awareness, to paraphrase both a song title by Childish Gambino and the title of a short film by artist Manu Luksch (see also Haider and Sundin, 2022). Timing – that is, tuning into the rhythm of the service and its algorithms – is an essential part of its use and of making sense of one's role in it and that of other people. This manifests itself in various temporal tactics. In the example above, it is about finding the best time to post for the algorithm to boost it in the feeds of followers. But it could also be about what time periods to avoid or when to post to hide content, how to interpret the timestamps given, when to check for updates, when to engage, and so on. This is enabled by experiential theories of how the temporal regime supported by the service's algorithms operates and what conditions for action such a regime might create. The rhythmicity of information practices is structured around the temporal regimes that algorithmic information systems enable and constrain (see also Tana et al., 2019; Bucher, 2020). Algorithm awareness entails an understanding of these temporal dynamics and regimes and is thus implicated in infrastructural meaning-making.

Indisputably, all this is far removed from the checklist approaches that we discussed earlier. Yet, it is also very different from what various official bodies and organisations promote as media and information literacy, how the media draw attention to it, or how it is taught or described in the curriculum, as we expand on in Chapter 5. Can these complex, multi-layered strategies of anticipation and infrastructural awareness even be discussed under the umbrella of media and information literacy? We argue – and hopefully succeed in making our case – that not only can they be considered under this label, but also that they need to be, if media and information literacy is to remain a meaningful category to be included in teaching, policymaking, or other attempts to address what we term "the crisis of information". Today, media and information literacy involves the creation of meaning from content shaped in the context of and by algorithmic systems that implement predictive decision-making. It thus increasingly involves ways of anticipating the shape of prediction in relation to particular forms of governance, and this typically includes the platform-specific algorithmic governance of corporate actors, such as social media, search engines, or recommender systems.

The next section touches upon a different type of temporal relation that constitutes media and information literacy and how it is imagined. Ideas of generational
characteristics are implicated in dominant narratives of people's relations to media
and information and in how they are thought to engage with it. Here, too, a distinct
future-orientation can be discerned, albeit operating in a different way.

Generational relations: between the times

In interviews with teachers, that we discuss more in Chapter 5, we encountered
the following statement: "it feels like you are always a step behind them" (see also
Carlsson and Sundin, 2018). Another teacher uses the same image when describing
pupils as "always [...] one step ahead" and teachers as "too old." This thinking is not
uncommon, and it is best expressed in the notorious metaphor of the digital native
(Prensky, 2001). The notion of digital natives, and variants of it, has been criticised
and its validity has been dismantled many times over, but it stubbornly sticks around.
Many teachers imply it, as this example illustrates, the media like it, and politicians
appreciate its straightforwardness. Yet, what is more, our own experience of engaging with young adults at university, indicates that the metaphor is attractive even to
the generation it describes, which by now is likely generations in the plural. One of
the authors remembers assigning the book *Search Engine Society* by communication
scholar Alexander Halavais (2017) to a class of first or second-year students in the BA
programme in the humanities at a Swedish University. Most of the students engaged
with the book in the way intended and we discussed it together with other readings
and reflections on their experiences at the seminar. However, it appeared that some
students found the reading unnecessary. It was too basic for them, they maintained,
and what's more, it was out of date. One student in particular brought in the notion
of the *digital native*, not as theoretical concept, but an identity. The student seemed to
apply it literally, as providing an accurate depiction of themself and her contemporaries in the seminar room that distinguished them from the lecturer, and also from
the author of *Search Engine Society*. Requiring them to read this book was a waste of
their time, the student explained. To explicate the position the student was speaking
from, an analogy was provided: "For us, this is like teaching us how to eat an apple."

Evidently, the intention with assigning the book was never to teach the students
how to use a search engine, but to enable understanding of various historic and
societal dynamics that Halavais (2017) addresses in his discussion of search engines.
We eventually addressed this miscommunication and could even use it as a basis for
discussion. The point of recounting this incident is not to specifically engage with
research on the concept digital native as such or whether is justified or not: rather,
here, it serves to highlight how deeply entrenched specific temporal relations that
advance normative ideas of what it means to belong to a certain age-group are and
importantly how these can be predicated on people's assumed relations to digital
information systems, most notably search engines and social media, but evidently
there are numerous others (see also Taipale et al., (Eds.)., 2017). These two self-
assigned positions, that of the teacher, who is always behind, and that of the young

university student, who is always ahead, can be seen to mark the extremes of the narrative of the digital native. Yet, if we want to understand the more nuanced expression of relations between members of different generations and their reasoning on media and information literacy in digital settings, we need to look elsewhere.

In series of family interviews, carried out as part of a research project led by one of the authors looking at notions of algorithms across generations (see Olsson Dahlquist and Sundin, 2020), the situation appears as considerably more nuanced. Consider the following exchange between a 39-year-old parent and their 13-year-old child, as part of a conversation on how Google orders search results, and whether that had been a topic of discussion in school:

CHILD: Have we? No, but I think it's a lot because what you searched for earlier. What they see that you have visited before and used, and so on

RESEARCHER: Right...

CHILD: Not because I have some prior knowledge about this, it's more like I am guessing that it's this. That they see what you have used earlier and what you visited. What would be a good fit for oneself, so they form it after one's personal... what you have visited.

PARENT: You make me proud (laughter). I am ashamed that we haven't talked about this.

The 13-year-old explains the search engine's way of determining relevance based on a rough, presumably experience-based understanding of predictive decision-making and an idea of a vague "they", who are watching and judging, and delivering content based on these observations of their users. Personalised relevance appears as the most important feature. This is interesting in itself. Google's personalisation of results – not adverts – is far less pronounced than such an account makes out. Yet, personalisation is a compelling narrative that tends to stick, and in the example above it appears as a deeply entrenched part of the infrastructural meaning-making. The relation between the parent and the child is nothing like the stereotypical digital native versus digital immigrant dichotomy: rather, the parent is pleased with the child's explanation, and wants to have a conversation about that topic, hinting that they are in fact competent to have such a discussion. Indeed, many parents in the family interviews seemed to have better understanding of the algorithmic mechanisms governing the circulation of information online than their children. Mainly because they are more experienced in looking for or dealing with information online, and often in important situations. Besides, parents often invoke their experience and general education that they can lean on to assess the credibility of media and information online. "It comes with age", a 49-year-old declares, while another person in their forties describes it as a civic duty to be critical, but that this duty requires being well-informed. For this parent, you need to be well-read and knowledgeable to be able to carry out the civic duty of critically evaluating information, which it is implied, is a matter of age, education, and life-experience.

A similar argument is made by a different parent, a 50-year-old. But the parent delivers it in way that is condescending of youth, who are accused of lacking general education. The other parent, who also participated in this interview, turns the tables. They frame being able to use mainstream digital tools – specifically, the conversation concerns Google Maps – into a matter of general education, more precisely a contemporary version of general education which the young possess and the old lack. This reintroduces the dichotomy between the young and the old, and makes it about a struggle over what counts as worthwhile knowledge and as being educated in the first place. Yet, if we extend this positioning to the information infrastructure itself, the question arises as to who is capable of perceiving and relating to it in the first place. A parent in their mid-fifties comments:

> I am thinking of [child's name]'s generation and those who are younger who entirely grow up in this digital society. That when it is so straightforward, then maybe you don't care as much about the background of it all and what it really is that steers. So, precisely because of this, it feels even more important to get knowledge about it.

Even though the term "digital native" is not mentioned directly, it is implied. Young people lack distance, the parent seems to say, which makes it difficult, not to say impossible, to perceive the infrastructure and oneself in it. Infrastructural meaning-making, we could argue, becomes difficult without frictions or disturbances that make the infrastructure perceptible in the first place. Being native to the infrastructure might reduce opportunities for friction and thus hinder rather than facilitate meaning-making, or at least some of it.

Let us return to the student, for whom using a search engine is as uncomplicated as eating an apple (of all fruits!). Self-confidently identifying as a digital native, the student skilfully navigates university and everyday life with digital tools, in ways that mark the student as different from those that were born in a non- or less digital world. These older people are perceived to be lagging behind, the same sentiment that was expressed by the teacher quoted at the outset of the section. At first sight, this appears to be a reversal of the typical depiction of how humans develop and mature, from children to youth to adults, an understanding which often informs metaphorical depictions of progress. Increasingly, workshops and training programmes specifically aiming to educate older people and to enable them to function in a constantly transforming, digital society. Media and information, or digital, literacy are common labels under which such initiatives are organised. These are intended to enable older people to participate in society, as both citizens and consumers, and to facilitate on the one hand their independence, and on the other hand their sense of belonging. And for sure, this is also what many participants in the family interviews report experiencing. This is a valid and important outcome, which surely increases the quality of life for many participants. Yet, in a wider perspective, returning to the notion of *responsibilisation*, that we discuss in Chapter 2, adds a further dimension which supports situating such initiatives in societal development more broadly. They can be seen as societal interventions to enable the governing of the self and furthermore, we suggest, to accelerate and intensify it.

Thus, what at first glance, appears as a reversal of an established image of progress as maturing, where the young are more advanced, more highly skilled and more knowledgeable than the old, is, at a collective level, better understood as affirming a conventional understanding of progress. The specific *discourse of progress* that has been described as formative of how modern cultures anticipate the future, envisions progress as a continuous linear process of incessant improvement, advancement, and expansion (Urry, 2016). The idea of economic development and the division of the world into more or less developed countries and populations, essentially along colonial and racist lines, is fundamentally wedded to this much critiqued, but extremely powerful idea of progress.

In a 2020 *Evaluation of UNESCO's work in the area of Media and Information Literacy* (UNESCO, 2020, p. 1) the purpose is formulated as follows: "to enhance the Organization's potential contribution to the 2030 Sustainable Development Agenda through its work in MIL and to provide better support to Member States in this area". This is then followed up in the management's response:

> This increase in demand for MIL is not only consequent to the rising "disinfodemic," partially owing to the COVID-19 pandemic, but also a recognition that media and information literate societies enable the achievement of the sustainable development goals.
>
> *(UNESCO, 2020, Annex I, p. 1)*

For sure, neither of these statements contains any surprises, as we already argue in Chapter 3. Nevertheless, the self-evident connection that is claimed between media and information literacy and development, here sustainable development, is interesting as it is reminiscent of the profound interconnection between certain understandings of media and information literacy, and sometimes digital literacy, and the discourse of progress, constitutive of international development (see also Haider and Bawden, 2006; Pilerot and Lindberg, 2011), but also of the global knowledge economy's neoliberal timescape (Drabinski, 2014; Nicholson, 2019). The temporal paradigm that media and information literacy exists within the worlds of organisations like UNESCO where it is enlisted in the project of sustainable development is one of strict linearity. The striving for development goals governs the advancement of media and information literacy. Correspondingly, media and information literacy, since it is instrumental to this goal, has to have the same thrust and direction, namely that of a better future. The question, then, is, for this better future to arrive, whose life and which societies need intervention and support?

In particular, the response provided to one of the recommendations in the *Evaluation of UNESCO's work in the area of Media and Information Literacy* is noteworthy in the context of our interest in generational and related temporal relations and their embedding in this linear notion of progress. The report recommends: "Upscale MIL work with a focus on gender equality and the inclusion of the most vulnerable groups" (UNESCO, 2020, Annex, p. 3). The response, which accepts the recommendation, includes the following:

> MIL actions targeting and empowering youth as a vulnerable group will be sustained. Partnerships will be explored around MIL in support of other disadvantaged groups, such as older people, migrants, and people with disabilities. MIL in support of gender equality and empowerment of disadvantaged or marginalized groups will be a central theme in the first global forum on "Mobilizing Partnerships and Resources for Media and Information Literacy" mentioned above.
>
> *(ibid.)*

Both the young and the old are identified as disadvantaged, alongside migrants, the disabled, and women, although the actual phrasing concerns gender equality. Once again, there are good reasons for discerning these specific groups and attempting to equip their members with education, knowledge, and resources to act independently in an unequal world pervaded by digital platforms. Yet, there is a further interpretation that can be made, which sheds light on the way in which deficiency is diagnosed in contrast to a normative ideal of media and information literacy, whose place is left void in the statement. Given that the groups singled out in this paragraph easily make up the majority of the global population, at the very least we can conclude that their members are predisposed in ways that constitute an obstacle to assuming this position and the ideal aspired to is personified by a group that is missing from the list.

In 1983 anthropologist Johannes Fabian (2014[1983]) published his analysis of how *anthropology makes its object*, which is the subtitle of his influential book *Time and the Other*. Fabian compellingly shows how various forms of temporal distancing are fundamental to the construction of *other*s to objectify and study. To conceptualise this way of othering he coins the notion of *allachronism* (ibid., p. 32). This captures, in Fabian's words, "the denial of coevalness", as it is manifest in situating the societies studied in a different time frame, depicting them as behind, immature, savage, tribal, child-like, native, or whichever other, often racist and sexist, metaphor is employed. UNESCO's various media and information literacy programmes or those of similar organisations and their identifying of specific disadvantaged groups in the 2020s, does not work according to the exact same mechanisms that Fabian described in an analysis of nineteenth and twentieth century anthropology. Nevertheless, the devices employed work to a comparable effect. Development, including sustainable development, is of course goal-oriented. In other words, it has direction, a path leading to an anticipated future. It needs one to be discernible, measurable, and governable. Media and information literacy is but one mechanism recruited to discern, measure, and govern the objects for this regime of progress, who tend to be disadvantaged, historically oppressed groups. Often it is the same groups that are mentioned: women, the poor, immigrants, the young, and the old. It is implied that these need to be brought to the future, or more accurately perhaps, they need to be altered so the future can happen. In this narrative, media and information literacy through its intimate connection with digital technology, appears as a precondition for this form of progress to be possible.

How does the cultural trope of the digital native fit into this? The notion of the native is one of the temporal distancing devices that have been used in anthropology as a means for othering in precisely the way critiqued by Fabian. It is a label that, at least rhetorically, suspends a group in time. One cannot choose to become native, one is either native to a culture, a language, a society, and so on, or not. That means it cannot be taken away from one either. Reading through the lens provided by Fabian's (2014[1983]) analysis of how the invocation of certain temporalities creates distance between groups, lets the implicit temporality of the notion of digital natives shine through. It exists in relation to others who are excluded from the category by temporal distance. The distance is fixed, and the resulting temporality is one of stasis. Yet, as a cultural trope the digital native is anything but stagnant. On the contrary, it is characterised by constant change and endless renewal, often intensified by planned obsolescence. Library and information studies researcher Christine Pawley (2003), as we discuss in Chapter 3, speaks of information literacy as a contradictory coupling in which two conflicting goals are brought together: that of commodification and that of democracy and participation. The notion "digital native" is an even clearer expression of such a contradictory coupling. Its main tension arrives from its two parts – native and digital – which embody opposing temporal regimes, namely stasis and acceleration. Sociologist Hartmut Rosa (2015, p. 13) uses the notion of frenetic standstill to describe, in his words,

> the paradoxical basic structure of time in modernity (and, a fortiori, in late modernity), namely that experiences of acceleration can repeatedly flip over into their diametrical opposites, [which] can be observed not only on the level of historical time, but also on levels of lifetime and everyday time.

Talk of a generation of digital natives and self-identification along these lines appears as a coagulated manifestation of the very paradoxical structure of time, which Rosa refers to. The *native* is frozen in time and bound by tradition, while *the digital* races ever faster into a future that never arrives.

Media and information literacy as a moving target?

Where does this leave us? Thus far, we have discussed different types of future and anticipatory strategies involved in how media and information literacy is constituted. Anticipation of algorithmic decision-making has emerged as a possible strategy for infrastructural meaning-making as it enables pre-emptive and personalised information control. We could also see how age differences and generational identification are involved in how certain futures are implicit in media and information literacy narratives, yet in ways that are considerably more complex than it first appears. Rosa's (2015) notion of *frenetic standstill* helps to discern one particular aspect of the complexity that underlies these relations as it situates certain understandings of media and information literacy in a narrative of linear progress. Acceleration, specifically social acceleration, is an important, and much theorised, facet of the form of – collectively anticipated – progress, characteristic of modernity and late-modernity, and of capitalist society. It is also entailed in how media and information literacy, as it is tightly connected to digital society, is in constant need of upgrading. Rosa (2015, p. 301) talks of an "acceleration history of modernity" and distinguishes between three dimensions of social acceleration, namely, technical acceleration, acceleration of social change, and acceleration of the pace of life. For Rosa, *technical acceleration* "essentially represents a history of the progressive accelera-tion of transportation, communication, and production" (ibid.). The *acceleration of social change* pertains to an "escalation of the rate of social change with respect to associational structures, knowledge (theoretical, practical, and moral), social prac-tices, and action orientations" (ibid.). Finally, "the *acceleration of the pace of life* rep-resents a reaction to the scarcity of (uncommitted) time resources" (ibid., italics in original). Rosa further develops how,

> [...] technical acceleration and the acceleration of the pace of life stand in a peculiar paradoxical relationship to each other: the former frees up time resources by shortening the duration of processes and thus by itself leads to a decrease in the pace of life; prima facie it makes more free time available.
>
> *(ibid.)*

Yet, owing to the specific, and typically modern, linkage between growth and accel-eration, instead of slowing down, the pace of life accelerates in response.

Media and information literacy exists between and across these three forms of acceleration: technical acceleration, acceleration of social change, and acceleration of the pace of life. Its different expressions – as a practice, as an idea, as a narrative, as an object of policy and education – gain their meaning not so much from any one of these forms of social acceleration, but rather from how technical acceleration and the acceleration of social change and of the pace of life converge. In particular, the paradoxical relationship Rosa notes for technological change and the acceleration of the pace of life contributes to a distinctive facet of media and information lit-eracy and its role in society, namely its constant transformation. As many have noted, media and information literacy is a moving target, or more accurately, it aims at a moving target (see also Livingstone et al., 2008; Little, 2018; Livingstone, 2018). The close connection to the ever-changing digital technology is the obvious reason for this characteristic, which requires constant revision. The various courses for older adults that are frequently offered, not least by libraries, are indicative of this. In such courses, the focus is usually on skills and the use of specific tools and devices, either to be able to use public services or to maintain family and social relationships, but also to enable activities such as online banking or shopping.

But it is not only people of retirement age who experience the need to keep up to date as a constant requirement, but others as well. In research there is still often a focus on older people as *lagging behind* the younger generation (e.g. Karaoglu et al., 2021), which is seen as a problem to be overcome. In one of our interviews with teachers, a participant said the following: "We really have to be open to keeping up. To keep the pace and that. We teachers need to work really hard with keeping up in their world." Yet, the difference between members of different age groups may not be due to a lack of ability, but rather a lack of time, and also a type of fatigue in the face of constant and ever faster change. In the family interviews there was a clear sense among the adults that they spend too much time online and some were tired of having to constantly learn new skills for new services. In the words of a 29-year-old from the family interviews: "I have become more and more technophobic. I find it difficult with new forums and new things to learn. Somehow it's comfortable with what you already know." It was common to restrict the use of certain applications or to limit themselves to a few applications that had a specific function in their daily and social lives that was difficult to replace. This was especially true with regard to Facebook, which was described as "hard to quit because you have a social network on there", by a parent in their late thirties, who further described themselves as having turned into a luddite. Both the *compulsion to adapt* and *the fear of missing out*, that are articulated here, can be interpreted as subjective expressions of the acceleration of the pace of life (Rosa, 2015, p. 307). Another parent, a person in their early fifties, expressed a similar sentiment, stating:

> Yes, I would like to avoid Facebook too, but because… On the desktop, Messenger is connected to it, and its calendar and events and stuff. This is what pulls you in and keeps you there and that feels really good to have.

The children and young people who participated in the family interviews did not generally share the same sense of wasting time or of losing control over time. Nonetheless, the parents' generation felt that the young were wasting their time and their lives by staring at screens. Indeed, how to regulate the time they and their children spent in front of screens, usually a shorthand for time spent online, was a recurring topic of discussion in most families. As expected, the young expressed opposition to the concept and its rules. Media and communication researchers Alicia Blum-Ross and Sonia Livingstone (2018) highlight the dilemma associated with expectations of contemporary parenting. On the one hand, parents are expected to ensure that their children develop relevant skills for a society steeped in media and digital technologies, not least in form of media and information literacy. On the other hand, they are expected to provide their children with a childhood similar to their own (or an idealised version of it) in a less media-saturated world.

These conflicting expectations, we suggest, are linked to the temporal paradox in which media and information literacy is caught. It could be argued that family discussions about screen time convey the experience of a loss of time and control over time from one generation to the next, and that this represents an attempt to decelerate time, or more specifically to decelerate the pace of life. This highlights two issues of relevance for understanding media and information literacy that nuance its conception as a moving target or as aiming at one, First, the issue of information avoidance, and second, its complicated association not only with technical acceleration, but with the acceleration of social change and the acceleration of the pace of life. To start with, the struggle over screen time – one's own and that of family members – can be interpreted as a struggle for the control of time. Moreover, as we suggest, it is implicated in attempts to decelerate. In a society characterised by a ubiquitous networked, corporate information infrastructure that constantly demands the production of user data and provides near-constant access to media and information, efforts at deceleration necessarily involve this infrastructure. They are articulated here as attempts to withdraw from the information infrastructure or at least limit participation in it. Media and information literacy not only emerges in regard to the media and information one actually encounters or interacts with, but also encompasses competencies to avoid getting involved in the first place. Control of information takes shape through the control of time, and vice-versa. In a pervasive information infrastructure, media and information literacy includes resources for the control of downtime and active time. Yet, social media, recommender systems, and similar platforms obstruct this possibility, by their very design, constantly withdrawing and making it an almost unattainable goal (or target). As the parent quoted above explains, "it pulls you in and keeps you there". This can be experienced as a denial of control, especially control over time and the acceleration of the pace of life. The mushrooming of software applications to help control screen time – one's own and that of one's children – must be seen in light of this close connection between information control and control of time.

Second, the image of media and information literacy as constantly lagging behind the increasingly faster development of digital tools, while intuitively plausible, also obscures other important aspects. In particular, it obscures the view of the fundamental integration of media and information literacy into social structures and practices, and their increasingly rapid transformation; what Rosa (2015) refers to as the acceleration of social change. This includes the ever faster changing of norms, values, knowledge, and also of "lifestyles, work, family structures, political and religious ties" (ibid., p. 301). Undoubtedly, media and information literacy is caught up in the acceleration of knowledge production and circulation, in changing values and social structures through which to enact and consider what it means to be media and information literate. However, there is also a profoundly material element that is rarely considered. The example of negotiating screen time, which we discussed above, works as a case in point. Regulating when and in which form to be online and when to disconnect is part of how to behave, how to have a conversation, how to have a family dinner, how to be a student, a friend, a parent, an employee, and so forth. An ever-changing etiquette has emerged that governs the use of information tools, be they screens, smart home assistants, or sound devices, and it intersects with various norms and values, including family structures and other social relations that are being modified in the process. From a broader perspective, as we tried to develop, media and information literacy cuts across the different forms of social acceleration, technical acceleration, acceleration of social change and of the pace of life. Thus, rather than imagining media and information literacy as aiming at a moving target, we can modify the metaphor to imagine that it is involved in moving and reshaping the target itself.

Social acceleration goes far beyond technological progress and also entails acceleration of the pace of life and of social change (ibid.). As we have tried to elucidate, various anticipatory mechanisms are involved in how media and information literacy is enacted, imagined, and promoted. The relationship between media and information literacy and the material-discursive expressions of the different forms of social acceleration is one of co-constitution. That is, media and information literacy – as a practice, as an idea, as a narrative, as an object of policy, education, and research – is not an outcome of social acceleration, but is involved in its production, which in turn is involved in the formation of media and information literacy.

In Chapter 2, we came across the United Nations-supported *Verified* project, with the aim to provide trustworthy, vetted information on COVID-19 that is explicitly tailored for social media dissemination in order to stem the tide of problematic content on the subject. *Verified* included a so-called *#pledgetopause*, that was introduced by a short video urging people not to spread outrageous content – mis- or disinformation – on social media, as this could have unintended consequences (Verified, n.d.). Leaving aside the irony of encouraging people to share a video on social media, which in turn encourages people not to share content on social media, this is interesting for another reason. It relates to a number of similar campaigns that all have the same message, which can be roughly summarised as follows: Stop before you share, consider the consequences of your actions, take responsibility.

This call for self-restriction ties into a general discussion that further complicates the contradictions around which responsibility evolves, namely the role and meaning of non-engagement, the refusal to share, the meaning of not searching and so on. The importance of *strategic ignoring* has been highlighted by scholar of education and psychology Sam Wineburg and digital literacy researcher Sarah McGrew (2019) in their discussion of lateral reading for civic online reasoning, where they convincingly show that expertise depends as much on the ability to ignore as it does on content intake. We return to lateral reading in particular in more detail in Chapter 5. For now, we want to point out that strategic ignoring, which requires, or even emerges from, the need to manage and conserve attention (Breakstone et al., 2021), is related to social acceleration. To evaluate large amounts of material and weigh different claims and sources, as is often required to determine the credibility and trustworthiness of information, attention must be drawn to some issues while others will be disregarded. In a media-saturated environment, with rapid production of content and a wealth of information available on almost any topic, it is essential to ignore large portions of information, but to do so in a strategic way that contributes to the creation of meaning. In this sense, media and information literacy in digital cultures already depends to a significant extent on strategic ignoring. Yet, we suggest, there is more to it. In part, initiatives like #pledgetopause can be understood as an extension of this notion of strategic ignoring to include what might be called strategic infrastructural constraint. The point is that information control concerns, of course, the selecting and vetting of information, but it is also about withdrawal, strategic ignoring, and constraint, both to enable understanding and meaning-making under time pressure and to resist the pull of infrastructural desires.

Conclusion: the temporal paradox

There is a disconnect between understanding media and information literacy as responding to existing information sources in order to evaluate them, and people's reasoning about media and information literacy as entailed in social practices that involve digital intermediaries and which have implications for their future information encounters and those of others. We suggest that media and information literacy needs to be both future-oriented and historically aware; however, the latter aspect is usually assigned more significance, which is reflected in the focus of teaching material or guides. Conceptualising media and information literacy in terms of its future-orientation helps us to clarify that it also involves anticipating future information flows and includes ways of understanding how present and past engagements shape future information. Given that the invisible rules that govern contemporary information intermediaries are adaptive, mutable, and dynamic, anticipation necessarily means negotiating multiple levels of uncertainty.

Further, attention to regimes of anticipation helps to identify more precisely how media and information literacy is enlisted in the dominant narrative of progress and development. There is, however, a negative dynamic arising from the fact that media and information literacy education and policymaking today frequently focuses on the mastery of digital skills that are often outdated in relation to the technology available only a short time later. The reader might remember the quote, "it feels like you are always a step behind them". The dynamic is also reflected in the way in which different generations are pitted against each other in different ways due to deficits in skills, general education, or access, most prominently expressed in the notion of the digital native, but there are other forms too. Anticipatory intervention and the setting of normative, progress-oriented goals, while different in many regards, both help emphasise the central role of information avoidance, be it in form of pre-empting the prediction of predictive decision-making, as regulating screen time in attempts to control time and slow down the pace of life, or be it by identifying and averting mis- or disinformation.

This sheds light on a further dimension regarding how anticipation and media and information literacy connect, namely on the level of what it means to be a responsible citizen. Adams et al., (2009, p. 254) write:

> Anticipation calls for a heralding of the emergent 'almost' as an ethicized state of being. Being ready for, being poised awaiting the predicted inevitable keeps one in a perpetual ethicized state of imperfect knowing that must always be attended to, modified, updated. The obligation to 'stay informed' about

possible futures has become mandatory for good citizenship and morality, engendering alertness and vigilance as normative affective states.

If we consider media and information literacy through the lens this reasoning provides, and in light of social acceleration, we can see how the incessantly delayed emergence of the media and information literate citizen rests on controlling the relationship between encountering and avoiding information. Information control intersects with time control at the level of anticipation. Knowledge and ignorance are not opposites, but adhere to the same rules as part of the same commitment and obligation (McGoey, 2012; Greyson, 2019). Likewise, avoiding and engaging with media and information are both encapsulated in the same responsibility, yet since the former is often rendered invisible a lopsided relation emerges. The anticipatory stance is embedded in a complex temporal paradox: a disconnect that makes media and information literacy necessary, but also always insufficient, that demands full immersion and also self-restriction, and that is involved in society's constant acceleration and technical progress at the same time as it is instrumental to attempts at decelerating the pace of life.

References

Adams, V., Murphy, M., & Clarke, A. E. (2009). Anticipation: Technoscience, life, affect, temporality. *Subjectivity, 28*(1), 246–265. doi:10.1057/sub.2009.18

Blum-Ross, A., & Livingstone, S. (2018). The trouble with "screen time" rules. In G. Mascheroni, C. Ponte & A. Jorge (Eds.), *Digital Parenting: The Challenges for Families in the Digital Age* (p. 179–1879). Nordicom.

Breakstone, J., Smith, M., Wineburg, S., Rapaport, A., Carle, J., Garland, M., & Saavedra, A. (2021). Students' civic online reasoning: A national portrait. *Educational Researcher*, May. doi:10.3102/0013189X211017495

Bucher, T. (2017). The algorithmic imaginary: Exploring the ordinary effects of Facebook algorithms. *Information, Communication & Society, 20*(1), 30–44. doi:10.1080/13691 18X.2016.1154086

Bucher, T. (2018). *If… then: Algorithmic power and politics*. Oxford University Press.

Bucher, T. (2020). The right-time web: Theorizing the kairologic of algorithmic media. *New Media & Society, 22*(9), 1699–1714. doi:10.1177/1461444820913560

Carlsson, H., & Sundin, O. (2018). *Sök- och källkritik i grundskolan: En forskningsrapport.* Department of Arts and Culural Sciences, Lund University.

Clarke, A. E. (2015). Anticipation work: Abduction, simplification, hope. In G. Bowker, S. Timmermans, A. E. Clarke, & E. Balka (Eds.), *Boundary Objects and Beyond. Working with Leigh Star* (pp. 85–119). MIT Press.

Dahlquist, O. & Sundin, O. (2020). *Algoritmmedvetenhet i mötet mellan generationer: En forskningsrapport inom ramen för Digitalt först med användaren i focus.* Department of Arts and Cultural Sciences, Lund University.

Drabinski, E. (2014). Toward a kairos of library instruction. *The Journal of Academic Librarianship, 40*(5), 480–485. doi:10.1016/j.acalib.2014.06.002

Fabian (2014[1983]). *Time and the Other: How Anthropology Makes Its Object.* Columbia University Press. doi:10.7312/fabi16926

Gran, A. B., Booth, P., & Bucher, T. (2021). To be or not to be algorithm aware: A question of a new digital divide?. *Information, Communication & Society, 24*(12), 1779–1796.

Greyson, D. (2019). The social informatics of ignorance. Journal of the Association for Information Science and Technology, 70(4), 412–415. https://doi.org/10.1002/asi.24143

Haider, J., & Bawden, D. (2006). Pairing information with poverty: Traces of development discourse in LIS. *New Library World, 107*(9/10), 371–385. doi:10.1108/03074800610702570

Haider, J. & Sundin, O. (2022). Information literacy as a site for anticipation: temporal tactics for infrastructural meaning-making and algo-rhythm awareness. *Journal of Documentation, 78*(1) 129–143. https://doi.org/10.1108/JD-11-2020-0204

Halavais, A. (2017). *Search Engine Society*. John Wiley & Sons.

Karaoglu, G., Hargittai, E., Hunsaker, A., & Nguyen, M. H. (2021). Changing technologies, changing lives: Older adults' perspectives on the benefits of using new technologies. *International Journal of Communication, 15*, 3887–3907.

Little, H. B. (2018). Media literacy: A moving target. *Knowledge Quest, 47*(1), 16–23.

Livingstone, S. (27-7-2018). *Media Literacy – Everyone's Favourite Solution to the Problems of Regulation.* https://blogs.lse.ac.uk/parenting4digitalfuture/2018/07/27/media-literacy-problems-of-regulation/ [24-8-2021]

Livingstone, S., van Couvering, E., & Thumin, N. (2008). Converging traditions of research on media and information literacies. In J. Coiro, M. Knobel, C. Lankshear & D. J. Leu (Eds.), *Handbook of Research on New Literacies* (pp. 103–132). Lawrence Erlbaum Associates.

McGoey, L. (2012). Strategic unknowns: Towards a sociology of ignorance. *Economy and Society, 41*(1), 1–16. doi:10.1080/03085147.2011.637330

Müller, R. (2014). Racing for what? Anticipation and acceleration in the work and career practices of academic life science postdocs. *Forum Qualitative Sozialforschung / Forum: Qualitative Social Research, 15*(3), Art. 15. http://nbn-resolving.de/urn:nbn:de:0114-fqs1403150

Nicholson, K. P. (2019). On the space/time of information literacy, higher education, and the global knowledge economy. *Journal of Critical Library and Information Studies, 2*(1). doi:10.24242/jclis.v2i1.86

Pawley, C. (2003). Information literacy: A contradictory coupling. *The Library Quarterly, 73*(4), 422–452.

Pilerot, O., & Lindberg, J. (2011). The concept of information literacy in policy-making texts: An imperialistic project? *Library Trends, 60*(2), 338–360. doi:10.1353/lib.2011.0040

Prensky, M. (2001). Digital natives, digital immigrants: Do they really think differently? *On the horizon, 9*(5), 1–6. doi:10.1108/10748120110424816

Rosa, H. (2015). *Social Acceleration: A new theory of modernity*. Columbia University Press.

Taipale, S., Wilska, T. A., & Gilleard, C. (Eds.). (2017). *Digital Technologies and Generational Identity: ICT Usage Across the Life Course*. Routledge.

Tana, J., Eirola, E., & Eriksson-Backa, K. (2019). Rhythmicity of health information behaviour: Utilizing the infodemiology approach to study temporal patterns and variations. *Aslib Journal of Information Management, 71*(6), 773–788. doi:10.1108/AJIM-01-2019-0029

UNESCO (2020). *Evaluation of UNESCO's work in the thematic area of Media and Information Literacy (MIL)*. UNESCO.

Urry, J. (2016). *What is the Future?* John Wiley & Sons.

Verified (n.d.). About. https://shareverified.com/about/ [24-8-2021]

Wineburg, S. & McGrew, S. (2019). Lateral reading and the nature of expertise: Reading less and learning more when evaluating digital information. *Teachers College Record, 121*(11), 1–40.

5
EDUCATING FOR MEDIA AND INFORMATION LITERACY

"That you should not trust what you see or hear". This was the response of a teacher in a research interview when asked to explain what a critical evaluation of sources is. This answer expresses one of the biggest challenges that the advocacy of media and information literacy in the educational context often faces: how is it possible to encourage a critical approach to information and information sources and at the same time maintain a position of authority with regard to the critical evaluation of information itself? More than any other institution, school is the institution that is supposed to teach and support media and information literacy. In many countries, the teaching style and method has changed to focus more on the investigations made by pupils at the expense of what has been referred to as *chalk-and-talk* teaching, or teacher-centred versus pupil-centred pedagogy. This shift has gone hand-in-hand with a greater presence of constructivist and sociocultural theories of learning. These theories emphasise the need for pupils' individual development of knowledge (constructivist theories) or the need to learn together with others in natural settings (sociocultural theories). The focus on pupils' own enquiry and self-directed learning makes the teacher more of a mentor or supervisor, while traditional frontal teaching assigns the teacher the role of an authoritative truth-teller. In some places, such as notably England, the pendulum has swung back in favour of a more traditional view of schooling with an emphasis on the transmission and memorisation of factual knowledge (Buckingham 2017; Cannon et al., 2020). In reality, we rarely encounter either of these extremes, which are often used as scarecrows by the respective other side in the ongoing public debate about what and how the next generation should learn. Pupils have to some extent always had, or at least have had for a long time, school assignments that required them to acquire information by themselves, by, for example, visiting the library, or consulting an encyclopaedia. Conversely, even the

DOI: 10.4324/9781003163237-5

most progressive teachers have most likely helped their pupils to evaluate certain sources of information and their knowledge claims in terms of quality and trust-worthiness, and of course also factual accuracy.

During and since the 1990s, new digital learning technologies found their ways into schools. CD-ROM encyclopaedias, installed on stand-alone computers and other quality-controlled databases, were soon replaced by online versions accessible via networks. From the late 1990s, general-purpose search engines, and later, Wikipedia, made looking up information so much easier, at the same time as the responsibility for quality control to some extent was transferred from publishers and teachers to pupils. The growing research interest in pupils' independent information seeking has coincided with the emergence of learning technologies that support such activities. In line with this development, researchers have become increasingly interested in how pupils evaluate information sources (Alexandersson and Limberg, 2012; Limberg et al., 2008; Sundin and Francke, 2009). Expensively produced, curated, and controlled databases of encyclopaedias or articles have difficulties competing with a free search engine that often leads pupils to Wikipedia.

However, for information literacy researchers and librarians, information-seeking was not a new phenomenon. For example, Carol Kuhlthau (2004, pp. 29–52) developed her well-known information-seeking process model in a series of projects in a USA context, starting in the early 1980s where she explored pupils' information-seeking while working with school tasks. Kuhlthau's work was groundbreaking. She demonstrates the complexity and dynamics of information-seeking in more extensive learning tasks, involving not just cognitive processes and doings, but also how pupils' emotions changed throughout the task, and in relation to the success of their information-seeking. Yet, even if information retrieval facilities are mentioned – such as card catalogues, table of contents, libraries and, in her later work, also databases – her primarily cognitive approach treats the information infrastructure and information sources without considering their materiality and agency.

In many countries, educational institutions exhibit precisely the complexity we described in Chapter 2, namely, simultaneously promoting trust and mistrust, and distinguishing the latter from distrust. The teacher quoted in the introduction to the chapter apparently favours one over the other: mistrust over trust, which risks fuelling distrust as the dominant form of interrogation. Such an approach could, in certain situations, trigger reflective engagements with more traditional sources of information that are put out by established publishers or organisations. Yet, within the contemporary data-driven, algorithmic, and commercial information ecosystem in tandem with the political situation more broadly, this is unlikely to unfold in a way that benefits the balance of trust and mistrust. Educational settings also throw into sharp relief the difficulties involved in developing a sociomaterial understanding in media and information literacy. The rest of this chapter circulates around the question: *How can information literacy be taught while maintaining the necessary balance between scepticism and trust when the societal foundations for this balance are unmoored?*

In different countries

While various actors and organisations from different sectors advocate and promote media and information literacy in different ways, one institution in particular stands out – schools. Schools have a special role to play, not least because school attendance is compulsory in most countries. Each country's education system contributes to establishing norms and values and creates common standards. During education, pupils are expected to learn what is considered knowledge in order to participate in society. In democracies, school is usually seen not only as a place of learning, but also as a place to foster democracy. So, what is the role of media and information literacy, with regard to this dual objective? It turns out that it is not always that significant. The current crisis of information and the constant warnings from experts and politicians about how social media, search engines and recommender systems amplify political and religious extremism and access to illegal material have not always led to a change in how schools approach media and information literacy. Media literacy researcher David Buckingham says:

> Politicians are happy to buy into anxieties about online pornography and paedophiles, or young people watching Isis recruiting videos, or 'fake news', but are somehow unable to stomach the idea that we might teach young people to be critical of media. They are keen to pour lots of media technology into schools, but they resist the idea that we might use it as anything other than an instrumental tool.
>
> *(Buckingham 2017, p. 4)*

In the sometimes-fierce competition over space between subjects in the curriculum, media and information literacy (and the various concepts describing similar teaching and learning content) often has difficulty finding a place at the curriculum table – either as a subject in its own right or as an aspect of other subjects.

The development of a critical attitude towards what is taken for granted is generally encouraged, even though the so-called knowledge-based curriculum can be seen as challenging such a critical approach (ibid.). We will return to this point shortly. However, it is only recently (if ever) that a critical approach has been extended to the information infrastructure itself. It is one thing to be able to do a quick Google search, but it is another to understand the role of Google and how the "mundaneification" of search and the "search-ification" of everyday life (Sundin., 2015[7]) perpetually re-arrange the orders of knowledge in contemporary society. It is one thing to know how to evaluate a news article from a critical perspective, but quite another to understand the news ecosystem in which social media platforms act as de facto editors. The shift from print media to digital media has highlighted the extent to which infrastructures for knowing and getting informed are part of and shaped by algorithms, power structures, politics, and commercial interests. This is of course also the case for earlier information infrastructures, and there is a rich history of research on this topic. But for the wider public, including schools, this has remained mostly opaque in today's society, we believe. A challenge for media and information literacy, if we let it speak as an actor in its own right, is now to extend a critical approach to the information infrastructures themselves, while acting from within the infrastructures to support and facilitate the same critical approach. To locate this challenge, and also address how it is being dealt with differently, we briefly present how this is expressed in the curricula in Sweden, England, and in Common Core Standards for the USA.

The USA

In the USA, curricula and learning goals are formulated at the state level. At the national level, the education system is therefore less homogeneous compared to some other Western countries. Nevertheless, a Common Core State Standards (CCSS) initiative was launched in 2009 to define what should count as basic knowledge for years K–12. It is important to note that a standard is not a curriculum and "[t]he Standards must therefore be complemented by a well-developed, content-rich curriculum consistent with the expectations laid out in this document" (National Governors Association Center for Best Practices, Council of Chief State School Officers 2010, p. 6). At the time of writing in summer 2021, all but nine states have adopted the CCSS. The CCSS includes English Language, arts and literacy in history/social studies, science, and technical subjects, as well as mathematics. It is up to the states to provide guidance on how to implement the standards in teaching practice. Nevertheless, the standards provide us with an idea of what is considered basic school knowledge in the USA, from Kindergarten (4–5 years old) to Grade 12 (17–18). Media and information literacy, or at least aspects of it, seems to be included in all subjects:

> [S]tudents need the ability to gather, comprehend, evaluate, synthesize, and report on information and ideas, to conduct original research [...] The need to conduct research and to produce and consume media is embedded into every aspect of today's curriculum.
>
> *(ibid., p. 4)*

When taking a closer look at the CCSS, we find specific examples of evaluating information sources in *Reading Standards for informational texts*. At Level 4, pupils are supposed to be able to: "Integrate information from two texts on the same topic in order to write or speak about the subject knowledgeably" (ibid., p. 14). This comparison of sources gets more and more advanced throughout the grades. For instance, in Grades 9–10, pupils should be able to "[a]nalyze various accounts of a subject told in different mediums [...]" and "[d]elineate and evaluate the argument and specific claims in a text, assessing whether the reasoning is valid and the evidence is relevant and sufficient; identify false statements and fallacious reasoning" (ibid., p. 40). It is apparent that the comparison and evaluation described here pertains to content of information rather than to information sources.

In the section *Writing Standards*, the issue of finding information is addressed. Already in preschool education (K) pupils should be able to do the following: "[w] ith guidance and support from adults, recall information from experiences or gather information from provided sources to answer a question" (ibid., p. 19). Even this ability is supposed to get more advanced in the higher grades. For Grades 11–12, it is then phrased as:

> Gather relevant information from multiple authoritative print and digital sources, using advanced searches effectively; assess the strengths and limitations of each source in terms of the task, purpose, and audience; integrate information into the text selectively to maintain the flow of ideas, avoiding plagiarism and overreliance on any one source and following a standard format for citation.
>
> *(ibid., p. 46)*

Similar formulations about searching ("gathering") are repeated in the descriptions of other subjects. However, finding sources of information – searching – is not connected with evaluating sources. Searching is described as a practical and instrumental method, which is reflected in the use of the word "effectively" instead of "critically". As a result, technologies for finding appear as neutral technical tools rather than the highly complex fusion of technology, information, and information that organises, and prioritises much of what there is to know in the world today.

Scholar of education and psychology Sam Wineburg criticises the CCSS for focusing too much on close reading of individual sources instead of providing an understanding of how the Internet can be used to evaluate sources (Wineburg, 2021). According to Wineburg, close reading is appropriate when there is a "scarcity of sources". But today for most topics people experience an "overabundance of sources" (ibid.), as we have already touched on in Chapter 4 in relation to time constraints and the need for *strategic ignoring*. Instead, he and his colleagues have repeatedly called for a greater focus on *lateral reading* rather than what they call *vertical reading* (e.g. Wineburg and McGrew, 2017), terms to which we will return later in the chapter. Wineburg also explains that evidence, a concept often repeated in the CCSS, must always be linked to a source (Wineburg, 2021; see also McGrew et al., 2018). This argument aligns well with our own argument developed in Chapter 3 under the heading "Content of message or source of information?".

The *Common Core State Standards* initiative in the USA might be combined with other related initiatives or standards. In California, for example, the *Model School Library Standards for California Public Schools* were adopted (2011). This is an ambitious standard that, at least in the words of the California Department of Education (Ong, 2011), "[…] sets a groundbreaking vision for strong school library programs in California, including identification of the skills and knowledge essential for students to be information literate." They explicitly refer to information literacy and extend from Kindergarten all the way to Grade 12. The *Model School Library Standards for California Public Schools* identify information literacy as a subject that should be taught by librarians, but it is not mandatory. Nevertheless, many of the learning goals of the school library standards can be related to the more abstractly formulated standards of the *Common Core State Standards* initiative, which focus on individual sources rather than the complexity of the information infrastructure.

England

The current national curriculum in England (National Curriculum in England, 2014) was introduced in 2014. The following subjects are obligatory for all pupils: English, mathematics, science, design and technology, history, geography, art and design, music, physical education (PE), computing, ancient and modern foreign languages. This curriculum is intended to be a "knowledge-based curriculum", something which critics have accused of merely focusing on cramming of facts instead of fostering critical understanding (Buckingham, 2017). The idea of a knowledge-based curriculum is based on the work of educational philosopher E. D. Hirsh. Its advocates claim "that returning to a traditional, academic curriculum built on shared knowledge is the best way to achieve social justice in society" (ASCL, n.d., p. 6). However, critics, such as Buckingham, maintain that the underlying idea is that "[t]his 'powerful' knowledge is possessed by the elite, by virtue of their superior, traditional education; but if all children can be taught it, then they will somehow automatically become 'powerful' themselves" (Buckingham, 14-08-2019).

Compared to its predecessors, the 2014 curriculum in England has reduced the importance of the subject of media studies, but aspects of media and information literacy appear as content in other subjects. In English, for example, the need to evaluate information content (rather than sources) is emphasised. Pupils of age 10 to 11 should be able to, it is said:

- Distinguish between statements of fact and opinion
- Retrieve, record and present information from non-fiction

(National Curriculum in England 2014, p. 45)

The guidance accompanying the learning requirement recommends the use of "reference books", "indexes", and "content pages" (ibid., p. 46). It also states that these "skills of information retrieval" should be applied in other subjects. Undoubtedly, this is a very traditional and book-centred view of information retrieval. For older pupils (14–16 years), the curriculum maintains that pupils should "understand and critically evaluate texts" (ibid., p. 86). It should be noted that, unlike previous national curricula, "media" is not mentioned at all in the chapter concerning the subject English (Cannon et al., 2020), but features instead in the subject computing.

Computing is not just defined as narrowly as computer science, but assigned the broader task of ensuring that "'pupils become digitally literate – able to use, and express themselves and develop their ideas through information and communication technology – at a level suitable for the future workplace and as active participants in a digital world" (National Curriculum in England 2014, p. 230). Social psychologist and media scholar Sonia Livingstone (27-07-2018) doubts that computing even covers what is needed for such broader understanding (see also Cannon et al., 2020). Between the ages of 5 and 7, pupils should already be learning to "understand what algorithms are" (National Curriculum in England 2014, p. 231) and between 7 and 11 they should be learning to "understand computer networks, including the internet" (ibid.). The term "critical" is not used here or elsewhere in the chapter on computing. Instead, it goes on to say "how they can provide multiple services such as the world wide web; and the opportunities they offer for communication and collaboration" (ibid.). In addition, pupils at this age should learn to "use search technologies effectively, appreciate how results are selected and ranked, and be discerning in evaluating digital content" (ibid.). At ages 11–14, pupils should learn to "understand several key algorithms that reflect computational thinking [for example, ones for sorting and searching]; use logical reasoning to compare the utility of alternative algorithms for the same problem" (ibid., p. 232). Conversely, the subject Citizenship concerns democracy, politics, critical thinking, and social issues. However, it does not relate to the evaluation of information sources, media or aspects of the information infrastructure, or "computational thinking", while computing does not relate "computational thinking" to *societal* or *political thinking*, to mirror the term.

What we see in the curriculum is a disconnect between critical understanding, information infrastructure, and democracy, which makes for a weak situation for media and information literacy content in English schools. For computing, the curriculum includes aspects of media and information literacy, but these are perceived as functional skills (Cannon et al., 2020). The challenge is to connect computing issues to social and cultural issues, or even more specifically to understand computing as a social phenomenon, so that topics such as algorithms and search engine rankings are not treated solely as technical concerns in a narrow sense.

Sweden

Sweden has a national curriculum for compulsory education, ranging from Level 1 to 9. Among the 14 bullet points in the introductory chapter of the *Swedish Curriculum for Compulsory School* (Lgr11, 2018) for what pupils should acquire knowledge about, the following goal is mentioned: They should be able to "use both digital and other tools and media for attaining knowledge, processing information, problem-solving, creation, communication and learning" (ibid., p. 11). All syllabi are presented in the curriculum with an aim, core content for different age levels, and knowledge requirements for different grade levels. Issues related to news media are mainly addressed in the subject Civics (literally translated as "Societal Knowledge"). Undoubtedly, news media, critical evaluation of information sources and searching are given a stronger presence than in the curriculum of England or in the standards of the USA.

One of six aims for civics (which is a compulsory subject in Sweden) wants pupils to be able to "search for information about society from the media, the internet and other sources and assess its relevance and credibility" (ibid., p. 228). One of five goals for the subject Swedish is: "search for information from different sources and evaluate these" (ibid., p. 263). Critical evaluation of sources is included in the curriculum of numerous subjects (Nygren et al., 2019). For example, in biology, one of the core content bullet points for Levels 7 to 9 reads as follows: "Critical examination of sources of information and arguments encountered by pupils in different sources and social discussions related to biology, in both digital and other media" (ibid., p. 170). In other words, it is not only about acquiring knowledge of the subject as such, but also about being able to evaluate and critically examine different sources on it. The amount of space given to critical evaluation of sources in the Swedish curricula is quite remarkable, especially when compared to England and the USA. We will return to this in Chapter 6.

Searching for information is particularly emphasised in the syllabus for the school subject Swedish. Already in Levels 1 to 3 (ages 7 to 9 years), it includes the following core content: "Searching for information in books, periodicals and on websites for children using search engines on the internet" (ibid., p. 264). There is similar content at Levels 4 to 6 (10 to 12 years) and 7 to 9 (13 to 15 years). However, search, search engines and other material and technical parts of the information infrastructure are not viewed from a critical perspective. Instead, they are conceived as neutral tools for accessing certain information. The critical examination is only attributed to the sources themselves and not to the information systems that prioritise and provide access to the sources. In the public debate in Sweden, the current curriculum has also been criticised for focusing too much on the analysis and critical evaluation of sources rather than on teaching factual knowledge.

Similar but different

A comparison between the three countries is difficult. The texts discussed here emerged from different national contexts and have different lengths and formats. As mentioned earlier, there is no compulsory curriculum in the USA as there is in England and Sweden. Moreover, a curriculum does not necessarily tell us much about what actually happens in the classroom. That said, we can make one general observation. While evaluating information sources has a place in all three documents, the infrastructure of information, including the different systems involved, is much less visible. If we take a look at the very broad and certainly ambitious model from UNESCO in the publication *Think Critically, Click Wisely! Media and Information Literate Citizens* (Grizzle et al., 2021), which is the second edition of the *UNESCO Model Media and Information Literacy Curriculum for Educators and Learners*, we come across a different perspective. This 2021 framework, which also suggests concrete pedagogical approaches to be used for media and information literacy education, covers some aspects of infrastructural meaning-making and considers the role of algorithms and their functions in social media and search engines.

Broadening the perspective to countries outside the Western world, it becomes clear how deeply some of the assumptions underlying media and information literacy presuppose the democratic organisation of society and social values rooted in Western cultures. We are aware that in writing this book, we are of course contributing to and continuing this kind of framing. The UNESCO published a report entitled *Media and Information Literacy Education in Asia: Exploration of policies and practises in Japan, Thailand, Indonesia, Malaysia and the Philippines* (Kajimoto et al., 2020). It provides a highly interesting perspective showing that the challenges are both similar and different across countries, cultures, and political systems. Just like Sweden, the USA, and England, this small selection of countries in Asia are of course not representative of other countries. The notion that media and information literacy, with its focus on criticism and democracy, should be formulated as a universal good is clearly at odds with the actual situation, in terms of cultural norms and not least existing political systems. In countries with authoritarian governments the critical aspect of media and information literacy simply prohibits itself. Yet, even in societies where freedom of expression and democratic values are part of the political system, questioning and the critical agenda of media and information literacy "can be considered as disrespectful" (ibid., p. 10), as an author of one of the studies included in the report formulates the difficulty. The report also shows how technical and practical aspects are prioritised in the teaching of media and information literacy, not because the organisations working with them lack an understanding of the importance of situated and critical aspects, but simply because such a focus appears neutral and can therefore be promoted. The authors' of the report astutely conclude that "the lofty aspiration of citizen empowerment through education to mitigate polarisation, inequality, radicalisation, and other pressing concerns of our time is marred by political conditions, cultural norms, structures of education sectors and other factors" (ibid., p. 12). In Chapter 2 we raised a similar point when we discuss the role of responsibility and the problematic conflation of the ideal of the rational consumer with that of the enlightened citizen. As responsibility is embedded in particular political systems, the implications are of course very different. The report's conclusion goes on to say that "[t]he focus of media and information literacy education in the five countries tends to be about teaching individuals how to be discerning media users and communicators with adequate digital skills, without being holistic about its impact on society" (ibid., p. 12). Again, the problems mentioned in the report are not unique to these countries, but are a general problem, although the extent and exact manifestations obviously vary from country to country, or even within countries.

The content of national curricula and standards is one way of capturing what is considered important knowledge in society. The content of international literacy tests is another. The best known of these is certainly the test conducted by the OECD under the name PISA test, short for *Programme for International Student Assessment*. The next section deals with the PISA test and its various assumptions about information and media.

Performing media and information literacy in tests

National and international tests and measuring of schools' performance set much of the focus on teaching. In countries like Sweden, where the school system has transformed into a huge market, national test results are something individual schools boast about or play down. Schools often train their pupils for weeks for them to become 'test literate'. National tests function as an instrument for examining pupils and comparing different areas, cities, and schools. This directly affects the way a specific subject or topic is taught, but indirectly also which aspects of a subject are left out. The national tests focus on core knowledge, and what is regarded as peripheral topics run the risk of being rendered irrelevant. In effect, the strongly hierarchical, centre-periphery relations between subjects or aspects within them is at least partially created through these test regimes. A combination of knowledge-based curricula and a focus on performance runs the risk of leaving media and information literacy out, particularly those aspects that involve doings in combination with critical understanding (Cannon et al., 2020).

International tests are used as benchmarking instruments in competition between countries and often serve as a weapon in domestic political disputes about the school system. Let us take a closer look at PISA (Programme for International Student Assessment) – the international test that every three years tests a sample of 15-year-old pupils around the world in reading, mathematics, and science. Behind PISA is the *Organisation for Economic Co-operation and Development* (OECD). The results of PISA should serve as a basis for country comparisons to find weaknesses, but also to identify success factors. In PISA 2018, the focus was on reading and reading was defined more broadly than decoding texts in the narrow sense. According to PISA, the process of reading includes "locating information", "understanding", and "evaluating and reflecting" (OECD, 2021, p. 23). In particular, the meaning of the term "locating information" requires further explanation. In PISA 2018, two types of locating information were described:

- Access and retrieve information within a text – scanning a single text in order to retrieve target information consisting of a few words, phrases or numerical values.
- Search for and select relevant text – searching for information among several texts to select the most relevant text given the demands of the item/task.

(OECD 2019, p. 3)

The quotation illustrates how locating information is handled in two very different ways – within a particular text or within a larger universe of texts. The difference between the two ways may not seem that significant at first glance, but in a naturalistic setting, searching for texts usually and increasingly means using a search engine that makes decisions based on algorithms. We have previously proposed to call the first way of locating information for *intra-textual information searching* and the second method *inter-textual information searching* (Haider and Sundin 2019, p. 114). In schools, intra-textual information searching has a long tradition, which also can be seen above in the review of curricula and standards. It is about teaching pupils how to find information, often referred to as 'facts', in a text so that they learn to read effectively. Inter-textual information searching, in contrast, concerns locating relevant information from across different texts (and other media or documents). Inter-textual information searching is not new to education as it occurs in schools. The school library has long provided a space for inter-textual information searching of books and articles. However, with general-purpose web search engines, this type of searching has become much more important and widespread. The challenge for a test like PISA, as we will see below, is to translate this common, everyday activity into something testable.

In PISA 2018, pupils were asked the following, with "yes" and "no" being the possible answers:

> whether during their entire school experience they were taught a) how to use keywords when using a search engine such as <Google©>, <Yahoo©>, etc, b) how to decide whether to trust information from the Internet, c) how to compare different web pages and decide what information is more relevant for their schoolwork, d) to understand the consequences of making information publicly available online, e) how to use the short description below the links in the list of results of a search, f) how to detect whether information is subjective or biased, and g) how to detect phishing or spam emails.
>
> *(OECD, 2021, p. 2)*

The responses to the survey, together with scenario-based tasks, form the basis for the report *Are 15-year-olds prepared to deal with fake news and misinformation?* (OECD, 2021). Results varied from country to country, but on average only 41% of respondents said they had been taught how to recognise phishing or spam emails, while 74% said they had been taught about the possible adverse consequences of publishing information on the Internet. Percentages for the other questions were somewhere between these two figures. The countries we paid special attention to earlier in the chapter – USA, England, and Sweden – are all above the average. PISA 2018 also included scenario-based tasks to assess pupils' abilities to evaluate single and multiple sources and to distinguish opinion from fact. The results show that pupils who had indicated that had been taught about biased information generally performed better on the scenario-based tasks than their peers. Nevertheless, the tasks involved searching for information from multiple sources to a very limited extent, although PISA 2018 emphasises that there is "a greater emphasis on multiple-source texts" (OECD, 2018, p. 127) compared to previous PISA tests. However, some of the scenarios required students to "search for and select the relevant text" (OECD, 2019, p. 32), but there were few texts to search for and no search engine was involved.

In the foreword to the latest PISA report, Andreas Schleicher, Director for Education and Skills at UNESCO and responsible for PISA, argues for what he calls a "new digital literacy" (OECD, 2021). In particular, he advocates and justifies the need for this new digital literacy as a means to protect and develop democracy, drawing a comparison with "consumer protection" in other areas.

> Has the time come to extend consumer protection to people as absorbers of information, who are – let us not forget – voters? And if we do so, how will this restrict freedom of speech and creativity in knowledge creation? Transparency in political advertising in the social media sphere also merits closer attention given its increasingly prevalent use. The degree and sophistication of targeting techniques being deployed are astounding and they are poorly understood by the majority of social media users.
>
> *(ibid., p. 3)*

According to Schleicher, protecting "the consumer" – who is bizarrely imagined as an "absorber of information" – in the way this is normally done compromises the very democracy that the protection is meant to safeguard. Instead, for him, digital literacy is the answer. The report, to which Schleicher's text is the foreword, itself demonstrates some of the difficulties we highlighted above when discussing the presence of media and information literacy in curricula and standards in the US, England and Sweden: credibility evaluation and also distinguishing between opinions and facts are treated as detached from the infrastructure that amplifies the problem – the workings of social media, search engines, recommender systems and other platforms; including the role of user data, algorithms, information policy, and so on. The report mentioned describes the dangers of the so-called "post-truth climate", in which feelings are often given more weight than facts, as follows:

> Algorithms that sort us into groups of like-minded individuals create social media echo chambers that amplify our views, and leave us insulated from opposing arguments that may alter our beliefs. These virtual bubbles homogenise opinions and polarise our societies; and they can have a significant – and adverse – impact on democratic processes.
>
> *(OECD 2021, p. 138)*

This is a bleak observation. Yet, even if the survey mentioned above, included questions asking pupils if they remembered having been taught about certain aspects of the information infrastructure – such as the role of keywords, understanding a search result list, and the need to compare with other sources – the scenario-based tasks did not address the problems identified in the survey. How could they? By its design alone, the PISA test, or other similar tests for that matter, cannot successfully determine how pupils act from within the information infrastructure.

Teaching evaluation or teaching searching?

Regardless of whether we speak of information literacy, media literacy, or digital literacy, there is a typical difference to a narrower view of literacy that focuses on letters and numbers. Since the nineteenth century at least, it has been the task of compulsory schools to teach children how to use these. For a long time, the literacy of the masses was seen as important for industrialisation and later for fostering democracy. Accordingly, it became the purview of schools to support it, and it still is of course. Information, media, and digital literacy too are promoted by schools, at least to some extent. But as educational researchers Julian Sefton-Green, Helen Nixon and Ola Erstad write, "schools, and the academy more generally, do not control access to digital literacy" (2009, p. 109). This means that we learn digital literacy (as well as other literacies discussed in this book) continuously while we are online, even if certain aspects are learned in the classroom. There seem to be two types of information, media, or digital literacy that overlap only to a certain extent – one that is learned in everyday life and one that is learned in formal educational institutions. Talk of a 'digital generation' or 'digital natives' suggests that the former type of literacy is something acquired simply by virtue of growing up in a certain culture, at a certain time.

However, the enactment of media and information literacy in the classroom is often very different from everyday life practices. This is also why research has highlighted the so-called digital generation's limited abilities in terms of information literacy (Gross and Latham 2012; Julien and Barker 2009; Julien et al., 2018; Mahmood 2016). To some extent, as we briefly touched on in Chapter 4, it seems that the persistent narrative of a digital generation and even more so of digital natives makes it difficult to assign media, information, and digital literacy a place in schools and other formal educational settings. How can one motivate the use of resources and space for teaching information, media or digital literacy in the classroom if it is seen as a *natural* outcome of belonging to a particular generation in a country with high Internet penetration? In what is generally considered to belong to the domain of media and information literacy, there is a considerable discrepancy between what is learned and practiced in everyday life outside of these situations (e.g. Andersson, 2017). Yet, to a substantial extent, exactly the same tools, or more precisely, platform services, are used. This situation further complicates teaching about, for instance, searching or evaluating online information and information sources.

It is not only in national curricula that searching is given low priority or even made invisible. When interviewing teachers about their instruction practice in relation to some aspects of media and information literacy, it becomes clear how difficult it is for the profession to make search part of the teaching content (Carlsson and Sundin, 2018; see also Limberg and Sundin, 2006; Sundin and Carlsson, 2016). Pupils were often expected to search for information when completing their schoolwork, but very little attention was paid to the activity of searching itself.

One Swedish teacher argued that they prioritised the task of critically evaluating sources over searching as such: "Yes, there is probably an emphasis on source criticism, exactly. That's it, it's absolutely so." If the pupils were to search for sources on their own, the teacher explained, the critical evaluation part of the task would have suffered in quality:

> In and of itself, it was like this when I think about the fact that some students had some difficulty finding actual sources, or they only took certain sources that were quite similar, so then the source criticism discussion did not become the same, did not get the same depth perhaps. [...] it was a focus on that they had to critically evaluate them, they had selected and, yes, it was really so. There was probably not much talk about searching for information like that, actually.

As shown above, searching for information is given a place in the Swedish curriculum, but in the interviews with teachers, search was mainly treated as a straightforward, unproblematic activity leading to a supposedly more complex critical evaluation of information sources. One teacher argued: "[I]nformation searching is more like a method sort of, where you find information, and then when you start judging the information, then it turns into source criticism. That's how I think." An interesting observation made by one teacher is that the digitisation of educational resources has exacerbated the invisibility of search: "We had a period when we were into looking things up in encyclopaedias and so on, but we had to give that up". When searching for information is possible anytime, anywhere, it becomes difficult for teachers and school librarians to help. When pupils were confined to the computers in their classrooms or in the school library, the searching could be more easily observed and supported by teachers and librarians.

Although the Swedish curriculum stipulates that searching abilities should be tested, this was not often the case among the teachers who participated in the interviews. The pupils' search skills were only assessed indirectly by evaluating which sources the students made use of:

> You can search and compile, that's also what you show when you discuss in ways that are critical of sources, that you have found these sources and that you have found information in them, so it's not really possible to distinguish between them, so to speak, in the assessment.

Another quote illustrates how search must take a back seat to critical evaluation of sources, both as teaching content and as assessment:

RESEARCHER: But is it often the case that you give them some material or do they have to search for the material themselves?

TEACHER: No, I test the ability to critically evaluate sources, so it usually happens that I give them the material and that I have questions about it.

Another teacher explains that they "usually recommend websites to them, mainly because I want them to get started and so I provide them with the sites". In the interviews, searching predominantly emerges as a technical practical skill, and because the technical knowledge needed to be able to google is seen as so low, searching is not seen as something that one needs to learn more about. At the same time, Google, Bing, Baidu, and Yandex – the four dominant search engines in the world – hold considerable sway over how what is considered relevant, or even true, through their indexes and algorithms, and they are neither impartial nor passive. Searching for information always takes place within a power structure that includes the economy, technology, people, the flow of data, and the many knowledge claims of the large institutions at the centre and numerous actors on the periphery.

General purpose web search engines are new learning technologies, if the word new can be used for a 30-year-old technology, while the practice of critical evaluation is something the teacher considers traditional academic practice. That said, it is curious how proficiency in a profoundly technology-dependent practice like using a search engine is equated with a natural ability that children are born with, an ability that most humans develop as they mature, like walking or speech, while other ubiquitous and pervasive – and much older – technologies and practices like reading and writing are not seen as something that develops naturally in the same way.

The very phenomenon of pupils' searching for information online by themselves has brought the need to be critical, not to trust everything you come across, to look for weakness in a source of information to the fore. One way of handling this situation is to draw on checklists, such as the CRAAP test that we described in Chapter 3, when evaluating sources. It is easy to scorn ostensibly simplistic solutions for evaluating information. The mechanical way of evaluating information and also the evaluation of information without considering the ecosystem of information on the web have been subject to repeated criticism (e.g. Meola, 2004; Wineburg and McGrew, 2017). In many ways, this criticism is valid and well founded. At the same time, considering the enormity of the task at hand, the use of protocols to guide processes for assessing information can functions as a way of managing responsibilisation and can thus also be understood as introducing a type of institutional and societal accountability, however abstract it may be.

As mentioned earlier, Sam Wineburg and Sarah McGrew (2017) suggest two different strategies for evaluating online sources: vertical reading and lateral reading. *Vertical* reading means carefully going through the website from beginning to end. Because it relies on close reading, vertical reading is time-consuming. Lateral reading, on the other hand, is better suited to situations where you are confronted with large numbers of information sources, which is, after all, usually the case on the Internet. Lateral reading is fundamentally different from close reading and relies on the quick comparison of sources through the use of search engines and the tab function of the browser. It can be seen as a way of taking advantage of the formative nature of the information infrastructure as we have outlined in this book. What is particularly interesting about Wineburg and McGrew's study is that not only was lateral reading more successful, but it was also the method used by professional fact-checkers (see also McGrew et al., 2018). As Wineburg (2021) reminds us, with regard to the US Common Core State Standards mentioned earlier, close reading has been the focus of many curricula and close reading is also the ideal of methodical academic work. The two types of reading are not an either–or. Evidently, vertical reading is still important, but it is primarily the method of lateral reading that is being adapted to the online environment. Sarah McGrew and her colleagues (2018), in proposing what they call *online civic reasoning*, have emphasised how students should be prepared to evaluate information by considering who the author is, what the evidence is, and what other sources say. That is, students need to take advantage of the Internet and find information about the author and other sources for corroboration online (see also Nygren and Guath, 2021).

In Chapter 3 we develop a critical understanding of information infrastructure and infrastructural meaning-making in a sociomaterial understanding, which allows us to foreground the various material-discursive formations at play and to consider how people and their practices are integral to the information infrastructure (Barad, 2003; 2007; Orlikowski and Scott, 2015). Thus, meaning-making has to account for the implications of this sociomaterial understanding for the distribution of agency, something which media and information literacy education needs to consider. Librarians and information literacy researchers Alaina C. Bull, Margy MacMillan, and Alison Head make a similar point:

> Once we shift the understanding of who is acting upon whom, we can shift our approaches and techniques to reflect this perspective. This change in thinking allows us to move from reactive evaluation, that is, "Here is what I found, what do I think of it?" to proactive evaluation, "Because I understand where this information came from and why I'm seeing it, I can trust it for this kind of information, and for this purpose."
>
> *(Bull et al., 14-07-2021)*

The important point to make here is how information is not just linked to sources. Information sources are never isolated, but exist in a constantly changing information infrastructure, integrating search engines, social media, recommender systems, and various other old, new, and emerging technologies, institutions, and people.

Teaching media and information literacy must include opportunities, not only to create awareness of this complex situation, but also to act and create meaning from within it. Infrastructural meaning-making needs to be approached through an explorative and performative framework that permits experience-based understanding of the sociomaterial agency that situates the self within and through the infrastructure. We suggest approaching this by means of what could be described as *performative probing*. That is, with performative probing we refer to teaching media and information literacy in a playful, explorative way with a starting point in the pupils' own information situation and the agency of their information infrastructures. If TikTok is the primary social media for pupils, then TikTok should be the starting point for conversations with them, for instance on how their feeds, and the feeds of others, come to be constituted in specific ways. This includes not least asking how certain doings effect certain arrangements and in particular takes advantage of experimentation with anticipatory strategies to support algorithm awareness and possibly to identify openings for resistance. Performative probing includes addressing the role of algorithms and how they work with data in order for sources to find their way to users. It is about advancing a sociomaterial understanding of media and information literacy in order to render infrastructural meaning-making possible.

Teaching trust, mistrust, or distrust?

Schools have always stood for established knowledge in society. The somewhat simplified idea is that a scientific consensus that slowly emerges and stabilises finds its way into encyclopaedias and textbooks, which in most cases and in most countries are considered trustworthy sources of information. There is a scientific consensus that the earth is a planet orbiting the sun, despite the conspiracy theory about a flat earth, but also that vaccines work (in principle), that twenty-first-century climate change is antropogenic, that structural racism exists, and that discrimination on sexist grounds is real. In this way, schools are a calibration tool for a society in terms of what should be known, what is considered important knowledge in a society, what should be included or excluded, and how it should be presented. So, they also set and reinforce norms and values. For this reason, there are also struggles about what should be included in textbooks and encyclopaedias and from which perspective it should be told; for example, the role of women in history, homosexuality, racism, and wars, slavery and colonialism, labour movements, or the safety of power plants. In Wikipedia, the struggle over what counts as worthwhile knowledge becomes visible in real time, even beyond issues that can be decided on the basis of scientific consensus (Tripodi, 2021). Nevertheless, in many areas consensus in science is constantly evolving, and in the case of many issues reference to scientific consensus is either insufficient or inappropriate.

If any pupil can find information to support a claim and build on it in an essay, the ability to distinguish a trustworthy source from the opposite is crucial from the schools' perspective. An important effect of teaching in schools is that pupils learn which sources are trustworthy. Through teaching, schools can promote trust in standard textbooks or their digital equivalent, but also in online resources and institutions that provide certain types of statistics. These include websites with official open data from national and international institutions such as UNESCO, the World Bank, or WHO. In traditional chalk-and-talk or frontal teaching, the teacher is seen as a trustworthy authority, and the books and websites pupils are asked to read are not questioned. When pupils are asked to engage in independent investigations, teachers may still recommend or even require that they include some compulsory texts. One Swedish teacher interviewed explains: "Yeah, well. Then I try to steer a little bit and after they have been at it for a while, I give some sources that are considered good." This is of course a valid and effective strategy to support learning on a particular topic. However, when it comes to supporting learning about how to conduct one's own investigation and how to search for and eventually find information by controlling access to reliable sources, this is a limitation.

Chapter 2 explores different ways of being critical of information and information sources based on pair interviews with older teenagers. We identify three different positions, the non-evaluator (also naïve evaluator), the pragmatic evaluator and the sceptical evaluator (see also Haider and Sundin, 2020), and how the notion of trust is always related to questioning and doubting. Here we return to these positions, but we reverse the perspective. Instead of starting from the experiences of young people, we take the experiences of teachers as a starting point when discussing how they try to make this issue of critical evaluation of information sources the content of teaching and the implications of this for education in terms of trust, mistrust, or distrust.

The way the educational system works, media and information literacy must become a part of teachers' assessment and grading if it is to be considered important for teachers and students. Therefore, teachers were asked how, if at all, a particular aspect of media and information literacy – critical evaluation of sources – is part of what they assess and grade (see also Carlsson and Sundin, 2018). One teacher talks about the role of evaluating information sources as part of more important writing assignments.

> And then there is usually an addition, with the source-critical reasoning. So, the references and sources themselves and so on, but this source-critical reasoning becomes like a task to the task.
>
> *Interviewer: Right.*
>
> If you say you write a paper and then you also have to submit your source-critical reasoning, why did you choose these sources? Why did you not choose others? So, it's not part of the essay task, but it comes as an appendage.

In the critical evaluation of information, the sources of information are taken so seriously here that the evaluation is to be reported in a short essay attached separately. This kind of assignment is quite common in contemporary Swedish schools and shows how much value is placed on questioning sources. The same teacher continues by explaining the role evaluation plays for grading, with A being the highest grade and F being the lowest. The teacher describes using a combination of the qualitative ability to evaluate sources and the actual number of sources used in the written work: "First of all, an A-student always has many different sources [...] Obviously, when evaluating sources, an A-student always finds [...] what would make it [the source] less credible. [...] They almost always show both sides." The focus of the exercise is on weighing sources against each other, with an emphasis on finding reasons for doubt, not certainty – but how can we weigh sources without norms for how to recognise a 'good' source? According to the teacher, the most able pupils [A-students] can always argue why a source, any source, is less credible, less trustworthy. The question of why we should trust a source is turned on its head here and is now why we should not trust a source, why it is not credible. Trust becomes a corollary to mistrust or even distrust. The teacher goes on to explain that pupils with lower grades have "more difficulty finding the negative parts of sources". The teachers interviewed were all highly competent professionals. They were simply trying to navigate between trust and distrust in a challenging information landscape, without any support from their curriculum or most likely from their teacher training.

After telling the interviewer that they recommend certain websites, a teacher suddenly questions their role as an authority in assessing the trustworthiness of these websites:

> And NE.se [Swedish professional online encyclopaedia], I've told them that you can trust it. And I have said that you can trust teachers when it comes to what I say, but you should still be critical of what I say, because I'm still just a teacher, I'm not a professor.

The teacher should also be critically evaluated as a source of information. At the same time, the quotation reproduces a very traditional hierarchy of knowledge and expertise, in which the professor is at the top, while the teacher and students are below. Later in the interview, the teacher describes what they consider critical evaluation of information sources to entail: "Do not trust what someone says or writes. That's the first thing you should talk about when it comes to source criticism." Later in the same interview, the issue of trust comes up again when the teacher stresses the importance of questioning and sums up the argument by saying: "Yeah, you cannot trust anybody anymore." Trust is replaced by mistrust as a guiding principle, and with so much emphasis that it runs the risk of leading to generalised doubt and distrust.

When teachers communicate the need to always be critical, pupils may naturally adopt a critical attitude that is also directed against the one who teaches them. Being critical does not necessarily mean being critical only of conspiracy theories and the like, but could also extend to criticism of the official version of knowledge and its promoters, such as the school itself. In contemporary culture, the ideal of being critical of what is taken for granted has often been misappropriated, leading to a shift in emphasis from mistrusting and justified scepticism of what one reads or sees to distrust and cynical disbelief. Put somewhat simplistically, instead of looking for trustworthy sources of information, pupils are taught to look for signs of why they should *not* trust a source. Political scientist Patti Tamara Lenard (2008, p. 313) comments on the differences between mistrust and distrust in the following way: "Distrust refers to a suspicious or cynical attitude towards others […] Mistrust refers to a cautious attitude towards others; a mistrustful person will approach interactions with others with a careful and questioning mindset". But how can one avoid fostering distrust by teaching critical evaluation of sources, focusing solely on questioning and criticising?

One way to challenge this form of distrust might be to find ways to admit to the complexity of how knowledge is constructed – including for example, how professional journalism works, or how scientific consensus emerges – yet without stopping at the obvious, namely that knowledge is rarely stable and that our understanding of the world is in constant flux. For the domain of science and scientific knowledge, history of science scholar Naomi Oreskes refers to this as the "instability of scientific truth" and asks, "[h]ow are we to evaluate the truth claims of science when we know that these claims may in the future be overturned?" (Oreskes, 2019, p. 74). In her answer, she highlights the need to understand the difference between trust in individual scientists and trust in science, "as a social process that rigorously vets claims" (ibid., p. 141). Although it is impossible to eliminate the central role trust plays in and for science, she writes, "scientists should not expect us to accept their claims solely on trust. Scientists must be prepared to explain the basis of their claims and be open to the possibility that they might be wrongly dismissing or discounting evidence" (ibid., p. 141).

Let us apply Oreskes' line of reasoning to the teaching of critical evaluation of sources. In this case, we could say that students should not learn to trust individual teachers or particular sources, but the social processes of scholarship, professional journalism, and the educational system. It is possible to refute Holocaust deniers, climate change sceptics, and the anti-vaccine movement without falling into the trap of naive trust in all scientific, journalistic, or educational authorities and each and every teacher. The promotion of trust in science, journalism, or schools, requires understanding of how professional knowledge development occurs, and how it differs between fields, rather than promoting unconditioned trust in individuals and their sources. This means teaching why one should trust, which in turn includes methods, processes, and other means of refuting, correcting, or re-evaluating knowledge claims. Knowledge is constituted by social relations and processes. But rather than seeing this as a problem to be solved or avoided, it must be seen as productive, after all it's what we have. This in turn requires an understanding of the social character of the rules by which knowledge is constituted, and in particular, as Oreskes emphasises for scientific knowledge by drawing on standpoint epistemology, that diversity of demographics and life experiences is central to the creation of knowledge. It is therefore not surprising that one of the main ways in which knowledge – and certainly, scientific knowledge – is created; i.e. through the creation of consensus among experts, is challenged through the creation of misinformation and disinformation. Likewise, source criticism can be twisted to be directed against the authorities who advocate for it, and the often ironic, condescending, and even cynical tone is part of the popularisation of this position. We will return to this in more detail in Chapter 6.

So far so good, but what is the role of media and information literacy for this and how does it relate to society's dominant algorithmic information infrastructure? Media and information literacy requires an understanding of the social constitution of knowledge including the centrality of consensus and diversity for the stabilisation of scientific knowledge in particular, and the ability to accept a certain level of ambiguity and pluralism for other forms. But it must also include, or at least aspire to, an awareness of how exactly knowledge claims are challenged and that media and information literacy plays a role in this.

Public libraries and the problem of the raised index finger

The compulsory school system is supposed to make sure that everyone has the same basic knowledge in a society. However, other societal actors also take on educational roles of significance for media and information literacy outside of school. Some are public, such as government agencies, many libraries, and public service journalism; others are private, such as news media, foundations, and social media companies. These educational initiatives focus both on critical evaluation of sources in the narrow sense and on what we refer to as infrastructural meaning-making. Initiatives are often motivated by the need to reach not only school pupils but also adults and older people. The school has the law on its side and a curriculum by whose content pupils are tested and graded. In this way, media and information literacy contains obvious elements of normativity; some sources of information are simply seen as better than others and some ways of searching for information are perceived as more appropriate. In other words, there are strong incentives to learn that actors who are outside the formal education system do not have when they try to encourage media and information literacy.

Efforts to promote media and information literacy can be seen as a raised index finger with disciplinary intent, and not without reason, as we also argue in Chapters 2 and 6. Once again, media and information literacy must be seen in the context of trust. Limited trust in public institutions and other actors promoting media and information literacy can hardly be 'educated away' by the same actors who are the target of distrust. COVID-19 provides us with numerous examples that illustrate this point. When health authorities issue calls reminding us that we should always critically evaluate information on the virus and the disease, the recommendation could also be made to apply to information coming from these health authorities themselves. Media and information literacy entails a critical attitude towards blind trust. However, advocating criticism always carries the risk of the advocate biting their own hand. We have shown this above, where teachers risk promoting general scepticism, doubt, and uncertainty. A combination of declining trust in established media and a high confidence in Google as a neutral tool for finding truthful facts, behind what is sometimes seen as a filter of political correctness, could be a toxic combination. Indeed, promoting media and information literacy with an exaggerated focus on criticism and doubt can be re-appropriated to distrust science and public authorities who try to raise awareness of, for example, the importance and benefits of vaccination, the harmful consequences of racism, or the benefits of sex education (see also boyd, 2017; Tripodi, 2018).

We illustrate some of this unintended, inverse outcome of media and information literacy by relating the history of the early public library movement to the contemporary notion that trust in libraries is somehow tied to their presumed neutral position. Public libraries are a fascinating example since they have a long tradition of balancing the controlling of access to 'dangerous' information while at the same time supporting freedom of speech, freedom of information, Bildung, and the emancipation of citizens. In the USA, the public library movement took off in the second half of the nineteenth century and reached Europe a few decades later. At that time, countries experienced social unrest, strikes for universal suffrage, large-scale migration, and huge economic inequalities, with many impoverished people living in the shadow of modernity and industrialisation (Hansson, 2010; Harris, 1999; Skouvig, 2007; Torstensson, 1995). In the Nordic countries, as working class voices became stronger, the idea of the early public library movement, inspired by the USA, was for the library to be a place for members of all classes (Hansson, 2010; Skouvig, 2007; Torstensson, 1995). On the one hand, the public library was a tool for the common man and woman to educate themselves with the aim of emancipation. As such, the public library movement contributed to educating the masses for modern society and developing democracy. Yet, clearly, and this is often forgotten, it also excluded large groups of the population and was steeped in racism as not least the segregation of US public libraries until the civil rights movement goes to show (Wiegand and Wiegand, 2018). On the other hand, the public library had a disciplining function, especially aimed at members of the working class. The public library was, in other words, also supposed to contribute to controlling the workers. Emancipation competed with disciplining. The library historian Laura Skouvig describes this disciplining role of public libraries in the following way: "The control of the user was direct and demonstrated a certain view on decent clothes and what the user was able to consume. The aim was to prevent revolutionary thought by restricting working class access to 'anarchistic' literature" (Skouvig, 2007, p. 227).

The seemingly impartial approach of the public library described here had its contrast in, for example, libraries of the workers' movement and its drive for education which always included libraries, also outside the Nordic and Anglo-American countries. To take an example from central Europe. In the capital of Austria, at the time called *Red Vienna* in the 1920s and 1930s, almost all newly built council houses, of which there were many, included spacious and beautifully designed workers' libraries (Pfoser, 1994). In the year 1932, just a couple of years before they were dissolved, there were 60 such libraries lending over 3 million items that year (Kolar, 2008). For the hundreds of people staffing those, librarianship was unsalaried political work. Needless to say, the purge of large parts of the collections, as well as the steering of readers and the ethnic and political cleansing of readers and librarians, was brutal both during the Austrofascist regime (1934–1938) and even more so during the Nazi regime (1938–1945). After World War II, the remnants of the former workers' libraries formed the basis for the new public library system, which was under the control of the City of Vienna, yet it bore the name chosen by the National Socialists. While the librarians running the workers' libraries were part of the adult education movement and worked on a voluntary basis, professionalisation occurred during the National Socialist dictatorship. This destroyed the democratisation efforts rooted in the adult education movement, but also led to a library school being established that public librarians had to attend. Strict rules applied as to what could be borrowed, with the aim of controlling the worldview of the population by regulating their reading habits and steering them in a national–socialist direction. For example, from 1941 onwards, only one book of fiction was allowed to be borrowed at a time, as the collection policy dictated a reduction in fiction texts and the expansion of a collection of non-fiction books that confirmed the national–socialist worldview. After the war, the social democratic municipal government rebuilt and expanded the network of public libraries, this time with a strong focus on children and their educational needs and demands on them. (SPÖ Wien, n.d.-a, SPÖ Wien, n.d.-b, Pfoser, 1994)

The point we want to make with this brief historical touch-down is that these struggles over libraries and the information they controlled were in keeping with the political turmoil and devastation, not to say horror, of the twentieth century. The same is true of the training of librarians, the rationale for their activities, their rules for collection building, controlling patrons' reading habits, and educational ambitions. Nothing was unpolitical, and nothing could be, and neither is neutrality unpolitical. Likewise, when during the civil rights era in the USA activists fought for the desegregation of public libraries in the South, this was clearly political and immersed in the period's social justice movements (Wiegand and Wiegand, 2018) and certainly incompatible with an idea of neutrality as disengagement (Gibson et al., 2017).

Today, the notion that public librarianship should be neutral is an established one and it has found its way into various codes of conduct, most notably IFLAs code of ethics. However, clearly not only is the history of librarianship anything but neutral, but neutrality itself is also a profoundly political concept that, it has been suggested, tends to hide its own political assumptions that originate in liberal thought (de Marneffe, 1990; Merrill, 2014). As we briefly touch upon in Chapter 3 and expand on in Chapter 6, neutrality is always complicated, not least in relation to libraries and librarianship (Macdonald and Bird, 2019; Schmidt, 2020) or outright complicit in enabling and sustaining racism (Gibson et al., 2017). How can public libraries advocate for media and information literacy in general and critical evaluation of sources in particular without some norms and values of what constitutes good information sources and appropriate information searching? Clearly, they cannot. Why then does the idea of neutrality persist so tenaciously when it comes to maintaining trust in libraries and other knowledge and memory institutions, and thus in the practices they support?

More than 100 years after the beginnings of the public library movement, (Western) society is undergoing a new upheaval with growing inequality and enormous economic disparities, accompanied by a severe crisis of information. In many countries, the public library is again seen as an institution of emancipation and disciplining. Public libraries offer workshops and courses about the Internet, the workings of algorithms, and the challenges of online mis- and disinformation. Schools have a curriculum that is set by a conglomerate of politicians, bureaucrats, and academics. Instead, the tradition of public libraries often includes a bottom-up approach, with impartiality (or neutrality) and freedom of expression as guiding principles.

Once media and information literacy goes beyond skills, some kind of evaluation of information sources takes place, and evaluations must be made in terms of a shared understanding of knowledge. Part of the success of some conspiracy theories depends on people believing them to be true or that they could be true (although of course part of their success might be due to the fact that they are entertaining in a strange way). There are definitely good reasons for libraries to take on an educational role and talk about the dangers of conspiracy ideologies and their proliferation in the information ecosystem. But for someone who believes a complex system of conspiracy theories, many of which are racist and antisemitic, to be the truth, a raised finger of rationality and enlightenment by representatives of the established order runs the risk of decreasing trust in the public library as such, and thus in public institutions more broadly.

In a July 2021 strategy paper, the UK government presented an Online Media Literacy Strategy (DCMS, 14-7-2021). Along with teachers, youth workers, and carers, librarians are assigned the role of training the public (young people and disabled people) to resist disinformation. It is hard not to support the intention behind the policy paper, but the paper also contains contradictions. It says that libraries are a "source of objective and accurate information to help guide users through the evolving information landscape and to help build the skills needed to thrive in a changing world" (ibid., p. 93). However, objective and accurate information has never been a feature of the collections of today's public libraries in democratic countries. Apart from fiction, which makes up the bulk of most collections, libraries, as we have pointed out above, unlike schools, have not traditionally had the same kind of normative approach to what they should hold or what they should offer training on. The policy paper goes on to emphasise that "[l]ibrary staff are specialists that help point users towards the best sources of information and help them understand how to assess and handle it" (ibid.). What the text overlooks is that media and information literacy must include a normative understanding of what constitutes the best sources. So while neutrality is often seen as a hallmark and justification for public libraries and a rationale for the inclusive public library for all (e.g. Macdonald and Birdi, 2019), it falls short when it comes to its own premises, simply because it never seems to account for its own social, historical or for that matter material situatedness (Elmborg, 2006; Gibson et al., 2017).

Conclusion: the trust paradox

The example of the public library reminds us of some of the difficulties of neutrality in relation to trust and that education always has some form of disciplinary agenda, including media and information literacy education. There are some benchmarks for what kind of information sources should be avoided and what sources should be trusted. If there is no agreement on what and where these benchmarks are, any form of media and information literacy shared between communities that goes beyond skills is extremely difficult to imagine. The many examples of all kinds of actors inside and outside formal school education that intend to teach people media and information literacy face the same challenge as the public library. The underlying idea is that people who search for, share, or believe in conspiracy theories or adhere to racist ideologies, for example, can be educated to stop doing so, that the crisis of information simply caused by ignorance and lack of education. This idea is based on the primacy of rationality and enlightenment, but it would be a mistake to assume that everyone wants to be just that; rational and enlightened.

A classic definition of information literacy is: "To be information literate, a person must be able to recognise when information is needed and have the ability to locate, evaluate, and use effectively the needed information" (ALA, 1989). Let us assume that we leave aside the normative dimension involved in evaluating information. In this case, someone may well exercise media and information literacy, and do so successfully by searching for, say, antisemitic conspiracy theories, and sharing the result with all their acquaintances. They might see the established representatives of knowledge and education as their antagonists, and rightly so. If they come across guidance on how to avoid said conspiracy theories, if anything, they are likely to exploit them for their own interests. In Chapter 2, we referred to Tarleton Gillespie (2020, p. 230) and how a "parasitic" type of disinformation is spread by people who know exactly how algorithms work and exploit the functionality of platforms. Indeed, disinformation and certainly disinformation campaigns depend on the active role of ordinary users who strategically enact the rules of social media. Human-computer interaction scholar Kate Starbird and her colleagues (2019) refer to this as the "participatory nature of strategic information operations". Once again, if we are concerned about the spread of misinformation and disinformation and how this spread could undermine trust in society and expose individuals to political, religious, and other forms of extremism, potentially harmful health information or the like, then neither the ability to evaluate sources nor, in fact, awareness of algorithms – both important components of media and information literacy – are enough.

If media and information literacy is a response to the current crisis of information, the formal education system has an important role to play. However, the different curricula and standards we present at the beginning of the chapter show that this is not always the case. Firstly, it is not self-evident that media and information literacy will be found in formal school education at all. A knowledge-based curriculum that relies on books and chalk-and-talk teaching is likely to give less consideration to the many important aspects of media and information literacy, although this is of course not impossible. Critical evaluation of information sources runs the risk of becoming obsolete and infrastructural meaning-making is not made the content of teaching and learning. At best, media and information literacy in this form has the potential to promote trust in established sources of knowledge, but it hardly equips pupils for their everyday lives or for civic participation. Promoting a critical agenda without relying on a shared and reasonable trust in society's knowledge institutions, despite good intentions, risks reinforcing distrust, and the volatility of information more generally. The ramifications of reinforcing a 'trust-no-one narrative' may be to strengthen distrust rather than to establish causes for trust or even reasons for justified mistrust.

The paradox highlighted in this chapter is a trust paradox. Media and information literacy challenges the unconditional trust in information, but at the same time relies on trust. Is it possible to maintain authority as a teacher when questioning everything and everyone? The answer, of course, is negative. In teaching media and information literacy, and more specifically in evaluating information sources, there is a fine balance between supporting constructive mistrust and fomenting cynical distrust. Media and information literacy will not be a shield against radical extremism or conspiracy theories – and certainly not against a combination of the two – if it is re-appropriated and turned against itself. Media and information literacy in the education system as a response to the crisis of information will not work if it is not linked to a fundamental trust in society and its knowledge institutions, and if it does not also provide opportunities to help make these institutions worthy of that trust. This is even more difficult if media and information literacy is to be promoted outside formal schooling. Without at least a basic, shared trust, the repercussions of media and information literacy could be quite different from outcomes originally intended. That is, if we go beyond skills, media and information literacy must be linked to trust, but also to norms and values, beyond a poorly understood notion of neutrality. It is apparent that while media and information literacy may well support values such as democracy, equality, and freedom, it can also be used against these very values. The potential ramifications of this perhaps obvious observation cannot be overstated. Chapter 6 is devoted precisely to this issue of media and information literacy's apparent proclivity for self-destruction. In doing so, the complicated relationship between trust and neutrality is examined more closely and in some more detail.

References

ALA (1989). *American Library Association Presidential Committee on Information Literacy, Final Report.*

Alexandersson, M., & Limberg, L. (2012). Changing conditions for information use and learning in Swedish schools: A synthesis of research. *Human IT: Journal for Information Technology Studies as a Human Science, 11*(2), 131–154.

Andersson, C. (2017), "Google is not fun": An investigation of how Swedish teenagers frame online searching. *Journal of Documentation, 73*(6), 1244–1260. doi:10.1108/JD-03-2017-0048

ASCL (n.d.). *The Question of Knowledge: Practicalities of a Knowledge-Based Curriculum.* The Association of School and College Leaders.

Barad, K. (2003). Posthumanist performativity: Toward an understanding of how matter comes to matter. *Signs: Journal of Women in Culture and Society, 28*(3), 801–831. doi:10.1086/345321

Barad, K. (2007). *Meeting the Universe Halfway: Quantum Physic and the Entanglement of Matter and Meaning.* Duke University Press.

boyd, d. (2017). Did media literacy backfire? *Journal of Applied Youth Studies, 1*(4), 83–89.

Buckingham, D. (2017). *The Strangulation of Media Studies.* https://ddbuckingham.files.wordpress.com/2017/08/strangulation-final-2.pdf [8 9 2021]

Buckingham, D. (14-8-2019). *Rewriting Education: The Legacy of Michael Gove.* https://davidbuckingham.net/2019/08/14/rewriting-education-the-legacy-of-michael-gove/ [9 9 2021]

Bull, A. C., MacMillan, M., & Head, A. (21-7-2021) *Dismantling the Evaluation Framework.* https://www.inthelibrarywiththeleadpipe.org/2021/dismantling-evaluation/ [9 9 2021]

California Department of Education (2011). *Model School Library Standards for California Public Schools.*

Cannon, M., Connolly, S., & Parry, R. (2020). Media literacy, curriculum and the rights of the child. *Discourse: Studies in the Cultural Politics of Education.* doi:10.1080/01596306.2020.1829551

Carlsson, H., & Sundin, O. (2018). *Sök- och källkritik i grundskolan: En forskningsrapport.* Department of Arts and Cultural Sciences, Lund University.

DCMS (14-7-2021). *Online Media Literacy Strategy.* Department for Digital, Culture, Media & Sport, UK.

Elmborg, J. (2006). Critical information literacy: Implications for instructional practice. *The Journal of Academic Librarianship, 32*(2), 192–199. doi:10.1016/j.acalib.2005.12.004

Gibson, A. N., Chancellor, R. L., Cooke, N. A., Park Dahlen, S., Lee, S. A., & Shorish, Y. L. (2017). Libraries on the frontlines: neutrality and social justice. *Equality, Diversity and Inclusion, 36*(8), 751–766. doi:10.1108/EDI-11-2016-0100

Gillespie, T. (2020). Content moderation, AI, and the question of scale. *Big Data & Society.* doi:10.1177/2053951720943234

Grizzle, A., Wilson, C., Tuazon, R., Cheung, C. K., Lau, J., Fischer, R., Gordon, D., Akyempong, K., Singh, J., Carr, P. R., Stewart, K., Tayie, S., Suraj, O., Jaakkola, M., Thésée, G., & Gulston, C. (2021). *Think Critically, Click Wisely! Media and Information Literate Citizens.* 2nd ed. of the UNESCO Model Media and Information Literacy Curriculum for Educators and Learners. UNESCO.

Haider, J., & Sundin, O. (2019). *Invisible Search and Online Search Engines: The Ubiquity of Search in Everyday Life.* Routledge.

Haider, J. & Sundin, O. (2020). Information literacy challenges in digital culture: Conflicting engagements of trust and doubt. *Information, Communication & Society.* doi:10.1080/1369118X.2020.1851389.

Gross, M. & Latham, D. (2012). What's skill got to do with it? Information literacy skills and self-views of ability among first-year college students. *Journal of The American Association for Information Science and Technology, 63*(3), 574–583. doi:10.1002/asi.21681

Hansson, J. (2010). *Libraries and Identity: The role of Institutional Self-Image and Identity in the Emergence of New Types of Libraries.* Chandos.

Harris, M. M. (1999). *History of libraries in the Western world.* 4th ed. Scarecrow.

Julien, H. & Barker, S. (2009). How high-school students find and evaluate scientific information: A basis for information literacy skills development. *Library and Information Science Research, 31*(1), 12–17. doi:10.1016/j.lisr.2008.10.008

Julien, H., Gross, M., & Latham, D. (2018). Survey of information literacy instructional practices in U.S. academic libraries. *College & Research Libraries, 79*(2), 179–199. doi:10.1177/0961000619891762

Kajimoto, M., Kularb, P., Guntarto, B., Salleh, S. M., Tuazon, R. R. Torres, T. P. S., & Palcone, G. M. C. (2020). *Media and Information Literacy Education in Asia Exploration of Policies and Practices in Japan, Thailand, Indonesia, Malaysia, and the Philippines.* UNESCO.

Kolar, Gisela (2008). Ein "Vorspiel": Die Wiener Arbeiterbüchereien im Austro-faschismus. Diplomarbeit. Universität Wien/University of Vienna.

Kuhlthau, C. C. (2004). *Seeking Meaning: A Process Approach to Library and Information Services.* Libraries Unlimited.

Lenard, P. T. (2008). Trust your compatriots, but count your change: The roles of trust, mistrust and distrust in democracy. *Political Studies, 56*(2), 312–332. doi:10.1111/j.1467-9248.2007.00693.x

Lgr11 (2018). *Curriculum for the Compulsory School, Preschool Class and School-age Educare.* Swedish National Agency for Education.

Limberg, L., Alexandersson, M., Lantz-Andersson, A., & Folkesson, L. (2008). What matters? Shaping meaningful learning through teaching information. *Libris, 48*, 82–91. Literacy. doi:10.1515/libr.2008.010

Limberg, L. & Sundin, O. (2006). Teaching information seeking literacy education to theories of information behaviour. *Information Research, 12*(1) 280. http://InformationR.net/ir/12-1/paper280.html [9 9 2021]

Livingstone, S. (27-7-2018). *Media Literacy – Everyone's Favourite Solution to the Problems of Regulation.* https://blogs.lse.ac.uk/parenting4digitalfuture/2018/07/27/media-literacy-problems-of-regulation/ [24 8 2021]

Macdonald, S., & Birdi, B. (2019). The concept of neutrality: A new approach. *Journal of Documentation, 76*(1), 333–353. doi:10.1108/JD-05-2019-0102

Mahmood, K. (2016). Do people overestimate their information literacy skills? A systematic review of empirical evidence on the Dunning-Kruger effect. *Communications in Information Literacy, 10*(2), 199–213. doi:10.15760/comminfolit.2016.10.2.24

McGrew, S., Breakstone, J., Ortega, T., Smith, M., & Wineburg, S. (2018). Can students evaluate online sources? Learning from assessments of civic online reasoning. *Theory & Research in Social Education, 46*(2), 165–193.

de Marneffe, P. (1990). Liberalism, liberty, and neutrality. *Philosophy & Public Affairs, 19*(3), 253–274. https://www.jstor.org/stable/2265396

Meola, M. (2004). Chucking the checklist: A contextual approach to teaching undergraduates Website evaluation. *Portal: Libraries and the Academy,* 4(3), 33–344. doi:10.1353/pla.2004.0055

Merrill, R. (2014). Introduction. In R. Merrill & D. Weinstock (Eds.), *Political Neutrality: A Re-evaluation* (pp. 1–21). Palgrave MacMillan.

National curriculum in England (2014). *The National Curriculum in England: Framework Document.* Department of Education.

National Governors Association Center for Best Practices, Council of Chief State School Officers (2010). *Common Core State Standards for English Language arts & Literacy in History/ Social Studies, Science, and technical Subjects.* National Governors Association Center for Best Practices, Council of Chief State School Officers.

Nygren, T., & Guath, M. (2021). Students evaluating and corroborating digital news. *Scandinavian Journal of Educational Research.* doi:10.1080/00313831.2021.1897876

Nygren, T., Haglund, J., Samuelsson, C. R., Af Geijerstam, Å., & Prytz, J. (2019). Critical thinking in national tests across four subjects in Swedish compulsory school. *Education Inquiry, 10*(1), 56–75. doi:10.1080/20004508.2018.1475200

Ong, F. (2011). *California Department of Education (2011). Model School Library Standards for California Public Schools.* Kindergarten Through Grade Twelve. California Department of Education.

OECD (2018). *PISA 2018 Results: What Students Know and Can Do.* Volume I.

OECD (2019) *PISA 2018: Released Field Trial New Reading Items.* Version 2.

OECD (2021). *21st-Century Readers: Developing Literacy Skills in a Digital World.*

Oreskes, N. (2019). *Why Trust Science?* Princeton University Press.

Orlikowski, W. J., & Scott, S. V. (2015). Exploring material-discursive practices. *Journal of Management Studies, 52*(5), 697–705. doi:10.1111/joms.12114

Pfoser, A. (1994). *Die Wiener Städtischen Büchereien: Zur Bibliothekskultur in Österreich.* WUV-Universitätsverlag.

Schmidt, N. (2020). The Privilege to Select: Global Research System, European Academic Library Collections and Decolonisation. Lund University.

Sefton-Green, J., Nixon, H., & Erstad, O. (2009). Reviewing approaches and perspectives on "digital literacy". *Pedagogies: An International Journal*, *4*(2), 107–125. doi:10.1080/15544800902741556

Skouvig, L. (2007). The construction of the working-class user: Danish free public libraries and the working classes, 1880–1920. *Library History*, *23*(3), 223–238. doi:10.1179/17458 1607x233850

SPÖ Wien (n.d.-a). Wiener Städtische Büchereien. In *Dasrotewien.at: Weblexikon der Wiener Sozialdemokratie*.

SPÖ Wien (n.d.-b). Arbeiterbüchereien. In *Dasrotewien.at: Weblexikon der Wiener Sozialdemokratie*.

Starbird, K., Arif, A., & Wilson, T. (2019). Disinformation as collaborative work: Surfacing the participatory nature of strategic information operations. *Proceedings of the ACM on Human-Computer Interaction*, *3*(127), 1–26. doi:10.1145/3359229

Sundin, O. (2015). Invisible Search: Information Literacy in the Swedish curriculum for compulsory schools. *Nordic Journal of Digital Literacy*, *10*(04), 193–209. doi:10.18261/ ISSN1891-943X-2015-04-01

Sundin, O., & Carlsson, H. (2016). Outsourcing trust to the information infrastructure in schools: How search engines order knowledge in education practices. *Journal of Documentation*, *72*(6), 990–1007. doi:10.1108/JD-12-2015-0148

Sundin, O., & Francke, H. (2009). In search of credibility: pupils' information practices in learning environments. *Information Research*, *14*(4) paper 418. http://InformationR.net/ ir/14-4/paper418.html [9 9 2021]

Sundin, O., Haider, J., Andersson, C., Carlsson, H. and Kjellberg, S. (2017). The search-ification of everyday life and the mundane-ification of search. *Journal of Documentation*, 73(2), 224–243. https://doi.org/10.1108/JD-06-2016-0081

Tripodi, F. (2018). *Searching for alternative facts: Analyzing scriptural inference in conservative news practices*. *Data and Society*. https://datasociety.net/library/searching-for-alternative-facts/ [24 08 2021]

Tripodi, F. (2021). Ms. Categorized: Gender, notability, and inequality on Wikipedia. *New Media & Society*. doi:10.1177/14614448211023772

Torstensson, M. (1995). Expectation and a worthy, respectable position in society: Means and aims of library work within the early Labour Movement in Sweden. *Swedish Library Research*, 1, 16–26.

Wiegand, S. A., & Wiegand, W. A. (2018). *The Desegregation of Public Libraries in the Jim Crow South: Civil Rights and Local Activism*. LSU Press.

Wineburg, S. (2021). *The Case for Elementary Social Studies: Social Studies in the age of Disinformation*. InquirEd Webinar, January 19th with Sam Wineburg, Shanti Elangovan and Martin Andrews. https://www.socialstudies.org/professional-learning/case-elementary-social-studies-social-studies-age-disinformation [3 8 2021]

Wineburg, S. & McGrew, S. (2017). *Lateral Reading: Reading Less and Learning More when Evaluating Digital Information*. Stanford History Education Group Working Paper No. 2017-A1.

6

POLARISATION OF MEDIA AND INFORMATION LITERACY

The case of Sweden

Critical evaluation of information and information sources is assigned an important and prominent role in dealing with mis- and disinformation in Sweden. There is one special word for it in Swedish, similar to that in other Germanic languages – *källkritik* – which verbatim translates into source criticism or source critique. It is taught in school, endorsed on public service television, promoted by government agencies and libraries, and made fun of on social media. Even if this amount of attention might be unique to Sweden, to such an extent that it warrants a chapter for itself the trend can also be detected in other countries. Yet, the Swedish preference for one word, rather than a host of different expressions as is the case in many other languages, makes for a particularly useful case for study. It works like a magnifying glass for exploring the contemporary crisis of information. We will use the translation *source criticism*, if nothing else is stated, but we want to underline that the word cannot be translated simply without losing many of the connotations we describe and analyse in this chapter.

To devote a whole chapter to the case of Sweden may also be justified on other grounds. Along with other Nordic countries, Sweden combines a strong tradition of public service with a relatively high level of social trust (Schroeder, 2020). However, as elsewhere, trust is declining, and the influence of so-called alternative online news media from the far-right spectrum is growing. In relation to the 2018 Swedish general elections, no less than three studies were conducted on the spread of disinformation (Colliver et al., 2018; Fernquist, et al., 2018; Hedman et al., 2018). Two of them were funded by the Swedish Civil Contingencies Agency (MSB) and the Swedish Defense Research Agency (FOI), respectively, indicative of the concern of the Swedish authorities. These studies reported, among other things, that news from alternative online media from the far-right were shared more on Twitter than in other European countries, that Twitter bots played an important role for the communication of these alternative media as well as for supporting the country's far-right party, the Sweden

DOI: 10.4324/9781003163237-6

Democrats (Fernquist et al., 2018). They also found that "[i]nternational far-right and Russian state-sponsored media are attempting to smear Sweden's reputation internationally" (Colliver et al., 2018, p. 5). The report by the Swedish Civil Contingencies Agency (MSB) somewhat pompously concludes: "The Swedish election provided these international actors with an opportunity to wreak havoc in the heartland of Europe's liberal, social democratic consensus" (ibid, p. 5).

A search for the Swedish word *källkritik* (from here on mostly translated to "source criticism") on YouTube results in page after page of instructional videos developed by teachers, librarians, and public authorities (April 2021). Some are professionally produced; others are simply screen recordings of PowerPoint presentations with voice-overs. You can tell they are aimed at different age groups. However, most seem to be for middle and high school pupils. Some use the languages of different immigrant communities, and not infrequently, source criticism remains untranslated in the subtitles, creating strange dissonance. The videos tend to have few or no comments, and hardly any likes. Often, the material presented favours a traditional approach to evaluating the trustworthiness of an information source as it has developed since the nineteenth century with roots in the academic discipline of history. Most films repeat the same guidelines regarding authenticity, time, dependency, and tendency. Is the source what it claims to be (authenticity)? How close in time is the source to the event it describes (time)? What is the relationship between the different sources that depict an event (dependency)? Is the source biased (tendency)? These elements of source criticism are translated into a school approach and adapted for the evaluation of online information in critical ways, with varying degrees of success. Increasingly, the specific conditions that social media, and to a lesser degree search engines, create are reflected on and considered.

By default, YouTube search results are presented in order of what they call *relevance*. This setting can be changed. In the case of our search on source criticism, changing the ordering to "number of views" leads to a significantly different ordering of results (April 2021). While the videos topping the relevance order are fairly widely watched, they are not the most-watched ones on the topic. The relevance criterion works in favour of what could be called the school approach to source criticism. Yet, here, relevance is clearly not equivalent to having the highest view count or even the most comments. The most-watched video that tops the list is very different. A fast-talking YouTuber presents source criticism to advance what can be described as a political agenda consistent with that of many far-right or right-leaning populist parties. The YouTuber offers the traditional criteria for source criticism and uses them to criticise the basis for anti-racist movements and specifically their manifestations in Sweden. Another video in the top three (April 2021) is produced by the same YouTuber, who describes their channel as the country's largest political channel, emphasising their own immigrant background as a former refugee. A perspective in line with far-right politics is applied to ostensibly dismantle the very concept of source criticism itself. This is attempted by showing how what is presented as its mainstream version of source criticism always falls short of fulfilling its own principles, thus irrationally privileging a centre-left worldview. The clip is awash with irony and cynicism, clearly intending to humiliate political opponents and naïve believers in source criticism as it is promoted by the establishment. The video has hundreds of thousands of views and more than a thousand comments, mostly positive, rooting for the presenter. The views, likes, and comments must be described as a considerable amount considering the topic and the limited spread of the Swedish language. Towards the end of the video, the YouTuber summarises their take on source criticism in the following words: "Don't trust anyone." The resemblance to the stereotypical sceptical evaluator we presented in Chapter 2 is no coincidence.

Critical assessment of information and information sources, in this chapter described as source criticism, is a central tenet of media and information literacy. Yet, in whose interest is it put to use? Who decides where its limits are? And what can be known through the filter its techniques provide? This chapter explores these questions through the case of Sweden. It does so by drawing attention to the concept of source criticism, which has, as we will show, a unique position in Swedish society, education, and policymaking. We start by briefly tracing the historical roots of source criticism from academia to the way it was taken up outside the university and adapted to the circumstances of online information that began to develop from the 1990s onwards. In an age when – at least, it seemed so – anyone could publish anything, a great responsibility was placed on the shoulders of source criticism. Media and information literacy is most often presented as something neutral, but in this chapter, we argue that this neutrality entails the risk of achieving exactly the opposite of the goals of many media and information literacy initiatives. Rather than supporting the grounds for society's accepted knowledge base, it might contribute to undermining it. *Therefore, we put forward the question: how can media and information literacy, if seen as a neutral concept and method, actually facilitate a strategic spreading of misinformation and the creation of doubt?*

Tracing the historical roots of source criticism

Source criticism is not a contemporary invention, and neither is it a Swedish one. The roots of source criticism lie in the academic discipline of history and are usually traced back to the German historian Leopold Ranke (1795–1886). He is known for his view on the role of sources in historical research, influential for the emergence and success of what is now known as the empiricist school. According to Ranke, historians should describe what happened, in a disinterested manner, without speculating or passing moral judgements influenced by their era. The duty of the historian is encapsulated in Ranke's much-cited dictum to "tell how it really was" [sagen wie es eigentlich gewesen] (Ranke, 1824, p. xi, translated from German by the authors). While this aphorism has been highly successful in expressing the intention of the empiricist historians coming after Ranke, it originated from an ongoing debate at the time. Indeed, it is very similar to a phrase formulated by an even earlier German historian (see Burke, 2016, p. 71). In the

1750s, Johann Friedrich Burscher published a treatise in which he reflected on common mistakes of historiographers. He expresses a very similar criticism to that of Ranke, which in a comparable vein demands a more distanced, less partisan treatment of sources and the clear distinction between fictional and non-fictional sources as well as between first-hand accounts and other reports. The historian, he declares, "has to report the matter as it has happened" [Er muss die Sache so vor-stellen, wie sie geschehen ist"] (Burscher 1754 in Kurth, 1964, p. 340, translated from German by the authors). Moreover, Burscher's treatise contains another, at the time noteworthy, view of which competencies a historian should display, namely, "knowing how to distinguish gold from cinder or the true from the false" [Gold von Schlacken, oder das Wahre vom Falschen, zu unterscheiden weis] (ibid., translated from German by the authors). We will return to this analogy after delving into some of the situations and context in which source criticism appears in contemporary Sweden.

While Ranke's contribution was profoundly influential in the development of the historical method of source criticism, it did not go unchallenged in the century that followed. The Swedish historian Fredrik Bertilsson (2021) describes how, especially in the Scandinavian countries, "a more radical form of source criticism emerged in the early 20th century", which turned around the burden of proof: "sources should be rejected unless there were clear reasons for trusting them. This principle was used against established or traditional historical scholarship paving the way for new modes of historical research." (Bertilsson 2021, p. 2) There were different ways of being source-critical even then, and the quotation addresses only one of them. But at the same time, it is obvious that source criticism was very present in Scandinavian historical research. However, this has changed. As a leading Swedish historian wrote in the mid-2000s, "[u]nfortunately, over the last couple of decades, source criticism has gradually become less practiced in our profession and has today been pushed to the margins of Swedish historiography" (Jarrick 2005, p. 232). Ironically, interest in source criticism in society outside of narrow historical research seems to have increased almost simultaneously with its decline in historical scholarship itself.

To better understand the many faces of source criticism in contemporary digi-tal culture, specifically as they manifest outside academia, there is one criticism of Ranke and the empiricists following his path, which is deserving of particu-lar attention, namely, *the issue of selection*. This extends not only to the selection necessarily made by the historian, but also to the many decisions preceding it and making it materially possible at all. It is expressed most vehemently by US historian Edward H. Carr in his influential work on historiography and the role of historical research, first published in 1961 under the title *What is History?* Carr complicates the relation between historians and facts and challenges the very possibility of historical facts (which he distinguishes from other facts of the past) existing without a historian assigning them this role in the first place. He points out that a focus on the historian as a disinterested and objective narrator of the past whose duty is to simply present the facts, as called for by Ranke, falls short of acknowledging that the historian actively chooses which facts to present and through which documents or with which language this should be done. The act of choosing alone gives weight to some sources over others, Carr notes. He also points to the need to consider that a source itself always already incorporates a perspective to the exclusion of others. "The historian is obliged to choose: the use of language forbids him to be neutral", Carr (1990, p. 25) writes. From today's vantage point, this seems an uncontroversial statement, easy to transfer to spheres outside historiography and academia.

Carr's approach to historiography has been debated in the discipline since then (e.g. Jenkins, 1995). Source criticism as a rigorous method is still used and advocated in the discipline, of course in a more nuanced way than in the early twentieth century (e.g. Jarrick et al., 2016). At the same time, Carr's statement above points to a contemporary dilemma facing source criticism as a key element of media and information literacy in terms of how it is legitimised and delegitimised. At least some of the impasses concerning the application of source criticism outside academia in dealing with bias and normative assumptions can be understood by considering the early understanding of source criticism and which problems it was meant to solve. These were: *to separate gold from cinder, or the trues from the false* and *to tell how it really was*, to paraphrase both Burscher and Ranke, who made these statements at times when the writing of history and the writing of fiction were not clearly distinguishable.

The concerns historians expressed over the historical method cannot just be expected to directly apply to the new media and information literacy demands in a twenty-first-century society permeated by algorithmic information systems. The original conception of source criticism emerged for a particular purpose and in reaction to specific challenges at a certain time. Still, there is a simple reason why reflecting on the roots of one of the key elements of media and information literacy is worthwhile. The original, empiricist notion of source criticism continues to infuse some of the more popular understandings of what it should concern today; the establishment of facts and the ability to judge the truthfulness of a statement. Yet, the disciplinary development and discussion of source criticism relating to selection, neutrality, and objectivity have found their way into its manifestation outside academia to a much lesser extent.

The contemporary version of source criticism outside historical research, which has entered the common vocabulary mainly in Swedish, but also in Danish and Norwegian (but not in German), can be described as a continuation of the tradition of the "what really happened" school, and is often translated as "what is really true". The discussion surrounding how we establish what is true and the various material conditions and sociopolitical interests that play a role in this have often been ignored. As algorithmic systems are increasingly involved in automating the very selection and make its materiality and interests even more opaque, this neglect is becoming more and more acute. The terminology for articulating the political values and normative assumptions that are necessarily implicated in source criticism (outside of historical research) is, if not entirely absent, underdeveloped.

Source criticism as psychological defence

The transferring of source criticism in Sweden from historical research to society at large noticeably intensified in the 1990s. In Chapter 2, we introduced a Foucauldian understanding of the role of media and information literacy promotion. Here, we continue this discussion by drawing on Bertilsson (2021), who elucidates how fostering a specific relationship with information among the general public became a central tenet of the Swedish psychological defence strategy quite early on. Bertilsson argues that source criticism in Sweden has evolved into a form of governmentality, a way of governing the population through technologies of the self:

> Source criticism is seen as an example of a contemporary form of government that entails a redistribution of responsibility from the state to the individual, who is provided with certain "technologies of self" to master an unpredictable political environment.
>
> *(Bertilsson, 2021, p. 2)*

Encouraging the general public to adopt a source-critical stance should enable the country to defy influence operations carried out by foreign powers. The strategy emerged increasingly clearly in the 1990s, with the Internet becoming more easily accessible through the first generation of web browsers. Since then, as Bertilsson (2021) convincingly shows, source criticism has been transferred to the web and found its way into curricula and to public authorities. Source criticism should be situated in a tradition of *responsibilisation*, that we discussed in Chapter 2, where the state instigates behavioural changes to shift specific responsibilities to the individual citizen in order to enable the upholding of open and democratic societies (Juhila and Raitakari, 2016). Bertilsson presents a number of examples of how different Swedish governmental bodies promote source criticism as a tool against foreign influence operations, a few of which we present below.

A key milestone was when the National Board of Psychological Defense funded a book on source criticism for the Internet in the year 2000 (Leth and Thurén, 2000). In it, its authors translated source-critical methods from the academic discipline in a way that made them meaningful to audiences outside the research community, not least journalistic practice in an increasingly digital world. "A key task of the Swedish Psychological Defence", writes Bertilsson (2021, p. 6), "is to safeguard, organise and distribute the flow of information in all directions between the government, media, and the population in crisis or war."

In 2018 a brochure called *If Crisis or War Comes* was distributed to all Swedish households. It was sent by the Swedish Civil Contingencies Agency (MSB). The purpose of the booklet was to prepare the population for a variety of threats: large-scale accidents, military conflict, environmental hazards, terror attacks, natural disasters, and also the breakdown of the IT infrastructure. The introduction reads: "Although Sweden is safer than many other countries, there are still threats to our security and independence. Peace, freedom, and democracy are values that we must protect and reinforce on a daily basis." In other words, everyone in Sweden is called upon to protect the country, and to do so every day. The brochure continues by emphasising that "everyone who lives in Sweden shares a collective responsibility for our country's security and safety". An entire page in the short brochure is dedicated to false or misleading information and how to best deal with it. It is explained as follows:

> States and organisations are already using misleading information in order to try and influence our values and how we act. The aim may be to reduce our resilience and willingness to defend ourselves. The best protection against false information and hostile propaganda is to critically appraise the source.
>
> *(MSB, 2018, p. 6)*

To enable people to carry out the required critical appraisal, or source criticism, six questions are posed as guidance.

1. Is this factual information or opinion?
2. What is the aim of this information?
3. Who has put this out?
4. Is the source trustworthy?
5. Is this information available somewhere else?
6. Is this information new or old, and why is it out there at this precise moment?

> *(MSB, 2018, p. 6)*

We recognise the criteria of source criticism, as they emerged as a historical method, slightly adapted to suit general purposes online. It is more or less identical to what a Swedish pupil would be taught in how to assess the sources for a project or what an undergraduate student would be advised on by the teaching librarian. Even the Swedish Military Intelligence and Security Service (MUST) promotes the method of source criticism. In 2020, during the first months of the COVID-19 pandemic, they specifically put out a warning alerting people to the *infodemic*, which can, in their words, "contribute to general polarization and instability and cast doubt on the actions of authorities" (Försvarsmakten 6-4-2020, translation from Swedish by the authors). As a response, they call for the population to adopt a source-critical stance. Indeed, while not always expressed that way, the idea that source criticism is implicated in governing the populace is well established. In Chapter 5, we show how source criticism plays a significant role in the Swedish compulsory school curriculum. But it is also dispersed across numerous other relevant institutions, policies, and professions.

Also, public and media interest have grown in tandem with the Internet developing into the undisputed forum for more or less all mediated information. A way of grasping the growing public interest in source criticism is to consider its use in the media. Below is an illustration of the increasing frequency with which it is used in a selection of Swedish print and audiovisual media (Figure 6.1).

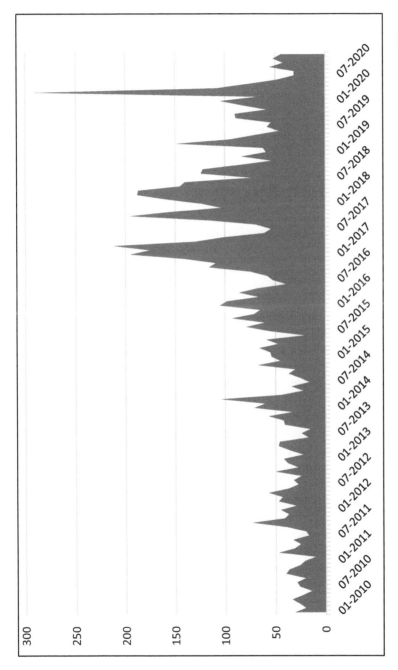

FIGURE 6.1 Presence of the term källkrit* over time in Swedish print media (n=217), 1 January 2010–31 December 2020, as indexed in Retriever.

The chart on the previous page shows how many times the term "källkrit★" appeared in a selection of Swedish print media each month between the years 2010 and 2020. The asterisk is a truncation mark, here used to retrieve as many different forms of the word källkritik as possible. It is noticeable that usage fluctuates, but also that it increased especially from 2014 onwards, peaking in 2017, the year in which the so-called "Day of Source Criticism" was introduced, to which we will return in due course.

In the next section, we focus on how the promotion of source criticism, considered a neutral method by official bodies in Swedish society, has been taken on by actors on the far-right-wing of the political spectrum and has been turned into explicit politics.

The politics of Swedish source criticism

March 13th each year has been designated as Sweden's Day of Source Criticism. The designation of the day is usually marked by things such as contributions in children's public service TV programmes, articles in newspapers, and events at public libraries. The joint Swedish Government website for crisis information (krisinformation.se) repeatedly warns against misinformation and communicates the message of source criticism on Twitter and Facebook. In 2021, the joint government website for crisis information drew attention to the occasion by publishing a Facebook post on March 13th on the importance of adopting a source-critical stance. Considering that it was the Facebook page of a public authority, the post attracted an unusual number of comments. While many commenters were appreciative of the message, a large number were very negative. A condescending and ironic, slightly humorous tone was characteristic of many of them. Many remarked that it was indeed necessary to adopt a source-critical position, but towards the government itself, which was deliberately covering up the truth. Of course, this should not come as a surprise, but can be interpreted as a form of "what aboutism" that has become something of a trope for how public authorities are met on social media.

Another high-profile example can be found in October 2019, when Swedish public service television released a three-minute video to raise people's awareness of the role of public service journalism. The film is titled *Höna av en fjäder [Mountain out of a molehill]* (SVT, 2019) and is about how rumours can be spread on social media. The video was accompanied by the text: "In a world where news spreads faster and faster, often magnified or distorted along the way, factual journalism has never been more important" (translation from Swedish by the authors). The video is well produced and has a humorous touch; at least that is the intention. It shows how an innocent prank (children filming how they tickle someone sleeping on a sofa with a feather) becomes a worldwide news story in a short time, discussed on all journalistic platforms and causing outrage – a text message gone absurdly wrong and blown out of all proportion. What is interesting for our argument, however, is not the content of the video, but rather the way it has been mangled in the machinery it seeks to criticise. The video was posted on YouTube, among other places, and within a short time received thousands of "thumbs down", hardly any "thumbs up", and hundreds of negative, cynical comments, some of which accused the public service broadcaster of carrying out propaganda against other opinions.

A common theme in many of the negative comments in both cases was the extension of source criticism to the very authorities behind the message, as well as to other bodies normally tasked with providing trustworthy information, an approach also promoted by the popular Swedish YouTuber we mentioned earlier in the chapter. These examples illustrate some of the challenges for traditional authorities – the so-called 'establishment' – in society when trying to encourage media and information literacy. In the cases described here, it is about critically evaluating sources of information that people come across in their social media feeds. As we already show in Chapter 5, good intentions concerning media and information literacy seem to run the risk of having detrimental effects. These cases are excellent examples of how media and information literacy can be turned around or reverse-engineered in ways that invite it to be reappropriated to do the opposite of what was originally intended. This is exactly what many advocates of conspiracy ideology, but also significant parts of the political far-right so often demonstrate: that they are highly capable of acting within the information infrastructure to spread their messages or even to re-orient general discourse. Indeed, the strategic use of techniques to strengthen one's position by ensuring that one's ideas show up in the social media feeds of large numbers of people and in search results around the world requires a considerable degree of expertise in media and information literacy and algorithm awareness.

Tweeting and googling

Source criticism has its own, fairly popular hashtag on Swedish Twitter. We collected almost 6,000 unique tweets (5,930) that were posted between October 2016 and October 2019, which contained the specific hashtag #källkritik. Our intention was merely to obtain a rough understanding of the terms connected to the notion on Twitter during this period, not to deliver a detailed network analysis of the various tweets or different Twitter profiles and their connections. A simple term frequency analysis allowed us to create the visualisation (in Swedish) shown in Figure 6.2.

Most of the frequently used terms are such as would be expected to appear: fake news, the Day of Source Criticism, media, facts, news, rumours, science, to mention a few of the most frequent ones. Several relate to education: school, teachers, pupils. The name of a party leader also appears frequently enough in the material to appear in the visualisation: Åkesson. This is the surname of the long-time leader of the Sweden Democrats, a far-right populist party that has been represented in parliament since 2010. However, one term, in particular, stands out: the abbreviation *svpol*. #Svpol is short for "Swedish politics" and it is a very prominent hashtag in the Swedish political discussion as it plays out on social media, especially on Twitter (Gunnarsson, 2016). This strong presence of a hashtag used to comment on politics

FIGURE 6.2 Wordcloud, tweets containing #källkritik on Twitter, 1 October 2016–30 September 2019 (created in Voyant).

in a set of tweets collected exclusively by searching for a hashtag that pulls together the Twitter discussion on source criticism is noteworthy. It is, we suggest, not so much indicative of the politicisation of the topic, but to highlight the contestation and polarisation of its societal foundation.

What else do people look for when they search for source criticism in Swedish, or more specifically, what does Google consider to be related searches that should be displayed? Google Trends is a tool maintained by Google itself that provides a comparison of search volume for certain terms over time and can be used country-specific. It only provides data on relative search volume and its settings are limited and also opaque to the end user. Nevertheless, it can help to gauge how certain searches fluctuate, how they relate to other terms and what people are searching for in relation to a term, at an aggregate level. Submitting the Swedish word for source criticism to it thus provides some indications of how the word as a search term evolves over time in terms of related search queries and fluctuations in search volume (April 2021): perhaps unsurprisingly, terms indicating an interest in educational topics or definitions of source criticism dominate in the five years preceding April 2021. This corresponds very well to the observation that source criticism is a school-related topic. Furthermore, the rhythm of search intensity also confirms this. The graph visualising the search volume displayed by the Google Trends tool shows an up and down that follows the same pattern every year. It is lowest each year in July and the week around Christmas and peaks in May and September. If you expand the time span in Google Trends to include all available data from 2004 onwards, this is confirmed further. In Sweden, Google searches for the term source criticism follow the pattern of the school year. And although the pattern is less pronounced for parts of the 2020 and 2021 pandemic years, it is still discernible;

overall interest drops sharply in the summer and rises when school starts again in the autumn. Dips are also evident for the late winter, the easter, and the autumn holidays. We can only speculate whether those entering the search term are students or teachers, but it is obvious that Google searches for source criticism follow the rhythm of the school year: low interest during holidays, high interest during school months (Figure 6.3).

In addition to the graph visualising search volume during selected periods, Google Trends also provides lists of related queries. In our case, these are terms that users searching for "source criticism" also search for. As mentioned earlier, most relate to school, or how to define the concept. However, in April 2021, two related queries stand out, namely searches for *Bamse* and searches for *Samnytt*. They top the list of so-called *rising* related queries, meaning these are queries whose search volume has increased significantly in the period before April 2021, one for a children's comic (*Bamse*), the other one for a right-leaning online news site with a clear anti-immigration and anti-establishment stance (*Samnytt*). What do we find if we follow these two search terms as suggested?

The first related search query we would like to focus on is for the term *Bamse*. This is a popular Swedish children's cartoon about a strong, kind, community-minded brown bear, by the name of *Bamse*, which has appeared weekly since the 1970s. The *Bamse* cartoons are known for their strong moral values and ideals of inclusion, equality, and non-violence. In 2017, a special issue of the *Bamse* magazine was published that specifically addresses the issue of source criticism, addressing younger children, and providing material for teachers to support their work. In the cartoon, source criticism is placed in the context of harmful rumours that spread about people. There are clear oppositions between true and false, good and bad. We are presented with a largely individualised and moralising form of source criticism (see also Abalo and Nilsson, 2021). That said, it is then extended to the fabric of the community, which is portrayed as threatened when certain individuals are exposed in this way. In this understanding, behaviour that adheres to the rules of source criticism becomes a matter of respect for personal integrity and by extension of community cohesion and solidarity. A Google search for the specific query "Bamse källkritik" returns results that correspond to the position of the *Bamse* series for school and education. At the top of the search results page are links to supplementary material for using the special issue in the classroom. School libraries report that they have added it to their collection and give advice on how it can be used. The list of related searches suggested at the bottom of the search results page further confirms this close connection between schools and the *Bamse* special issue on source criticism. Suggested search queries include lesson planning and the use of comics in the classroom.

One related search query suggestion for *Bamse* is particularly interesting. It leads to a series of short educational films produced by the Swedish Educational Broadcasting Company (UR), which is part of the country's tax-funded public service. The title of this series translates as "Is this true?" (UR, 2012, translated from Swedish by the authors) and the target audience is 10-to-12-year-old pupils and

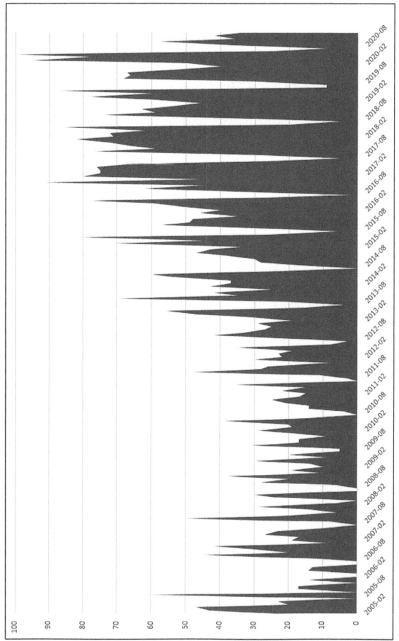

FIGURE 6.3 Search volume for query "källkritik" in Google web search (all categories), relative interest over time, location: Sweden, 1 anuary 2005–31 December 2020, data retrieved from Google Trends.

their teachers. The series consists of six humorous14-minute films in which a self-assured, but incompetent news anchor, and an equally incompetent reporter, make repeated mistakes in the production of a news programme. These mistakes then provide an opportunity to discuss, among other things, source criticism, which is addressed in the first and tone-setting episode. The other episodes deal with advertising, news, cheating with pictures, girls and boys in the media, and the final episode is called "Being on the Internet". In the episode on source criticism, emphasis is placed on its role in establishing truth. Accordingly, the audience encounters oversized "truth glasses" – which are, however, of limited use – receives "truth advice", and learns that primary sources are usually better than secondary sources. We meet an expert on source criticism, who is interviewed in a library amidst bookshelves. The expert is introduced as follows: "But did you know that anyone can write anything on the Internet? How can you know what is true?" The viewer learns that probing information with the help of five questions – Who? What? When? Why? How? – should help to determine whether something is based on fact and therefore true or not. Facts are contrasted with opinion, personal views, entertainment, and also content that is produced for the sole purpose of making money. The intended audience inevitably affects the way source criticism is approached and what problem source criticism is meant to solve: determining whether something is true or false. It also rubs off on the way the problem is presented, with funny, relatable examples, like rat meat in pizza, or a burger chain presenting a report on the low quality of a competitor's product. To criticise this is the last thing we want to do. Rather, by this example, we want to highlight that the prevailing version of source criticism in Swedish education not only follows the thinking of the empiricist school as it goes back to Ranke and even earlier to Burscher and his contemporaries, but also that it is indeed very close to the roots of this tradition. If we go back to the Google search that led us to these educational films in the first place, and to the search term that Google Trends showed as rising in April 2021, namely *Bamse*, then it is safe to say that the version of source criticism that appears here is firmly linked to the classroom and also that it continues the tradition of early historiography.

Let us now turn to the second search term that stood out as related to source criticism in the Google Trends tool. The other rising related query term in April 2021 was for the right-wing online magazine *Samnytt*. Following the Google search as suggested in Trends leads to an article from March 2019 with an intentionally self-contradictory title that translates as: "Kids are drilled in source criticism – shall uncritically take in public service content" accompanied by the picture of a children's television presenter, in what seems like a screenshot from a news programme (Putilov, 15-3-2019a, translated from Swedish by the authors). As its title promises the article condemns public service children's television for their programming on the occasion of the Day of Source Criticism. Specifically, the text strongly opposes the host's claim that established traditional media adhering to journalistic principles are more trustworthy than unnamed social media posts or websites. According to the social media buttons next to the article, it is widely shared on Facebook. It also has over 300 (mostly positive) comments below it. Again, for a small language such as Swedish, this is not a low number. A search for "source criticism" on the page of the magazine *Samnytt* itself produces 26 results between 2017 and April 2021. Not all deal with the issue in-depth, but those that do have the same thrust. Source criticism is presented as part of the control structure that mainstream media and the establishment, explicitly including libraries, employ to indoctrinate the population. This interpretation of source criticism in society is indeed consistent with the Foucauldian reading we presented in Chapter 2 and with Bertilsson's (2021) analysis of the role of source criticism in civil defence. But where many see a somewhat blunt method, developed with a lack of nuance but with good intentions, *Samnytt* sees an unacceptable indoctrination of society from the left.

However, there is another dimension to this, namely the use of source criticism by the authors of *Samnytt*, where they explicitly use the term to describe how they apply well-established techniques, such as checking different sources, to confirm their narratives. One example is a fact-check to show that Swedish media reports on the then US president, Donald Trump, obscure his achievements and misrepresent his statements on contentious issues such as racism and immigration. In other cases, they accuse other journalists or media of not adhering to the principles of source criticism, for example in the context of the #metoo movement or when others criticise *Samnytt's* reporting. That said, other news media – across the political spectrum – in Sweden write and report about source criticism too. And they do so at least as frequently as *Samnytt*. Usually in connection with the Day of Source Criticism on March 13th, and occasionally when relevant research is published. However, there is only one other media outlet that appears on Google Trend's list of related searches, with which we started our journey, and that is Swedish public service television. Clicking on the link provided by Google Trends activates Google Search and results in a list of links to various pages describing the broadcaster, its purpose and organisational structure, a Wikipedia page, a student paper in a university repository, and similar. The public service pages, which come first in the search results, do not address source criticism as a topic, either critically or positively. However, the results page does include videos and links to YouTube. These are short clips from public service television, mostly from the news, reporting on activities in particular schools where children and teachers are interviewed, or where parents are encouraged to talk to their children about source criticism. They are, in short, very similar to the activities and content criticised in *Samnytt*.

The library

In 2018, in the run-up to the elections, the journal of the Swedish Library Association (*Biblioteksbladet*) approached the eight political parties already represented in parliament with a series of questions gauging their positions on issues of importance for the sector. One of these questions concerned source criticism. It read: "It is the task of the library to provide sources such as books, databases, moving images, and the Internet. What role should libraries play in increasing knowledge about how sources should be valued, about source criticism and fact-based knowledge?" (Biblioteksbladet 4-9-, 2018, translated from Swedish by the authors). All parties from left to right responded, albeit in varying degrees of detail. All but one acknowledged the importance of source criticism in affirmative terms and all but two mentioned libraries as central to the issue in a positive sense. The two longest answers were provided by the Social Democrats and the Sweden Democrats. On the political spectrum, these can be placed to the centre-left and the far-right, respectively. The Social Democrats have a long, though by no means continuous, history of governing Sweden and in 2018 they led a minority government together with the Green party. At the time of the survey, the Sweden Democrats, built on what they call "a social conservative, nationalist foundation" (Sverigedemokraterna, 2019, translated from Swedish by the authors), had never been in government. However, with their strongly anti-immigration position, they had a visible presence in the public debate and still do at the time of writing in 2021. In the years between 2006 and 2018, the Sweden Democrats rose from a fringe party to third place, from 2.93% to 17.53% of the national vote. By comparison, the Social Democrats went from 34.99% in 2006 to 28.26 % in the 2018 parliamentary election that had prompted the survey carried out by the Library Association's journal.

The responses in the Library Association's journal concern the attitudes of the various parties to source criticism and the role of libraries. The Social Democrats mention several budget proposals and comment on how they support the National Library in creating and improving conditions for the promotion of digital competencies and source criticism. In their response, they affirm their role in providing financial incentives that enable libraries to act as catalysts for source criticism, a need they implicitly link to digital development and information technology. The Social Democrats refer to source criticism as an issue that is a priority for them and their government. They also explicitly refer to the Swedish Library Act and what tasks libraries should fulfil: "The libraries in the public library system shall promote the development of a democratic society by contributing to the transfer of knowledge and the free formation of opinions" (SFS, 2012:801). In short, their answer is quite technical, and reflects on the government's role in creating conditions for policy implementation. The Sweden Democrats' answer to the same question, namely "What role should libraries play in increasing knowledge about how sources should be valued, about source criticism and fact-based knowledge?", could not be more different. It is an interesting answer that deserves to be quoted in full:

> When it comes to source criticism, libraries should not make their own assessments, it would be downright undemocratic. However, libraries must have a broad selection so that source criticism can be carried out. It is a dangerous road to travel on if libraries are to tell the public how different sources should be assessed. We do not believe that this is the task of libraries in a democratic state. It is completely undemocratic for libraries to talk about what is right and wrong, concerning both history and politics. We strongly object to a

development where a librarian tells the public what is true or not of the material on the library shelf and it is reminiscent of the former GDR.

(Biblioteksbladet 4-9-2018, translated from Swedish by the authors.)

In particular, we want to highlight two points that stand out. Firstly, in the statement provided by the Sweden Democrats, source criticism is ostensibly moved from the institution to the individual alone. It appears in a liberal guise and is presented as an entirely personal responsibility. This appears to chime poorly with the nationalist, collectivist stance, founded in opposition to liberalism which the Sweden Democrats, like other right-wing movements, otherwise advance. Secondly, the notion of source criticism is unstable and moves between two understandings, one of which, however, is more pronounced than the other. On the one hand, source criticism is seen as providing instruments for evaluating sources from the outside. On the other hand, it is taken to mean the act of distinguishing true from false. At first, it appears the established understanding of source criticism, and media and information literacy more broadly, as providing techniques for establishing the trustworthiness of sources is advanced. This is a structural perspective. However, this is then shifted to infer that source criticism concerns the content itself and specifically its truthfulness (compare Chapter 3: Content of message or source of information?). At any rate, according to the response of the Sweden Democrats, libraries and librarians should have nothing to do with either.

The friction between the library sector and current far-right movements can also be illustrated with the release of the Swedish National Library Strategy proposal, initiated by the Swedish Government in 2015 and published in 2019 under the title *Treasury of Democracy* (translated from Swedish by the authors). The proposal was introduced thus: "In times when democracy is threatened by dark forces all over the world, the role and task of libraries is becoming increasingly important" (Nationell biblioteksstrategi, 2019, p. 6, translated from Swedish by the authors). Thereafter, the role of libraries was formulated as a crucial prerequisite for democracy with its basis in the Swedish constitution. The *Treasury of Democracy* continues,

[W]e must defend and promote our democracy and the rule of law against all internal and external actors who may wish to undermine them. These values have an inalienable intrinsic value. They form a basis for the prosperity and resilience of our society.

(p. 6, translated from Swedish by the authors)

What does *Samnytt* magazine have to say about this? The far-right publication is, unsurprisingly, highly critical, rejecting in no uncertain terms the prominent role the strategy proposal assigns to libraries: "The proposal calls itself the *Treasury of Democracy*, but aims to turn libraries into propaganda centres against 'dark forces'" (Putilov, 2-4-2019b, translated from Swedish by the authors). The article in which this statement was made elicited many approving reader comments, many of which associated libraries with a left-wing establishment trying to impose their ideology via, among other methods, source criticism.

Establishing a mechanism for gauging the reliability of a statement or a source and actually establishing its epistemic content are fundamentally different notions, but they are of course also connected. When Burscher in the 1750s expressed the need for historians to know how to distinguish true from false, this was probably obvious. However, in its origin as a research method, source criticism is about past events and thus usually concerns means for establishing the plausibility and trust-worthiness of second-hand evidence. Indeed, the turning of source criticism, and by extension media and information literacy, from being a matter of establishing the trustworthiness and plausibility of information *sources* by gauging the various mechanisms involved in their existences (and visibility), into being a matter of estab-lishing the truthfulness of the epistemic content itself is a major shift. We can see in our material that the latter is gaining ground. The proliferation of the notion of fake news, often as a shorthand for politically inconvenient messages, certainly plays a role in this understanding gaining ground. It is also easier to dismiss. But to dismiss something, you first have to make it a problem. It could be argued that framing source criticism as concerning the truthfulness of the content rather than the reli-ability of a source, also has the effect of turning it into a different type of problem, one which is easily recognised as having sociopolitical implications. This in turn makes it easier to dismiss source criticism as a form of information suppression or to adapt its methods to suit different biases and purposes.

The example of the YouTuber above turning source criticism against itself is a case in point, as are the ironic comments in response to public authorities posting on the need to be vigilant. Another example can be found in the case of a remade image called "source criticism for adults" (translated from Swedish by the authors). This appeared in our Twitter material as well as in *Samnytt* (Putilov, 29-5-2019c). The original was distributed by the *Swedish Media Council* and it presents, in an eas-ily recognisable graphical way, four steps to consider before sharing something on social media: *see, read, search, think,* and finally *share.* Advice is given for each category, including what is illegal to share, with a stop sign that says "Stop before you share." The step "think" is accompanied by two questions: "Which view of people/view of society/worldview do the headline and text reflect? Do you want your friends to associate you with it?" One of the articles *Samnytt* published on source criticism concerns exactly this image, more precisely a public library in a small town that had put up a sign displaying it (Putilov, 29-5-2019c). The point made in the article is that the sign bullies library visitors by insinuating they might have a reprehensible view of people if they share something on social media that might be considered inappropriate. The author of the article also explicitly raises the question of whether this call for caution is compatible with the library's legal mission to facilitate a diver-sity of views. In connection with this, the author also casts doubt – again explicitly in a question posed to the library director – on the library's claimed neutrality by portraying its call for caution towards certain worldviews as dismissive of those views and thus as menacing to their patrons. The Swedish Library Act at the time does not mention neutrality as a guiding principle. It speaks of "versatility", "quality", and of "promoting the development of a democratic society by contributing to the transfer of knowledge and the free formation of opinions" (translated from Swedish by the authors). Still, the argument presented boils down to showing that source criticism, at least in the version promoted on the poster, is not neutral. The advocacy of source criticism, the author implies, is therefore incompatible with the legal mandate of public libraries. It is interesting, however, that it is never made clear which worldviews this concerns. They are neither mentioned nor illustrated by the author nor in the quotes attributed to the various interviewees. Once again, the article is shared in the thousands on social media and receives hundreds of approving comments.

Shortly after the original was published in spring 2019, a parodic remake of the image mentioned above started to be shared on Twitter. All the advice is turned on its head. Instead of Google or Wikipedia, as in the original, people are advised to turn to a specific, unmoderated forum. Instead of considering what facts can be gleaned from an article, the advice is to check which immigration-related crimes can be identified. Who is behind the content? If it is mainstream media, then, the advice is, ignore it. The list of things you should not share includes climate alarmism, public service content, as well as the content of most other mainstream media and information from all but one political party in the Swedish parliament. And so it goes on. The graphics look just like the original, released under a Creative Commons licence, and it is easy to imagine how much fun it was to create them.

Media and information literacy reverse-engineered

In an influential lecture and subsequent publications, technology and social media researcher danah boyd (2017) discusses the risk of media literacy being weaponised. She takes her cue from author and journalist Cory Doctorow, and specifically his astute observation, "we're not living through a crisis about what is true, we're living through a crisis about how we know whether something is true" (Doctorow, 2017). Media and information literacy is routinely assigned a crucial role in establishing the truth of something, most often facts, as if this was what the current crisis of information was about. Just as misinformation is contextual, so is media and information literacy, and in Sweden this is most clearly seen through the lens of source criticism. Facts need to be agreed on. The mechanisms of how this agreement is reached must be relatively stable, accepted, and known by most of society. As we explain in Chapter 3, without this basic stability across society, the demand for critical evaluation of information – at least on certain issues – can be likened either to an invitation to wade through quicksand or to cherry-pick. Given the sheer amount of information available online that can be used to confirm more or less anything, this is no abstract concern.

What is more, media and information literacy is more than just an invitation to cherry-pick. It can be turned on itself too and used as a way to criticise enactments of media and information literacy and source criticism themselves. Thus, media and information literacy has a role to play in how individuals assess information or facts, but it might not always be in the way that literacy educators and organisations imagine. It could, as danah boyd (2017) puts it, "backfire". The "backfire effect" is a concept often used to capture a potential adverse effect of certain facts presented to a person that run counter to their strongly held beliefs (Nyhan and Reifler, 2010). Rather than changing one's position on an issue, the backfire effect means that the original position may actually be strengthened. The validity of this concept has been repeatedly challenged (Swire-Thompson et al., 2020). Regardless of whether the original backfire effect actually exists or not, we would like to emphasise the difference. Negative side effects of media and information literacy, such as fostering an unreflected cynical attitude towards everything, are not the same as a potential negative side effect of for example, fact-checking. In the first case, the potential side effect is built into a person's relation with the issue as such, while in the second case it is a potential side effect that is external to the issue. It is more similar to the so-called "hostile media effect" (e.g. Gunther and Schmitt, 2004; Perloff, 2015). This can roughly be described as resulting from a form of confirmation bias that affects a person's attitude towards media content depending on the medium in which it is published. However, when it comes to media and information literacy, it is even further removed from the actual content, which makes the adverse effects associated with its cynical expression even more far-reaching. Even if in particular the hostile media effect, certainly has a part in how this plays out. That being said, we would like to emphasise one point in particular: as we show in this chapter, the decrease of people's trust in society's established knowledge institutions should not be seen merely as a side effect of poorly understood source criticism. When source criticism, which is after all central to media and information literacy, is politicised in the way we have described, decreasing trust in society's institutions is indeed the intended effect.

Certain expressions of media and information literacy, which include critical evaluation of information and information sources, have been reverse-engineered and reappropriated, and have contributed to the destabilisation of trust in public knowledge. In Chapter 2 we identified the *sceptical evaluator*, and in Chapter 5 we wrote about the risks associated with teaching distrust. Bertilsson (2021, p. 3) notes the same problem in relation to Swedish promotion of source criticism when he remarks, "[I]t could be argued that source criticism helps to instil a general or methodological scepticism for protecting the population from being manipulated." His analysis shows how source criticism and critical thinking are seen as protecting democratic Swedish society. He continues:

> A problem nevertheless emerged as source criticism entails a critical stance towards all information, which also includes information produced and distributed by the government. This implies that source criticism advances a critical view of the population on government information and the statements of political parties and actors as well.
>
> *(Bertilsson, 2021, p. 9)*

The critical stance runs the risk of biting its own tail. Not infrequently, critics have accused a vaguely defined postmodernism of being the cause of a problematic form of relativism that sees no difference between different perspectives, interests, or knowledge. This, critics argue, then runs the risk of nurturing a kind of "post-truth" knowledge that allows facts to be challenged with "alternative facts" (e.g. McIntyre, 2018). This is not the place to initiate (or resolve) an epistemological debate. But looking at the problem with a critical-sceptical stance, it is hard to see how we can attribute responsibility for declining levels of trust and the proliferation of misinformation to a philosophical understanding that has made us aware of how (academic) knowledge must be related to power. To bring in power to the analysis or to include a sociomaterial or a discursive frame does not lead to *anything goes* or *cherry-picking of facts*. On the contrary, such a position, which never loses sight of the relationship between power and knowledge, is always acutely aware of the fact that it matters – in the most profound sense – how things and meanings are constituted.

Conclusion: the neutrality paradox

No doubt, source criticism can be approached from different angles depending on, amongst other things, who performs it, and who or what the source is. As we note in the introduction to this chapter, we need to bear in mind that the politicisation of information and information sources goes beyond their *aboutness* and includes the various mechanisms used for establishing the information's trustworthiness, and that it always has done so. These mechanisms, if we continue this metaphor for a moment, have to be applied, and also studied, from a position. This cannot be done from nowhere. There is, however, one position that seems to masquerade as a non-position, suspended in relation to the norms and value systems of society, namely neutrality. While it is of course more complex than this, at the very least it can be said that neutrality is poorly understood. Moreover, its colloquial meaning as not taking sides in a conflict complicates the situation even further, since there are obviously very many conflicts in which not taking sides is tantamount to moral abdication.

It is no coincidence that the far-right online publication we encountered earlier explicitly demands neutrality from libraries and from source criticism, considering that for far-right populists there is indeed a conflict that divides society. In this conflict, sometimes described as a culture war, they find themselves on one side, while the so-called 'mainstream' or the 'establishment', which includes in particular society's knowledge-producing institutions, is on the other. But as we have already touched upon in Chapter 5 in relation to the history of public libraries, neutrality is indeed a political position with its own history, far more complex than not-taking-side in a given conflict. As such, while neutrality is considered a hallmark of liberalism (de Marneffe, 1990), its strong position in political liberal thought can only be traced back to the 1970s (Merrill, 2014). Yet, even as a central tenet of liberalism, the actual meaning, and even the usefulness of neutrality, is far from uncontroversial. Not least, neutrality can imply different things. Coming from philosophy, Roberto Merrill (2014, p. 2) distinguishes between three meanings: neutrality of consequence, neutrality of aims, and neutrality of justification. For our purposes, it suffices to highlight what these three meanings have in common, namely that they relate the state to the conception of a good life and outline at which level the boundaries for the state's involvement in setting the conditions for such conceptions should lie.

Neutrality, then, is by no means a middle ground or a non-position from which to observe, but one that requires possibilities for the creation of conceptions of a good life. Yet, it is quite obvious that the notion *conceptions of a good life* or of the *human good*, central to liberalism, cannot be detached from the question of power and control of resources, including collective resources, and further that neutrality understood in this way, as regulating the relation between the state and conceptions of a good life, is in its foundations born out of a paradoxical ideal. In the words of political science scholar Peter de Marneffe (1990, p. 254), "liberal institutions have traditionally been defined as promoting the common good, and this aim clearly presupposes some conception of human good". Thus, neutrality, as a central concept for governing institutions in liberal democracies, must be aligned with this conception of the human good. Yet, the question remains whether this can be achieved without including or even advancing human goods that exclude neutrality itself and thus exclude other human goods and conceptions of a good life?

Considering that much of today's political turmoil is focused around challenging precisely liberalism, not least from the right, but of course also from the left, the implications for the human good and for neutrality as balancing different conceptions of it are likely to be profound. Interestingly though, while there is a tradition of critiquing neutrality from the left, in particular as part of its opposition to economic liberalism, but also in relation various structural injustices and inequalities, the right-wing commentators we encounter in our material aim to re-claim neutrality. After all, neutrality is a compelling concept, that most will instinctively understand as alluding to justice, balance, or moderation and inclusion. As such, at least in its colloquial understanding, it fits well with the pervasive tendency to frame most issues, even those where there is a large agreement, as having two sides, that are both equally valid. Thus, to understand how source criticism – along with other tools and methods of organising and controlling information – is currently being reappropriated by moving the position of neutrality and thus what it concerns, we must of course recognise that neutrality is political, but also that it seems to be moving away from its liberal roots in public discourse. Evidently, some techniques of source criticism are less politically motivated than others. For example, it is reasonable to argue that a text full of plagiarism is a less trustworthy source than a text which uses a proper referencing system, and that a poorly written text that is internally incoherent tends to be less trustworthy than a well-written one. However, all will agree that the idea of using a supposedly neutral method – source criticism – to weigh the trustworthiness of the content of two well-written texts on the same topic but with contradictory arguments is naïve, or at least ill-informed about contemporary online politics.

Tendency or purpose, both of which inquire into the bias of a source, are almost always included in the various criteria compiled in guidelines on the critical assessment of sources. The various instruments and means of establishing order and trustworthiness are products of specific value systems and exist within and through the society of which they are a part, and so is source criticism. The history of information control is political, as is the history of information, but so is the history of neutrality. Yet, history is unfolding as we write, and what we can see is the instrumental implication of source criticism in Sweden in an ongoing destabilisation of trust in institutions, and the concept of neutrality is caught up in this. Paradoxically, traditional societal knowledge institutions – schools, libraries, media, and public authorities – seem to regard source criticism only as a method, while right-wing actors identify the concept – rightly, we think – as a highly political one. We agree with the latter understanding of the concept, but draw completely different conclusions. The right-wing actors presented in this chapter use source criticism to raise doubts, with the overarching aim of weakening trust in established knowledge and other social institutions. We suggest that source criticism (or, for that matter, media and information literacy) must include means of making visible structures of trust, including their mechanisms for exclusion and oppression, historically and presently, with the ultimate aim of enabling and justifying shared trust. This means that building trust in institutions, which is a never-ending task, must be part of media and information literacy, but for this to work, it has to face up to its interestedness.

Control over information has always been political, as has source criticism, and also media and information literacy. Sometimes this is more and sometimes less obvious. Sometimes it may even be irrelevant. That said, if we remember Carr's problematising the issue of selection in his discussion of historiography, we can appreciate that source criticism is, and always has been, political in a fundamental way. In a pluralist understanding of democracy this poses no problem, but rather justifies the pluralist position on the value of antagonism. Yet, even if one accepts neutrality as an overarching guiding principle of democracy, it is still obvious that not all types of information sources are equal, if only because not all conceptions of the human good are, or should ever be, equal. Neutrality needs to be enacted from a standpoint, at the exclusion of others. We must be so bold as to say that it does not matter if a text follows academic rules for citations and similar formal criteria, if it has, for example, a racist agenda. It is not source criticism as a method that does not take sides, which helps us to assert that such a source is not to be trusted, but source criticism based on values, justified trust, and accountability.

References

Abalo, E. & Nilsson, J. (2021). Fostering the truthful individual: Communicating media literacy in the comic Bamse. Nordicom Review, 42(1), 109–123. https://doi.org/10.2478/nor-2021-0032

Bertilsson, F. (2021). Source criticism as a technology of government in the Swedish psychological defence: The impact of humanistic knowledge on contemporary security policy. *Humanities, 10*(1), 13. doi:10.3390/h10010013

Biblioteksbladet (4-9-2018). *Stor valenkät: Strid om källkritiken.* https://www.biblioteksbladet.se/nyheter/allmant/stor-valenkat-strid-om-kallkritiken/ [1-10-2021] boyd, d. (2017). Did media literacy backfire? *Journal of Applied Youth Studies*, 1(4), 83–89.

Burke, P. (2016). *What is the History of Knowledge?* Polity Press.

Carr, E. H. (1990). What is History? The George Macaulay Trevelyan Lectures Delivered in thw University of Cambridge January-March 1961. 2nd ed. Penguin.

Colliver, C., Pomerantsev, P., Applebaum, A., & Birdwell, J. (2018). *Smearing Sweden: International Influence Campaigns in the 2018 Swedish Election.* LSE Institute of Global Affairs. https://www.isdglobal.org/wp-content/uploads/2018/11/Smearing-Sweden.pdf [7-10-2021]

de Marneffe, P. (1990). Liberalism, liberty, and neutrality. *Philosophy & Public Affairs, 19*(3), 253–274. https://www.jstor.org/stable/2265396

Doctorow, C (25-2-2017). Three kinds of propaganda, and what to do about them. *Boingboing.* https://boingboing.net/2017/02/25/counternarratives-not-fact-che.html [12-10-2021]

Fernquist, J., Kaati, L., Schroeder, R. (2018). Political bots and the Swedish general election. In *2018 IEEE International Conference on Intelligence and Security Informatics (ISI)* (pp. 124–129). IEEE.

Försvarsmakten (4-6-2020). *Säkerhetsrisker och desinformation: Så kan du undvika att bidra till en infodemi i tider av oro [Security risks and misinformation: This way you can avoid contributing to an infodemic in times of worry].* https://www.forsvarsmakten.se/sv/aktuellt/2020/04/sakerhetsrisker-och-desinformation/ [9-9-2021]

Gunnarsson, D. (2016). *Following Tweets Around: Informetric Methodology for the Twittersphere.* University of Borås. Dissertation.

Gunther, A. C., & Schmitt, K. (2004). Mapping boundaries of the hostile media effect. *Journal of Communication, 54*(1), 55–70.

Hedman, F., Sivnert, F., Kollanyi, B., Narayanan, V., Neudert, L. M., & Howard, P. N. (2018). News and political information consumption in Sweden: Mapping the 2018 Swedish general election on Twitter. *Computational Propaganda Data Memo.* Oxford Internet Institute.

Jarrick, A. (2005). Källkritiken måste uppdateras för att inte reduceras till kvarleva. *Historisk Tidskrift, 125*(2), 219–235.

Jarrick, A., Janken M., & Wallenberg Bondesson, M. (2016). *Globalization and World History.* Nordic Academic Press.

Jenkins, K. (1995). *On 'What Is History?' From Carr and Elton to Rorty and White.* Routledge.

Juhila, K., & Raitakari, S. (2016). Responsibilisation in governmentality literature. In K. Juhila, S. Raitakari, & C. Hall (Eds.), *Responsibilisation at the Margins of Welfare Services* (pp. 11–34). Routledge. https://doi.org/10.4324/9781315681757

Kurth, L. E. (1964). *Historiographie und Historischer Roman: Kritik und Theorie im 18. Jahrhundert.*

Leth, G., & Thurén, T. (2000). *Källkritik för Internet.* Styrelsen för Psykologiskt Försvar.

McIntyre, L. C. (2018). *Post-truth.* MIT Press.

Merrill, R. (2014). Introduction. In R. Merrill & D. Weinstock (Eds.), *Political Neutrality: A Re-evaluation* (pp. 1–21). Palgrave MacMillan.

MSB (2018). *If Crisis or War Comes.* Swedish Contingencies Agency.

Nationell biblioteksstrategi (2019). *Demokratins skattkammare [Treasury of Democracy].* Kungliga Biblioteket, Stockholm.

Nyhan, B., & Reifler, J. (2010). When corrections fail: The persistence of political misperceptions. *Political Behavior,* 32(2), 303–330.

Perloff, R. M. (2015). A three-decade retrospective on the hostile media effect. *Mass Communication and Society,* 18(6), 701–729. doi:10.1080/15205436.2015.1051234

Putilov, E. (15-3-2019a). Barn drillas i "källkritik" – ska okritiskt ta in SVTs produktion. *Samnytt.* https://samnytt.se/barn-drillas-i-kallkritik-ska-okritiskt-ta-in-svts-produktion/ [9-9-2021]

Putilov, E. (2-4-2019b). Nationell samordnare vill göra bibliotek till propagandacentraler mot "mörka krafter". *Samnytt.* https://samnytt.se/nationell-samordnare-vill-gora-bibliotek-till-propagandacentraler-mot-morka-krafter/ [9-9-2021]

Putilov, E. (29-5-2019c). Bibliotek hotar besökare: "Vill du att dina vänner ska förknippa dig med dålig människosyn?" *Samnytt.* https://samnytt.se/bibliotek-hotar-besokare-vill-du-att-dina-vanner-ska-forknippa-dig-med-dalig-manniskosyn/# [9-9-2021]

Ranke, L. (1824). Geschichte der Germanischen und Romanischen Völker von 1494–1535. Erster Band. Reimer.

Schroeder, R. (2020). Even in Sweden? Misinformation and elections in the new media landscape. *Nordic Journal of Media Studies, 2,* 97–108. doi:10.2478/njms-2020-0009

SFS (2012:801). *The Swedish Library Act.*

Sverigedemokraterna (2019). *Principprogram: Sverigedemokraternas Principprogram 2019.* https://ratatosk.sd.se/sd/wp-content/uploads/2020/11/16092141/Sverigedemokraternas-principprogram-2019.pdf [9-9-2021]

SVT (2019). *Höna av en fjäder [Mountain out of a molehill].* Swedish public service television. https://www.youtube.com/watch?v=2Iz5vZX9hH0 [15-10-2021]

Swire Thompson, B., DeGutis, J., & Lazer, D. (2020). Searching for the backfire effect: Measurement and design considerations. *Journal of Applied Research in Memory and Cognition, 9,* 286–299. doi:10.1016/j.jarmac.2020.06.006

UR (2012). *Är det sant? [Is it true?].* https://urplay.se/serie/177413-ar-det-sant [5-10-2021]

7
CONCLUSION

In late 2020, a three-part documentary about the anti-vaccine movement, *The Vaccine Warriors* [*Vaccinkrigarna*], was broadcast on Swedish public service television (Dokument inifrån, 2020). In the documentary, the two reporters Anna Nordbeck and Malin Olofsson went undercover in the movement. They pretended to be filming a documentary on the dangers of vaccines, when in fact they were producing a highly critical film about the anti-vaccine movement. They obtained access to leading figures in both Sweden and the USA, as well as in the UK and Australia, and they even had the opportunity to join a group of social media 'savvy' representatives of the movement on a campaign bus touring the United States. Amongst other things, the documentary included scenes filmed on this bus, and also interviews with people involved in producing the highly successful anti-vaccine film *Vaxxed: From Cover-Up to Catastrophe* from 2016, and its sequel, *Vaxxed II: The People's Truth*, from 2019, most notably its director Andrew Wakefield. Incidentally, former physician Andrew Wakefield is one of the most celebrated figures in the international anti-vaccine movement, due to his 1998 research article on the connection between autism and what is known as the MMR vaccine, which protects against measles, mumps, and rubella. This much-criticised paper has since been retracted, and the research has been proven entirely unsubstantiated many times over. Nevertheless, it has become iconic of the anti-establishment position that the anti-vaccine movement tries to project, casting doubt over the institution of science itself and accusing, in particular, medical science of systemic corruption.

DOI: 10.4324/9781003163237-7

In the documentary, we get to hear a person responsible for the movement's social media campaign in the USA. Sitting on the campaign bus, she explains:

> Your goal is to plant the seed of doubt that they have done enough research. Simple, right? 'Have you done enough research?' without saying that. That's what I'm doing. I'm planting that seed of doubt about whether or not they've done enough on this thing. Right?
>
> *(Dokument inifrån, 2020, part 3, 5:37 min.)*

She refers specifically to parents of young children, who are in the throes of deciding whether or not to get their children vaccinated. She continues:

> If we get them to the clickbait stage, they click and then they go 'what is that? oh… What is that?' and everything they click on, is like a fact point that they just can't ignore. Like 'Half the kids are sick.' And they can't unlearn that.
>
> *(ibid., 6:28 min.)*

What she describes plays by the rules of conspiracy theory, where the first step is to create uncertainty, to sow doubt about established information on a specific topic. Once uncertainty and doubt are in place, the strategy moves to getting people to find their own information, but within the context of the anti-vaccine movement. In this way, people can bypass established sources of information and encounter a different information landscape of links, claims, and assertions – or, as the anti-vaccine activists would like us to believe, of facts.

The interesting point for us is how this resembles very closely a project to empower people to do their own research, not unlike how the need for media and information literacy is often justified. The anti-vaccine campaigner goes on to describe how the role that facts are assigned needs to be finely calibrated:

> You can't use those until you've opened the door to them doubting vaccines. You just can't do it. You can't just blast them with facts. It has to be some sort of clickbait, where they are curious, it's beautiful and they are clicking 'ah… I didn't know that'.
>
> *(ibid., 7:22 min.)*

The point is to help people form their own opinions, but to have them do it in an environment where the rules are made by those who oppose established knowledge: in this case, about vaccines.

Sowing doubt

In Chapter 1, we introduce the notion of the *trustworthiness chimera*, to highlight how some of the mechanisms for corroborating information are fundamentally destabilised in contemporary society. In particular, the notion that the visibility of an assertion can be used as a proxy for establishing trustworthiness or credibility is untenable, as a general rule. But the concept of *cognitive authority*, which we discuss in Chapter 3, does nothing to mitigate the destabilisation either. Rather, when people are encouraged to do their own research, as the person in the documentary calls for, the assumption is, or has to be, that the research will most likely lead in a certain direction. To enable this, everything is put in place, cognitive authorities, facts, statistics, professional presenters, and the right amount of emotional triggers. Established scientific knowledge and other traditional institutions and knowledge claims are assigned the role of dis- or misinformation and made to act as a necessary counterweight. The roles are inverted, or, from a standpoint of most media and information literacy initiatives, even perverted.

Following the trail of evidence that is laid out in front of them, people, it is assumed, will arrive at a certain conclusion. The anti-vaccine activist interviewed in the documentary talks of clickbait, to describe how she approaches the issue. This is certainly an accurate depiction of the strategy, yet it could be argued that what we see is more than just one bait. A more accurate image would be that of a *click trail* being laid out. While clickbait is almost inevitably followed by disappointment, here people are rewarded with a feeling of discovering truths, of being responsible, critical, and in control. The campaigner featured in the documentary is not only highly media and information literate herself, but she also steers the people she addresses, her target group, in a certain direction. She does that by letting them act in ways that affirm their media and information literacy. And, at least, if we understand media and information literacy as profoundly situated, this is not only highly effective, but considered from within her community, it is also appropriate for the situation at hand. Yet, how does such an understanding chime with other prevailing ideas of what media and information literacy is? Or perhaps better, what should media and information literacy enable and support in the current situation?

Media and information literacy can already be used for purposes that are exactly the opposite of the goals of many media and information literacy initiatives; namely, to sow doubt, support conspiracy ideology, and strategically recruit people to the project of spreading misinformation or disinformation. Evidently, there are certain types of information, or rather situations, where this is of little consequence. However, on the whole, a variety of societal and individual interests are involved and those may conflict. For instance, establishing what happened under slavery, during colonialism, and apartheid, or how to interpret the history of women's rights, are all issues that most people will agree are steeped in human suffering and different societal interests. But even topics such as nutrition, parenting, or travel planning, to name just a few less obviously political examples, are riddled with controversy. Assessing the credibility of claims that are more obviously anchored in scientific knowledge, such as how a medical treatment works or the composition of a chemical substance, may seem less contentious at first glance. Still, the question of whose expertise counts is clearly socially negotiated, agreed on, and – as the anti-vaccine community reminds us – also contended (Oreskes, 2019). The activists, the focus of the documentary, do not discount this close and socially embedded connection between expertise, norms, and truth claims. On the contrary, they clearly acknowledge it, but they also unpack and reassemble it. Media and information literacy plays, as we can see throughout the book, a central role in how this happens. There is a strategic element to it that is usually hard to pinpoint, but which is succinctly captured in the campaigner's description of her way of working. So instead of talking of a regime of 'post-truth' or 'fact-resistance', there is a need for acknowledging that these kinds of strategic misinformation and disinformation, as exemplified here, do not exist in a space or in a time beyond knowledge; nor do the people invested in them. Rather, they are successful and seductive because they are constituted by the reassembling of established, recognisable mechanisms for creating, disseminating, and verifying knowledge.

In addition, it is of course important to establish the factual accuracy of a statement, and therefore much attention is given to supporting this; for example, through fact-checking initiatives or the regulation of platforms, but also through how media and information literacy is justified. Yet, an important concern lies with the notion of fact itself and with its complicated relation with opinions, as we discuss in Chapter 1, drawing on the work of Hanna Arendt. Related to this is a further issue that also shines through in the anti-vaccine campaigner's account. It concerns the narrative that holds the facts together, the stories told to arrange facts and to make sense of the world. The emotionally exposed situation of a parent with a young child about to be vaccinated invites a specific story to be presented, as the campaigner also explains. Media and information literacy helps to make the story plausible and justifiable. Have you done enough research? Are you a responsible parent? These are not innocent questions, prompting an answer or specific actions, they are part of an emotionally charged and very contemporary narrative that works to glue facts or fact-like claims together.

In the previous chapters, we examine different facets of media and information literacy and formulate the associated contradictions and dilemmas in terms of paradoxes. Specifically, we propose five different paradoxes, each capturing the contradictory dimensions in a particular domain: responsibility, normativity, temporality, trust, and neutrality. Given the situation depicted in the documentary on the anti-vaccine movement, a number of questions suggest themselves when considering these paradoxical relationships that shape media and information literacy. Who is responsible for evaluating what information, and at what level of aggregation? Which norms shall be advanced and who decides on them? What temporal assumptions and demands are implicit in expressions of media and information literacy? What is the role of trust and what is the role of expertise? What values are vested in the mechanisms of evaluation? The following section briefly revisits the various paradoxes. Doing so allows us to highlight their interrelations and also their co-constitutive relations with what we term the crisis of information.

Paradoxical relations

Formulating a responsibility paradox help us shed light on how the rift between two dominant ideals of how responsibility should be implemented in media and information literacy, that of information consumers and that of rational citizens, contributes to shaping the concept. Despite their axiological and epistemological incompatibility, these ideals not only co-exist, but they also flow into each other. Moreover, they are increasingly bound by corporate information infrastructures that employ information control to support profit maximisation, primarily through data extraction. The notion of responsibility for a democratic decision versus consumer choice, and the intricate balance between trust and agency, increasingly exists only in the context of, or even within, this ubiquitous platformised information infrastructure. Individual responsibility through media and information literacy, as expressed in most policy texts and textbooks, is thwarted by the infrastructural conditions through which it is realised. The conditions for the control of information, for the volatility of information, for the regulation of access, and ultimately for the trust and stability of public knowledge are by and large set by global corporations with monopolising tendencies. Opportunities for citizen participation are extremely limited, as is accountability to democratic institutions or social control. Responsibility lies with the individual, yet accountability remains on hold. This leads to the paradoxical situation where people are accountable for their own behaviour in terms of information control, but have no way of demanding their participation in the mechanisms that make the dissemination of information possible in the first place.

The question of norms, or more precisely, of different normative assumptions regarding which values media and information literacy, underlies a schism between research, practice, and policymaking. Media and information literacy is characterised by a fundamental conflict between two narratives, namely the normative understanding that media and information literacy should promote democratic participation in society on the one hand, and notions of media and information literacy as situated in social practices on the other. The latter, often theoretically grounded and research-based, necessarily emphasises a plurality of media and information literacies and is critical of normative and prescriptive goals often pursued in policy or educational contexts. The paradox does not lie solely in identifying the gap between these two positions, but rather derives from the paradox of liberal democracy itself (Mouffe, 2000); namely, the problem that in order for a plurality of divergent and contradictory sources and for a variety of situated media and information literacies to be possible, certain normative assumptions must be advanced. These are not least assumptions about the legitimacy of plurality, including its limits. Unpacking this space of contradictory positions, and also positionings, is a necessary condition for the plurality of media and information literacies to become embedded in democracy and civic participation.

The notion of a temporal paradox helps identify how the incessantly delayed emergence of the media and information literate citizen rests on controlling the relationship between encountering and avoiding information. The intersection of information control and time control is especially manifest, we suggest, at the level of anticipation. That is, the dominant information and media platforms, such as social media, streaming services, and even search engines, use predictive analytics to customise their feeds, suggestions, results, or content in general. Control over information and the conditions for media and information literacy are tied up with the ability to anticipate and pre-empt the systems' likely predictions. Moreover, media and information literacy is deeply imbued with assumptions about generational differences and constant technological progress. This implies a future orientation and an inherent social acceleration to which one must simultaneously adapt and resist. The anticipatory stance is embedded in a temporal paradox, a disconnect that makes media and information literacy necessary but also always insufficient. It requires full immersion and also self-restraint, in order to balance the constant acceleration of society and technological progress while contributing to the deceleration of the pace of life. It is also in relation to this point that it becomes noticeable how knowledge and ignorance are shaped in relation to the same rules. The avoidance of media and information and engaging with media and information are both rooted in the same responsibility. This throws into stark relief how media and information literacy is constitutive of both knowledge and ignorance, not as opposites, but as necessities.

Throughout, we repeatedly return to the importance of trust, in particular the issue of social and institutional trust. Underlying the conflicting understandings of media and information literacy are different ways of associating trust with agency. This is quite evident in how media and information literacy is experienced and expressed. Several of our interview participants are aware of these contradictions and refer to the resulting epistemic uncertainties as a challenge. You are supposed to question what you read and what you see, but that questioning always runs the risk of becoming cynical and undermining the establishment of a point from which to judge conflicting knowledge claims. The formulation of a trust paradox provides a framing for this situation, in which media and information literacy relies on questioning trust in information while relying on trust in institutions and methods. In teaching media and information literacy, and especially in evaluating information sources, the balance between fostering constructive mistrust and avoiding cynical distrust is delicate. This is all the more difficult when media and information literacy is to be promoted outside the domain of formal schooling. But trust cannot just be assumed or established once and for all. It is an ongoing process that takes place between different actors. There are often valid reasons for people's lack of trust, and certainly for particular communities' lack of trust in the institutions of society, and in the grand narrative of a collective future based on trust. Naomi Oreskes (2019) asks the simple question, "Why trust science?", and sets out to sketch an answer that does not turn a blind eye to its history of exclusion and complicity in oppression. This question is very similar to the question we have also encountered with media and information literacy. It is difficult to articulate, and at times almost painful to phrase, but the question to which media and information literacy needs to be moored to is, "Why trust?" That said, in order to transform the paradoxical relationship between trust and mistrust (or even distrust) that characterises media and information literacy into a productive one, the question of *why* must be wedded to the questions of *how* and *when* to trust, and thus acknowledge the various causes, historic and present, for mistrusting the institutions involved in creating and scaffolding media and information in society.

Along with trust, the issue of neutrality is a recurring and equally contentious theme in the preceding chapters. Neutrality is a political concept grounded in political liberalism (de Marneffe, 1990; Merrill, 1990). As such, its importance, and indeed legitimacy, in areas such as journalism, librarianship, education, and by extension, media and information literacy, is closely linked to liberal democracy's imperative that its social institutions be impartial. However, not only are there several different meanings to neutrality, but also, since neutrality is inherently social, it is inevitably shaped by certain cultural values at the expense of others, as has been repeatedly pointed out in various fields (Macdonald and Birdi, 2019; Ojala, 2021). Neutrality is also part of various conceptions of media and information literacy and of the institutions involved in its promotion. However, as a liberal concept, neutrality regulates the relation of the state with conceptions of the human good. It is in other words a profoundly political concept that cannot be divorced from the question of human good and whose conceptions of it weigh more than those of others. The current crises, of which we focus on one, the crisis of information, all involve struggles over human good, present and future, and the power to define what counts as neutrality in relation to human good is at stake. The implications for media and information literacy cannot be understated. We introduce the notion of a neutrality paradox to elaborate on both the trust paradox and the normativity paradox, and to draw attention to the ramifications of obscuring the specific political roots and assumptions that are implicit in the neutrality principle, which, after all, guides much of media and information literacy and the institutions involved.

As we can see throughout, but particularly clearly in Chapter 6, the cynical rhetoric pervading current public debate paves the way for a discursive decoupling of neutrality from liberalism. We realise that this glosses over a number of complexities, yet we suggest that this is premised on the following: given that liberalism is undergoing severe challenges advanced from different sides of the political spectrum and is indeed facing opposition as the leading paradigm underpinning economics and many existing democracies, it comes as no surprise that upholding it in the context of media and information literacy gets increasingly harder, at least we would like add, if it is not justified and situated. Neutrality must include reflection on bias, which again is a meaningless notion if it is not open about who benefits and who is harmed and how. Indeed, unless media and information literacy is normatively and expressly aligned with human good and human good is clearly articulated beyond the customary dutiful nod to unspecified notions of democracy, it will inevitably be pulled in the direction of the political currents that prove strongest. Thus, if neutrality is to be an option for enabling a plurality of sources, media and literacies, it needs to be bounded and the boundaries need to be articulated and discernible. It requires a space within which to enact it.

Performative and anticipatory: infrastructure as action

We introduced the book by noting the convergence of various societal crises related to the increasing volatility of information, and argue that this amounts to a crisis of information. We further note that the crisis of information is most readily identifiable in terms of how solutions to it are imagined and who imagines them. Solutions vary across time, country, specific political situation, legal requirements, technical conditions, and so on. In this book, we focus on media and information literacy, which we hope we have been able to show is promoted as a solution that links different institutions, values, and actors in often contradictory ways. These contradictions are rooted in deep-seated epistemological conflicts, political thoughts and moral demands, institutional agendas, the chronopolitics of everyday life, and are co-constituted by the material-discursive assemblage of a platformised and increasingly corporate, algorithmic information infrastructure. All of this is shaped by the tide of contemporary political and social unrest and, to complicate matters further, by the existential threat posed by climate change.

Throughout the book, we come back to the institution of the library and that of librarianship. And this is also how we want to conclude. For millennia, libraries and librarianship have played a central role in organising knowledge in its material form, in making it accessible, and, not to be forgotten, in controlling it. The library is an institution whose materiality is shaped by society and which in turn shapes society, immersed in politics, social and technological change, and civil society. The point here is not to look to the library for solutions, and still less to present it as *the* solution to this profound crisis of information. That would be naïve. Yet, libraries and librarians have always been at the intersection of different interests. As an institution, the library is characterised by a profession-defining discussion that, when successful, stabilises relationships between different actors, interests, and agendas. It is the discussion itself that establishes and sustains libraries as legitimate information infrastructures. It cannot be resolved. In fact, it must not. Nor should the debate about media and information more broadly, and control over it, be resolved.

Media and information literacy is embedded in the wider social and political debate. In order to remain (or become) possible and productive as a form of critical engagement with media and information, media and information literacy must include an awareness of its own contradictions and normative assumptions and, above all, must not be based on cynicism. Addressing this issue opens up possibilities for *infrastructure as action*. By this we mean forms of performative and anticipatory engagement with the various material-discursive, and necessarily social and political, arrangements that make up the information infrastructure in order to create opportunities for bringing about change and to constantly engage in the process of building trust grounded in accountability, not re-building as if it ever was finished.

References

de Marneffe, P. (1990). Liberalism, liberty, and neutrality. *Philosophy & Public Affairs, 19*(3), 253–274. https://www.jstor.org/stable/2265396

Dokument inifrån (2020). *Vaccinkrigarna* [*The Vaccine Warriors*]. Part 1–3. Swedish public service television. https://www.svtplay.se/dokument-inifran-vaccinkrigarna [5-10-2021]

Macdonald, S., & Birdi, B. (2019). The concept of neutrality: A new approach. *Journal of Documentation, 76*(1), 333–353. doi:10.1108/JD-05-2019-0102

Merrill, R. (1990). Introduction, in R. Merrill & D. Weinstock (2014). *Political Neutrality: A Re-evaluation* (pp. 1–24). Springer.

Mouffe, C. (2000). *The Democratic Paradox.* Verso.

Ojala, M. (2021). Is the age of impartial journalism over? The neutrality principle and audience (dis)trust in mainstream News. *Journalism Studies.* doi:10.1080/1461670X.2021.1942150

Oreskes, N. (2019). *Why Trust Science?* Princeton University Press.

INDEX

Page numbers in *italic* indicate figures.

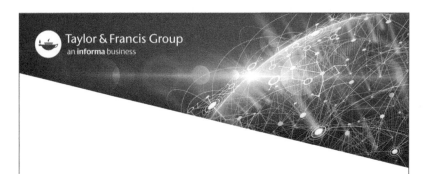

For Product Safety Concerns and Information please contact our
EU representative GPSR@taylorandfrancis.com Taylor & Francis
Verlag GmbH, Kaufingerstraße 24, 80331 München, Germany